SERVICEMEMBER'S LEGAL GUIDE

*Everything
You and Your Family
Need to Know about the Law*

3rd Edition

LTC Jonathan P. Tomes, USA (Ret.)

STACKPOLE
BOOKS

Published by
STACKPOLE BOOKS
5067 Ritter Road
Mechanicsburg, PA 17055

This book is not an official publication of the Department of Defense, nor does its publication in any way imply its endorsement by that agency.

Printed in the United States of America

10 9 8 7 6 5 4 3 2 1

All photographs by the author unless otherwise noted.
Cover design by Tina M. Hill.

Library of Congress Cataloging-in-Publication Data

Tomes, Jonathan P.
    Servicemember's legal guide: everything you and your family need to know about the law / Jonathan P. Tomes—3rd ed.
        p.   cm.
    Includes index.
    ISBN 0–8117–3089–1
    1. Soldiers—Legal status, laws, etc.—United States—Popular works.
2. Military law—United States—Popular works. I. Title.
KF7270.Z9T66 1996
343.73'01—dc20   95–25153
[347.3031]   CIP

For Colonel (Ret.) Jim Wosepka
and Colonel (Ret.) Michael Spak
for their wonderful support for many years.

Contents

PART I   MILITARY STATUS

PART II   YOUR LEGAL REMEDIES

PART III   WHAT YOU NEED TO KNOW
ABOUT CRIMINAL LAW

PART IV   PERSONAL LEGAL MATTERS

PART V   PROPERTY

PART VI   FINANCIAL MATTERS

PART VII
RESERVE COMPONENTS AND MOBILIZATION

Foreword

For quite some time there has been a need for a clear, comprehensive explanation of the rights of service men and women, and Colonel Tomes's book provides it.

Servicemember's Legal Guide begins at the onset of a military career and explains the delicate balance between individual rights and the rights of the military as an institution.

Each chapter covers a basic that someone new to the profession of arms should understand about rights and obligations. In the past, this legal information, if covered at all, was mainly provided orally, and little was available in written form. Even in those rare instances in which rights of servicemembers have been explained, the writing has often been too technical or too bureaucratic to be easily understood. This guide covers important legal information simply and adequately.

While I believe *Servicemember's Legal Guide* will be particularly useful to those entering the service for the first time, it also will be useful to old-timers who need a simple, comprehensive volume to refer to as the need arises. This volume covers a wide variety of issues ranging from sexual harassment to the provisions of Article 139 of the Uniform Code of Military Justice.

While military justice is covered in a relatively small section, the coverage is of value because it focuses on the commonsense application of the system to the individual rather than on the technical aspects of the military justice system.

I particularly like the coverage of the legal implications overseas. Even if someone entering the service has some understanding of his legal rights in these United States, he may know nothing about the application of law to him overseas.

Finally, the Glossary, with its clear explanation of legal terms, should be particularly useful as an aid to understanding.

> Hugh J. Clausen
> Major General (USA, Retired)
> Judge Advocate General, U.S. Army, 1981–85

Preface

During my three years as a military judge at Fort Campbell, Kentucky, I saw that many crimes occurred because a servicemember let a family problem, a conflict with a military supervisor, or a financial situation become so complicated that he committed an illegal act to rectify the problem. Many times, he or she had a way out of the problem without breaking the law but was unaware of the remedy. Often, soldiers who would never commit a crime, even under the most desperate circumstances, suffered needless worry and financial damage because they let a problem escalate instead of taking legal steps to solve it.

Although many other attorneys were qualified to write this book, my experiences as an infantryman, as a commander, and as a military lawyer gave me the insight to see how a lack of legal knowledge affects servicemembers in all ranks. These experiences also proved to me that servicemembers perform their mission if commanders and other supervisors make certain that they understand their rights and help them with their personal problems, legal and otherwise.

Thus, legal knowledge is important both to servicemembers and to the military. This book will tell you, the servicemember, how to recognize legal problems and how to solve them. Although it will not have the answer to every legal question that may arise, it will give you the knowledge you need to recognize the problem and to decide from whom to get help, if necessary. In addition, when you consult a lawyer, this book should help you understand his or her methods so that you can effectively use the advice.

This book should help the military as well. Soldiers who have legal problems tend, quite naturally, to worry about them. If their minds are on family or financial problems, their duty performance will suffer. If this book prevents a few soldiers from developing legal problems, it has been worthwhile.

Senior leaders of the armed forces have emphasized the reality that military members do not serve alone. They have families whose support aids the accomplishment of the mission. Consequently, this book is a guide not only to servicemembers' legal problems but also to those of family members. A legal problem affecting a spouse, for example, certainly harms the morale and effectiveness of the military member of the team. More recently, the downsizing of the military has resulted in an increased emphasis on retaining only the best-qualified servicemembers, leading to more discharges for conduct that would have been ignored in the past.

Although this book is as accurate as possible, you should not use it as a substitute for consulting an attorney. Because state laws vary and change frequently, only consulting an attorney can ensure a solution to your problem with current legal advice.

The views expressed in this book are those of the author and do not reflect the official policy or position of the Department of the Army, the Department of Defense, or the U.S. government.

Acknowledgments

This third edition would not have been possible without the help of many people. I would especially like to recognize the help of Alice McCart, Esq.; Captain John Bodle, USAF; and David Lee, Esq.

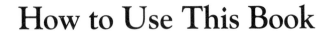

How to Use This Book

You should begin by reading the first chapter of this book, "Entering the Service," because it is a good introduction to how your military status affects your legal rights. The remaining chapters in part I discuss your constitutional rights, civil and other rights, and leaving the service.

Part II covers remedies you can use to solve problems that occur while you are in the military. If a problem worsens so that you end up in trouble, part III can help you understand how criminal law affects servicemembers and their families. Part IV covers personal legal matters, and chapter 9, "Your Legal Survival Kit," is especially important. Part V tells you what you need to know about property, and part VI discusses the legal aspects of money, such as debt and earning extra income. Part VII addresses special concerns of reservists. The Glossary explains military and legal terms.

Although this book contains some sample legal forms and letters, you should not use them because they may not be proper for your particular situation. To avoid confusion about forms, ask the agency that requires the form to give you the one it prefers for you to use.

The best advice I can give you is to see a lawyer early, before your problem gets out of hand. At worst, the lawyer will refer you to someone else, such as an inspector general or your commander.

Although a military legal assistance officer cannot help you with every legal problem, his advice is free. He may, however, need to refer you to a civilian attorney, perhaps because your problem is in an area in which the military does not allow him to advise, such as a business matter, or because your problem requires a court appearance with a civilian attorney. Military attorneys cannot represent you in civilian court in most cases. But in some states, by agreement with the State Bar, military attorneys in an expanded legal assistance program may represent low-ranking servicemembers, who earn little money, in civilian courts. If your problem requires a court appearance and you do not qualify for this expanded assistance, or if you are not in a state with this program, you may have to hire a civilian attorney.

If you read this book and consult a lawyer early, you will be better able to prevent most legal problems before they arise and to solve those that do.

PART I

Military Status

The *American Heritage Dictionary* defines *status* as the "legal condition of a person." You may change your status, or your legal condition, many times in your life, such as from child to adult, or from single person to spouse. Each change in status has different legal consequences. You also change status when you enter the military. Your legal condition changes when you become a member of the armed forces because your rights and responsibilities differ from those of civilians. Therefore, to get the most out of your military service, you need to know your duties and your rights.

Part I defines your duties and your rights as a servicemember. First, chapter 1 discusses how you get military status—how you become a servicemember—and how that status changes your rights and obligations. Next, chapter 2 outlines your constitutional rights, and chapter 3 discusses civil and other rights that are important to servicemembers. Finally, chapter 4 tells you about the legal consequences of leaving the service.

1

1

Entering the Service

You can become a servicemember on active duty in any one of several ways. Since the government is no longer using a draft, the most common way to come on active duty is to enlist. The government may also appoint you as an officer or may activate you from reserve status. No matter how you become a servicemember, you need to know the legal consequences of obtaining military status.

ENLISTMENT

On the face of it, enlisting is simple—sign an enlistment contract and take an oath of enlistment given by a commissioned officer of any U.S. armed force. Those two simple acts, however, involve important legal considerations for both the government and the person who enlists.

According to law, no one can enlist in the U.S. armed forces without being either a U.S. citizen or an alien who has lawful permanent resident status. The armed forces also may not enlist anyone who is insane or drunk, has a felony conviction, or is a deserter. And, in order for the enlistment to be legal, a prospective servicemember must be at least eighteen years old to enlist without parental consent or at least seventeen years old to enlist with parental consent. If the prospective enlistee does not meet these requirements, the enlistment is illegal. Thus, if a person who is less than seventeen enlists, the enlistment is void and of no legal effect, and the military will release him.

Because of these and other legal considerations, you should regard your enlistment as a contract, or an agreement, between you and the government in which each party to the contract agrees to do certain things. When you

ENLISTMENT / REENLISTMENT DOCUMENT
ARMED FORCES OF THE UNITED STATES

A. ENLISTEE / REENLISTEE IDENTIFICATION DATA

1. NAME (Last, First, Middle)	2. SOCIAL SECURITY NUMBER

3. HOME OF RECORD (Street, City, State, ZIP Code) | 4. PLACE OF ENLISTMENT / REENLISTMENT (Mil. Installation, City, State)

5. DATE OF ENLISTMENT/ REENLISTMENT (YYMMDD)	6. DATE OF BIRTH (YYMMDD)	7. PREV MIL SVC UPON ENL / REENLIST	YEARS	MONTHS	DAYS
		a. Total Active Military Service			
		b. Total Inactive Military Service			

B. AGREEMENTS

8. I am enlisting /reenlisting in the United States (list branch of service) _____ _____ this date for_____ years and _____ weeks beginning in pay grade _____ . The additional details of my enlistment / reenlistment are in Section C and Annex(es) _____ .

a. FOR ENLISTMENT IN A DELAYED ENTRY / ENLISTMENT PROGRAM (DEP):
I understand that I will be ordered to active duty as a Reservist unless I report to the place shown in item 4 above by (list date (YYMMDD))_____ for enlistment in the Regular component of the United States (list branch of service)_____ for not less than_____ years and _____ weeks. My enlistment in the DEP is in a nonpay status. I understand my period of time in the DEP is **NOT** creditable for pay purposes upon entry into a pay status. However, I also understand that this time is counted toward fulfillment of my military service obligation or commitment. I must maintain my current qualifications and keep my recruiter informed of any changes in my physical or dependency status, moral qualifications, and mailing address.

b. Remarks: (If none, so state.)

c. The agreements in this section and attached annex(es) are all the promises made to me by the Government. **ANYTHING ELSE ANYONE HAS PROMISED ME IS NOT VALID AND WILL NOT BE HONORED.**
(Initials of Enlistee/Reenlistee)_____ .

DD Form 4/1, MAY 85   *Previous editions are obsolete.*

An enlistment contract.

take your enlistment oath and enter the military, you agree to do the following:

- Obey the orders of your military superiors.
- Allow the military to punish you under the Uniform Code of Military Justice if you violate military law. (Many civilian crimes also violate military law.)
- Be assigned in accordance with the needs of the military, including combat duty, after the military has lived up to any agreement it made to give you an initial assignment or training.
- Remain six months past the end of a war that happens during your enlistment, even if your enlistment is supposed to end before the war is over.
- Lose some benefits the government promised you if the United States is involved in a war.
- Be aware that changes in the laws Congress passes while you are on active duty may change your rights.
- Lose military and veterans benefits and perhaps be unable to get a job if you receive a discharge that is not honorable.

In return, the military agrees to do the following:

- Pay you and give you allowances and benefits when you are eligible, such as quarters allowances and veterans benefits. You become eligible for quarters allowances, for example, by having a family you support, and you become eligible for veterans benefits by serving honorably for a sufficient time.
- Give you the assignment, the schooling, the training, or whatever else you enlisted for if you qualify. For example, to qualify for special training, you may have to achieve a certain score on an aptitude test or be in better physical condition than is necessary to enlist.

Because military status is different from civilian status, it is important that you understand that when you enlist, you do not merely agree to the terms of a contract, as you would if you signed an employment contract with a civilian company. When you enlist and become a servicemember, you also get a new status, a new legal condition. Because of that status, you cannot, for example, quit your job or go on strike the way a civilian can. In fact, even if the military does not honor its promises in the enlistment contract, you still have to accept your obligations under the contract because you still have the status of a servicemember until the military discharges you.

If you believe the military has broken its promises in the enlistment contract, do not quit or go AWOL (absent without leave). Even if the military has broken the contract, its breach of contract is no defense to a criminal charge if you violate its laws contained in the Uniform Code of Military Justice (see chapter 7), such as by going AWOL.

Your first step toward getting the military to honor its end of the deal should be to use your chain of command to discuss the problem. If the chain of command does not resolve the problem, you may consider consulting an inspector general or a military attorney. As a last resort, an attorney may advise you to bring a lawsuit in a federal court to enforce your rights under the contract. Remember, however, that you will continue to be a service-member—with all a servicemember's duties and responsibilities—until the military discharges you (see chapter 4). You must continue to work and to be productive, despite the circumstances, so that you won't aggravate the situation from which you are seeking relief.

Because many servicemembers do not realize that the military has violated their enlistment contract until they get in trouble and want to get out of the military, most challenges to enlistments occur in courts-martial. A servicemember charged with a military crime may argue that the military cannot court-martial him because his enlistment was improper, and he is, therefore, not a servicemember. While this defense has succeeded in the past, Congress amended Article 2 of the Uniform Code of Military Justice so that the military may try by court-martial any person serving in an armed force until he is discharged if he did the following:

- Enlisted voluntarily.
- Met the minimum mental and age qualifications at the time of enlistment.
- Received military pay.
- Performed military duties.

With this amendment, only rarely will a servicemember be able to avoid a court-martial because of an enlistment problem. Even if the servicemember avoids a court-martial because a military judge finds that he or she was not properly enlisted and, therefore, isn't a servicemember, he or she may be tried in a civilian court by a federal or state prosecutor, depending on whether the crime violated federal or state law.

COMMISSION

A person does not become an officer by enlisting—instead, a person becomes an officer by a *commission*. The U.S. Constitution says that the president may, with the advice and consent of Congress, commission, or appoint, officers. Of course, the president himself does not appoint every officer. He has delegated his authority, through the secretary of defense, to the service secretaries, such as the secretary of the Air Force, so that he personally appoints only very high ranking officers.

The office to which the president appoints an officer has two characteristics, both of which must be present for the commission to be legal. First, the appointment must be in a particular component of an armed force, such as the infantry branch of the U.S. Army or the Judge Advocate Corps of the U.S. Navy. Second, the appointment must be to a particular grade within that component, such as ensign or colonel. In fact, each time the military promotes an officer, it reappoints him to the higher grade in that component.

The appointment to such an office has three requirements:

1. The president or a service secretary must make the appointment.

2. The military service must offer the appointment to the person, usually by giving the person a letter of appointment and an oath of office.

3. The person must accept the appointment. Taking the oath of office is the most common method of accepting the appointment, but any act that shows that the person meant to take the commission may be good enough to be an acceptance and thus to finalize the appointment as an officer. Because the military cannot force a person to become an officer, the military cannot force anyone to accept an appointment. If, however, you have a service obligation because you were a service academy graduate or a military scholarship recipient, you cannot avoid it by refusing the appointment. If you have a service obligation and refuse an appointment, you must serve your obligated period as an enlisted person.

When a person accepts a commission and becomes an officer, he or she has a different status from that of an enlistee. In addition to the things an enlistment gives a person, such as status, rights, and obligations as a member of the military, a commission confers on the officer both the authority and the privileges of rank. This authority allows the officer to issue lawful orders to subordinates.

RESPONSIBILITIES OF SERVICEMEMBERS
Now that you understand how you enter the service and how your status changes when you do so, it is important to know what the military expects of you.

When you enter the service, your military status involves certain responsibilities that civilians do not have. Your obligation to defend your country carries with it a number of responsibilities to ensure that you can defend the United States when called on. While in the service, you must constantly be ready to do your part to defend your country, whether that means fighting as an infantryman, performing aircraft maintenance, or being a shore patrolman. Because this obligation means that you must always be ready to perform your assigned duties, your service requires you to remain fit, to be present in your unit or at your job unless a superior excuses you, to perform your duties efficiently, and to obey the lawful orders of your military superiors.

To Remain Fit
Your obligation to keep fit allows the military to require you to maintain height and weight standards, to pass medical examinations, and to pass physical readiness tests. This responsibility, however, means more than just maintaining a condition that's sufficient to pass a physical readiness test. You must also avoid using drugs or too much alcohol (any alcohol is too much just before or during duty hours) or doing anything else that would hurt your job performance. Any drug or alcohol abuse or self-inflicted injury is a crime in the military, as is simple possession or use of drugs (see part III). The mili-

tary's need to make certain that you are fit to perform your duties allows it to conduct urinalysis tests to determine whether you are using illegal drugs.

Your fitness obligation allows the military to require you to undergo medical examinations and medical treatment. Thus, an order to take a flu shot is a lawful order. The military can also require you to lose weight if you are overweight, or it can discharge you if you don't meet height and weight standards.

To Be Present in Your Unit or at Your Job

Your duty to be prepared to defend your country is a twenty-four-hour-a-day obligation. Thus, you must be at your place of duty unless properly excused. If a civilian is late for work, his boss may fire him or dock his pay. But in the military, being late for work or leaving early without permission is a crime called *failure to repair*. Leaving your unit or not returning from a leave or pass without permission is the crime of *absence without leave* (AWOL). Both failure to repair and AWOL are crimes under Article 86 of the Uniform Code of Military Justice. A car breakdown or a lack of money to get back, for example, would not excuse you because those problems are foreseeable. In other words, before you left your unit, you should have anticipated a possible breakdown and planned for alternative transportation. Make certain you also have some extra money for car repair or for a bus ticket before you leave.

If some problem such as an accident or a car breakdown should occur, however, you must contact your commander immediately and get permission to return late; otherwise you are AWOL. If you cannot contact your unit, turn yourself in to the nearest military base or even to a recruiting office to return to military control and thus not become AWOL. The only circumstance that could excuse you from an unauthorized absence would be a totally unforeseeable one beyond your control, such as becoming stranded by a July blizzard in Florida with no access to a telephone.

To Perform Your Duties Efficiently

Not only must you be present and able to do your duties, but also you must do them well. Failure to perform your duty well is a crime called *dereliction of duty*. You can also commit this crime by failing to do your duties at all.

If a civilian doesn't get his work done or does a poor job, his boss could fire him. Because of the need for a high degree of efficiency in defense of the country, however, the military has both higher standards of efficiency and more severe consequences for poor duty performance. Not only could you face a court-martial for dereliction of duty (see chapter 7), but also your service could discharge you for poor duty performance (see chapter 4) with a less-than-honorable discharge. In today's downsizing military, poor job performance will quickly result in a discharge, but if you always do your duty to the best of your ability, you will never be guilty of dereliction of duty.

To Obey Lawful Orders

You also have the responsibility to obey the lawful orders of superiors. Under the Uniform Code of Military Justice, disobedience of a lawful order is a crime punishable by up to five years' confinement and a dishonorable discharge. So you need to know both what a lawful order is and what to do if you suspect an order isn't lawful.

You disobey an order at your own risk under military law, which presumes orders to be lawful. Hence, a court-martial would assume an order was proper unless you proved that it was illegal. Therefore, if you disobeyed an order because you thought it was illegal and the judge ruled that it was lawful, the military could punish you for disobeying the order.

Conversely, if you do something illegal, it is no excuse that you were ordered to do it if you knew, or should have known, that the order was illegal. For example, because shooting an unresisting prisoner is a war crime, an order to do so would be illegal. If you shot and killed the prisoner, the order to do so would not be a defense in your murder trial because you either knew or should have known that it is illegal to kill a prisoner who is not attacking you (the Law of War does allow you to defend yourself).

What is the difference between a lawful order and one that is not? A lawful order must relate to the performance of military duties and have a proper military purpose, such as any of the following:

- To accomplish a military mission.
- To raise morale, such as an order to clean a sports field for a unit game.
- To maintain discipline, such as an order to "be at ease" to stop a subordinate from being disrespectful to a superior.
- To keep unit members able to perform their duties, such as an order to take a flu shot to prevent illness.

An order is illegal if it is unconstitutional or against the law, if it is unrelated to military duties, if it is unreasonable, or if a superior gives it solely to increase punishment for a crime he things you may commit. An example of an unconstitutional order would be an order to torture a suspect to get him to confess to a crime. An order from a superior to buy insurance from him would be an example of an order that is against the law, in this case the law that prohibits superiors from using their rank for personal gain (see chapter 16). Although an order to wash a unit military vehicle, for example, would be legal, an order to wash the commander's personal car would not, because it is unrelated to military duties and would be for the commander's personal benefit. An order restricting a whole unit to the unit area because one unit member went AWOL would be unreasonable and, hence, illegal.

Finally, if, after you disobeyed a noncommissioned or a petty officer, a captain gave you the same order *solely* to increase your punishment, the captain's order would be illegal. (The maximum punishment for disobeying a noncommissioned or petty officer is a bad-conduct discharge and confinement at hard labor for one year. The maximum punishment for disobeying a commissioned officer, however, includes a dishonorable discharge and confinement at hard labor for five years.) Of course, you could be punished for the original disobedience to the noncommissioned or petty officer.

You should also be aware that sometimes a junior-ranking servicemember, most commonly a military policeperson, may give you an order that you have to obey. Regardless of his or her rank, if an MP tells you to move your car because it is blocking traffic, that is a lawful order you must obey because his or her status as a military policeperson gives him or her the authority to issue orders to enforce law and order.

What do you do if someone gives you an order that you think is unlawful? First, you should ask the person who gave you the order to repeat it to make sure that you heard it correctly. Then, if you still think the order may not be lawful, ask him or her to explain it. If you cannot respectfully convince the person that it is illegal, obey any order requiring immediate obedience because you disobey an order at your own risk—unless you are certain that the order is illegal or that it would hurt someone. Remember, however, that you are not an expert on the legality of orders and that the military may punish you for disobeying a legal order even if you thought it was illegal.

After obeying such an order, you could complain first through the chain of command and then to the inspector general. If the order did not require immediate obedience, you could also use these means to find out its legality before deciding whether to obey it. If, for example, I were given an order to wash the commander's personal car, and if I could not convince him that it was an improper order, I would first wash the car and then complain because washing a car is not illegal or harmful to anyone. But, on the other hand, if I were given an order to kill an unresisting prisoner, I would disobey because the order is illegal under the Law of War, which prohibits killing unresisting prisoners.

Because most of your superiors should know how to give proper orders, you'll probably never receive an illegal one, and asking for clarification of the order would probably resolve any question in the few times that the order may seem improper.

CONCLUSION

Entering the service, whether you enlist or accept a commission, means that you take on the responsibilities to remain fit, to be present for duty, to perform your duties well, and to obey lawful orders. If you read this part of this book, apply common sense, and ask for help if you don't understand your responsibilities, you will do your military duties well and have a rewarding period of service.

2

The U.S. Constitution and the Servicemember

As a general rule, servicemembers have the same constitutional rights and protections as other Americans. The courts, however, interpret the constitutional rights of servicemembers in light of their unique military status.

The only passage in the Constitution that excludes servicemembers is in the Fifth Amendment, which, as protection against improper prosecutions, provides for the right to indictment by grand jury for serious crimes "except in cases arising in the land and naval forces." Thus, the military may try servicemembers by court-martial without first indicting them by a grand jury. But the Article 32 investigation (see chapter 7) provides much the same protection as the Fifth Amendment for a servicemember facing a general court-martial. When, however, a civilian prosecutor tries servicemembers in civilian courts, such cases do not arise "in the land and naval forces," and servicemembers have the same right to indictment by grand jury as other citizens.

Although all other constitutional protections apply to servicemembers, the degree of protection may differ from that which civilians enjoy because the military's need for a disciplined and ready fighting force justifies some restrictions on individual liberties. This chapter will discuss your constitutional protections as products of two competing interests: the need for the services to be ready and effective fighting forces and your constitutional rights as guaranteed in the Bill of Rights, the first ten amendments to the Constitution.

YOU AND THE FIRST AMENDMENT

The First Amendment to the Constitution guarantees everyone in the United States, including servicemembers, the freedoms of speech, religion, assembly, and the press. Again, the particular nature of military service may place more restrictions on exercising these rights than civilians have. These limitations apply because some speeches or assemblies may harm the loyalty, discipline, or morale of other servicemembers, or they may reveal classified information. Because this potential harm could conflict with the need for the military to be a ready and effective fighting force, the military may restrict these freedoms among servicemembers.

Although the military can limit your rights of speech and association while you are in the service, you still have many ways to express your legitimate concerns or complaints. The key to exercising these rights is first to discuss any complaint or problem you have with your superior. Then, if your superior does not solve the problem, use the chain of command to see your commander and, if necessary, his commander. If this method does not solve the problem, use other military remedies, such as Article 138 and the inspector general system (see chapter 5). At this point, you may wish to consult a military lawyer if you have not done so earlier.

Freedom of Speech

The Uniform Code of Military Justice (UCMJ) contains several articles that restrict the speech of servicemembers. In fact, in the following cases the UCMJ makes certain language a crime:

• Article 82 makes it a crime to advise another servicemember to desert.

• Article 88 forbids officers from using contemptuous words against certain civilian officeholders, such as the president of the United States or a state governor. This article does not make it a crime to criticize an official, unless the language used is contemptuous. So, if an officer criticizes the president in a respectful manner, he has not violated Article 88. Recently, the Air Force disciplined a general for making contemptuous remarks about President Clinton.

• Article 89 makes it a criminal act to be disrespectful to a superior commissioned officer.

• Article 91 is similar to Article 89 but protects warrant and non-commissioned or petty officers from disrespect.

• Article 107 forbids making a false official statement.

• Article 117 prohibits provoking speeches or gestures, known as "fighting words or gestures."

• Article 131 makes it criminal to lie under oath in a court-martial or Article 32 investigation. This crime is called *perjury*.

• Article 134, known as the general article, makes criminal those acts of speech that are prejudicial to good order and discipline or that could bring discredit upon the armed forces. These acts, which are not necessarily crimes for civilians, include the following:

1. Disloyal statements. This part of Article 134 prohibits statements made with the intent of promoting disloyalty to the United States. Examples of this type of speech would be talking against participation in a war the United States is fighting or talking against our form of government to cause other servicemembers to be disloyal to it.

2. False swearing. This crime involves making an untrue statement under oath.

3. Indecent language. Indecent language is offensive, vulgar, filthy, or lustful language.

4. Requesting or soliciting commission of an offense. This part of Article 134 makes it a crime to ask or to advise another to commit a crime.

5. Bomb threat or hoax. Under this part of Article 134, saying that someone planted a bomb when it is not true is a crime.

6. Communicating a threat. This crime involves communicating an intention to injure another.

As you can see, your rights do not allow complete freedom of speech while you are in the military. But the crimes listed above are proper restrictions on your free speech rights because they all could harm other persons or the morale, loyalty, discipline, or readiness of the armed forces.

Not all the restrictions on free speech are in the Uniform Code of Military Justice. Some are in laws enacted by Congress, and some are in regulations of the various services. For example, a federal law prohibits officers and noncommissioned or petty officers from trying to influence servicemembers to vote for a candidate for political office. Likewise, they may not, under a Department of Defense directive, become actively involved in political campaigns. A service may also require its members to submit written material about the service for clearance before publication in civilian media. Further, the military may control the distribution of literature, especially if the writings present a clear danger to loyalty, discipline, or morale.

Although some people may feel these restrictions prevent servicemembers from expressing their grievances, the law provides other avenues for servicemembers to express complaints. Of course, a servicemember should always go through the chain of command before using another method to correct a situation. Using the chain of command is the best way to resolve the problem. Other methods will simply result in transfer of the matter to the chain of command for its comments on the situation. These other means of expressing grievances include the following:

•   Article 138, Uniform Code of Military Justice. This article permits you to petition your commander to correct a wrong he has done you. If he denies the request, he must forward the complaint through channels to the service secretary for resolution (see chapter 5).

•　Inspectors general. Servicemembers may also see an inspector general when the chain of command is unable to resolve a complaint. Again, you should go to your commander before seeing an inspector general (see chapter 5).

•　Petitioning Congress. Servicemembers have the right to petition Congress. In fact, a federal law states that no one may prevent a person from communicating with any member of Congress unless the communication is illegal or violates a national security regulation. Thus, a commander may not lawfully order you not to write a letter to a senator. But he could punish you if the letter contained classified material in violation of a regulation prohibiting distribution of secret materials. Servicemembers have no right, however, to circulate petitions on military installations among other servicemembers to get signatures to send to Congress. In other words, you may send a letter to a congressman yourself, but the military can order you not to circulate the petition around the post to get other signatures on it.

Political Activity

Servicemembers' First Amendment rights are also more limited than those of civilians in the area of political activity. Of course, servicemembers may vote for any political party or candidate or on any issue on which any other citizen may vote. But because of the military's unique status and the powers that superiors have over subordinates, a federal law prohibits officers, both commissioned and noncommissioned or petty officers, from trying to influence servicemembers to vote for a particular candidate. A Department of Defense directive also prohibits military members from participating in political campaigns. Although these rules limit your freedom of speech while you are in the military, they are necessary to protect the integrity of the political process.

Freedom of Association

The First Amendment right to freedom of association relates to freedom of speech because it involves the right to gather peaceably with other people to discuss grievances. And, like freedom of speech, freedom of assembly is not an absolute right for servicemembers. The Uniform Code of Military Justice, other laws, and regulations limit the right to associate with others when necessary to protect the loyalty, discipline, and morale of servicemembers or to ensure mission accomplishment.

Two articles—116 and 134—of the Uniform Code of Military Justice restrict association:

•　Article 116 prohibits riot or breach of the peace. A *riot* is a violent or turbulent disturbance of the peace by three or more persons for a common purpose. A *breach of peace* is a disturbance of the peace by a demonstration of a violent or turbulent nature, even by just one person acting alone.

• Article 134, fraternization, prohibits commissioned or warrant officers from improper social contacts on terms of equality with enlisted persons. These improper contacts generally involve compromising the chain of command or showing favoritism. It compromises the chain of command, for example, for a commander to date someone who works for him or her. Favoritism, on the other hand, does not necessarily involve servicemembers in the same chain of command. For instance, favoritism would occur if a personnel officer got a better assignment for someone he or she dated. Even if no compromise of the chain of command or favoritism actually exists, the appearance of either can seriously harm morale if other servicemembers believe that another received better treatment because of a relationship with a superior. Consequently, not only is fraternization a crime under Article 134, but also each service has regulations that limit the circumstances under which superiors and subordinates may socialize. For example, all training units and military schools have regulations forbidding trainers from fraternizing with trainees and instructors from fraternizing with students. If you are assigned to a training unit or military school, you must familiarize yourself with these regulations.

Many service regulations also limit associations. Generally, the military cannot prohibit membership in organizations, except for military unions. But the military can forbid servicemembers from engaging in an organization's activities that would harm the mission or be prejudicial to good order and discipline.

All services have regulations that prohibit servicemembers from participating in demonstrations on post, on duty, in uniform, in foreign countries, when the activities constitute a breach of the peace, or when violence is likely to result. Of course, a commander could permit an on-post demonstration when it would foster morale, such as a veterans parade on Independence Day. All services require approval for any demonstrations on post. Thus, for example, the services may not be able to ban membership in the Ku Klux Klan, but they can bar participation in a Klan rally when violence is likely to result. Although the military cannot prevent you from belonging to an organization such as the Ku Klux Klan or the American Nazi Party, belonging to one of them may hurt your career—by causing you to lose your security clearance, for example.

Union Membership

Several years ago some federal civilian employee unions tried to extend union membership to servicemembers. Many servicemembers were interested in having a union represent them, thinking that the union could negotiate or even go on strike for better working conditions for servicemembers. The military has always resisted unionization of its membership because it feels that unions are incompatible with good order and discipline. It does not want servicemembers to go on strike, for example, when ordered to perform dangerous or unpleasant duty. Congress has also said that servicemember unions would be incompatible with the chain of command and would hurt the readiness of the armed forces. Because of these legitimate concerns, the right of servicemembers to freedom of association has been limited regarding union membership, much as the right to freedom of speech has been limited.

Because of the move toward unionization by federal civilian employees, Congress passed a law that made it illegal for servicemembers to join or to organize military unions or to take union actions, such as picketing and striking. The law does recognize, however, that soldiers may join other nonunion organizations and associations for servicemembers, such as the Association of the U.S. Army, the Air Force Association, or the Fleet Reserve Association. If you are considering joining an organization that you think may be a union, check with your commander or a legal assistance officer to make certain that you do not violate the law that prohibits joining a union.

Freedom of Religion

Servicemembers also have the First Amendment constitutional guarantee of religious freedom. This guarantee protects the right of servicemembers and their families to follow their own religious beliefs or to have no religious beliefs. But freedom of religion is not an unlimited right. Although military laws and regulations may not forbid a religious belief, the military may ban religious practices that are harmful to others or to the military mission.

Religious beliefs sometimes cause servicemembers to feel that they cannot serve in the military without violating their beliefs. These servicemembers are called conscientious objectors. A *conscientious objector* is one who, because of religious beliefs, objects to participation in war. That objection, however, may permit participation in a noncombat role, such as serving as a medic. Conscientious objection may be a ground for discharge from the military, or it may authorize a change from combatant status to noncombatant status. Class 1-O status qualifies a servicemember for discharge if he or she is opposed to military service. Class 1-A-O is reserved for those who may serve in a noncombat role.

For the military to recognize you as a conscientious objector, you must show objection to participating in war because of your sincere religious, ethical, or moral beliefs. If you object because of other beliefs than these, or if you object only to a particular war, you do not qualify for conscientious objector status. In other words, if your belief rests on a feeling that this war is wrong on political or practical grounds, instead of on religious or moral grounds, the military will not recognize you as a conscientious objector entitled to discharge or noncombat duties.

During the Middle East crisis in 1990–91, a number of servicemembers suddenly decided to avoid going to Saudi Arabia by becoming conscientious objectors. Sudden conversions to avoid deployment don't work. A sudden conscientious objection is very unlikely to be a defense in a court-martial for desertion, going AWOL, missing movement, or similar offenses.

Your beliefs do not necessarily have to be religious in nature to qualify you for conscientious objector status, but they must be equally as important to you as religious beliefs are to a religious person. In addition, your belief must be sincere enough to convince the military that you aren't falsely trying to get out of the service (Class 1-O) or to get noncombat duties (Class 1-A-O). The belief is not sincere if it is only a temporary one, if you hold the belief only to avoid military service, or if the belief is merely a restatement of someone else's belief.

If you are thinking about applying for conscientious objector status, you should first talk to a chaplain. Although the application procedures for this status vary somewhat from service to service, the process generally requires you to talk to your commander and to a chaplain and to have a psychiatric examination. An investigating officer then conducts a hearing, studies your case, and recommends whether you should receive conscientious objector status. Finally, after a judge advocate has reviewed the paperwork and report of investigation for legal sufficiency, your commander will forward the packet through command channels.

A commanding general or an admiral may make a decision that is favorable to you, but an unfavorable one must go to the Department of the Army, Navy, or Air Force (depending on your service) for final approval or disapproval. Service regulations require that you perform only noncombatant duties while your application is pending.

If your service disapproves your application, you may resubmit it with any additional proof of the validity of your beliefs, but resubmittal is unlikely to succeed. You can also petition your service's Board of Correction of Military Records (see chapter 5). Your final remedy is to sue in a federal court. Obviously, you will want to consult an attorney to find out whether you have grounds for a lawsuit.

If your conscientious objection application is approved, you will receive an honorable or a general (under honorable conditions) discharge, depending upon how well you have served. You will also receive whatever military and veterans benefits you would otherwise be entitled to, considering the length of your service. You must normally serve three years or more to receive most Department of Veterans Affairs benefits.

Religious beliefs and military service may also conflict when a particular religious practice conflicts with a military duty. For example, a conflict would arise when a servicemember believes his religion requires that he not work on Sunday and he is assigned Sunday duties. Another servicemember may believe he must wear a religious symbol that is incompatible with wearing a uniform. These examples illustrate that although the military permits free-dom of religious belief, the practice of that belief cannot interfere with the performance of the military mission or with good order and discipline. Thus, a conflict between a religious belief and an order is not a defense to a charge of disobeying a lawful order, and a court-martial could find you guilty regard-less of the sincerity of your belief.

The Department of Defense permits religious practices that do not have an adverse effect on readiness, health, safety, or good order and discipline. For example, your religion may require you to wear a beard, but your service will not permit you to have one because it would interfere with a protective (gas) mask. (Some bearded, turbaned Sikh servicemembers may still be serv-ing who entered the service before a policy barring them from entering mili-tary service if they refused to shave and to remove the turban became effective.) Your service may allow you to wear unobtrusive religious articles, however. Certainly, a small religious emblem on a neckchain worn under the uniform would not be a problem. But the military will not permit a head cov-ering, a beard, excessively long hair, special clothes, a special diet, or refusal to undergo certain medical treatments.

Again, you are free to believe or to disbelieve, but the practice of your beliefs must not interfere with military necessities. If you have a religious practice that you feel may interfere with your military service, talk to a chap-lain or to a military attorney before acting on that belief.

YOU AND THE FOURTH AMENDMENT

The Fourth Amendment to the U.S. Constitution protects servicemembers as well as civilians from "unreasonable" searches and seizures. A *search* is a hunt for evidence to use against a suspect in a criminal prosecution. An *unreasonable search* is one that a government official conducts without proba-ble cause, without a search warrant, or without other authority to examine you or your property. A *seizure* involves taking property to use as evidence against a person accused in a criminal prosecution.

This amendment protects you only from unreasonable searches and seizures by government officials. If a private citizen or a soldier who has no supervisory authority over you and is not performing law enforcement duties searches your car, seizes property there, and turns it over to the police, the government has not violated your Fourth Amendment rights. If the military police or your commander, however, searches your car in a unreasonable manner, they have violated the Fourth Amendment.

The Fourth Amendment protects you and your property only when you have an expectation of privacy in that area. This expectation of privacy requirement has two parts: Did you believe that the property was in a private place? Does society think that it was reasonable for you to believe that the place was private?

For example, one reasonable expectation of privacy case involved garbage. The suspect put evidence of his drug crimes in garbage bags and set them out for the garbagemen to pick up. The police told the garbage collector to give them the suspect's garbage bags instead of taking them to the dump. The police did not have a search warrant. At the trial, the suspect claimed that the evidence from the garbage bags could not be used against him because it resulted from an illegal search. He said he had an expectation of privacy because he thought that, since the evidence was tied up in garbage bags, no one could look at it. The court decided that once he had set his garbage out on the street, he had abandoned it and that society would not find his expectation of privacy to be reasonable. Thus, the police did not need a warrant and the evidence could be used against him.

Therefore, if a government official searches an area in which you have a reasonable expectation of privacy, the search must be reasonable or it violates the Fourth Amendment. You should note that the law does not recognize an expectation of privacy in the desk you use on duty. It is a government desk, and your supervisor can search it without your permission or a search authorization. The same holds true as to information in a government computer. You would have a reasonable expectation of privacy in a desk in your home or your barracks room, however. But how does the law protect you from unreasonable searches and seizures? The police cannot use the property they find or take from you as evidence against you if they violate your rights by an illegal search or seizure. This remedy is called the *exclusionary rule*. So, if military police search you or your property in an unreasonable manner, the military cannot use any evidence it finds in such a search against you in a trial by court-martial.

The key to the whole subject of search and seizure is the word *unreasonable*. The Fourth Amendment does not protect against all searches and seizures, just against unreasonable ones—those without probable cause, a warrant, or other authority. This rule is another example of the difference between civilians' rights and those of servicemembers. Although both civilians and military members have the right to be free from unreasonable searches and seizures, what is an unreasonable search of a civilian's home might be an entirely reasonable search of a servicemember's barracks room or berthing compartment. Again, this difference exists because of the military's need for good order and discipline and readiness to perform its mission—concerns that do not apply to a civilian's home.

Reasonable Searches
The law allows several kinds of searches, and each has different rules that the government must follow to make it "reasonable." It's important for you to know about the consent search because you must make decisions about this type of search. Anyone may waive (give up) the right to be free from unrea-

sonable searches and seizures. Thus, the law recognizes that you may consent to be searched (see the accompanying form). Not only may you consent, but also anyone who has control over the place to be searched may consent.

CONSENT TO SEARCH FORM

Date _____

Location _____

I, _____(1)_____ , having been advised of my constitutional right *not* to allow a search of my person, home, belongings, or property (including wall or footlockers) without a search warrant or commander's authorization, both of which would have to be based on probable cause, and having been advised of my right to refuse to consent to or to voluntarily allow such a search, hereby AUTHORIZE _____(2)_____ to conduct a complete search of _____(3)_____ for _____(4)_____ and to seize any or all of such item(s) if found within the areas I have allowed to be searched.

This permission is given by me to the above-named persons voluntarily and without threats or promises of any kind. I understand that I can refuse to give permission to search, that I can limit my permission to search to a specific area, and that I can withdraw my permission to search at any time.

_____
(Signature of individual granting permission)

_____
(Signature of witness)

_____
(Printed name, rank, and unit of witness)

Directions for Use

1. Insert name of individual whose person, property, or area is to be searched.
2. Insert names and titles of individuals who are to conduct the search.
3. Insert specific areas to be searched (e.g., individual's locker, quarters, person).
4. Insert items to be searched for with as much specificity as possible.

For example, your spouse could consent to a search of your home. Or your spouse could consent to a search of your car if you and your spouse owned it jointly. If law enforcement personnel found contraband, such as drugs or stolen property, after your spouse consented to the search of your home, they could use it as evidence against you in a trial by court-martial. Of course, the prosecution would have to prove that you had possession of the contraband, but if they found it in your house, it would certainly appear to be in your possession.

Before a court-martial judge would admit evidence found as a result of a consent search, the prosecution would have to show that you voluntarily gave consent. The law does not require that law enforcement personnel use any particular magic words when asking for your consent. The following factors would show a judge that the consent was voluntary:

• If the official asking you for consent told you that you had the right to refuse to consent.

• If the official asking you for consent told you what he was looking for.

• If the official told you the specific area that he wanted to search.

• If the official read you your rights against self-incrimination before asking you to consent.

• If you were not in custody.

On the other hand, the following factors would show that the consent was not voluntary:

• If the official told you that he would search with or without your consent because he had a search warrant.

• If the official threatened to harm you or a family member to force you to consent.

• If the official promised you that any evidence found would not be used against you or that the government official would not try to punish you.

• If you consented only because the official asking for your consent was your military superior so you thought you had to consent.

• If the official mistreated you to force you to consent.

By now you know you do not have to consent, despite what a military policeperson or other official may tell you. Furthermore, if you do consent, you may limit that consent. If, for example, an officer asked you to consent to a search of your car, you could say, "OK, but not the trunk." And, although you have given consent, you may withdraw it at any time. You may say, "Stop searching. I no longer consent." The law enforcement officer must then stop, unless he has another valid authority entitling him to search, such as a search warrant.

If you refused to consent, the prosecutor could not use your refusal against you at a court-martial to prove that you were guilty. A refusal to consent to a search is not admissible in court because it does not prove guilt. You may refuse consent for reasons other than to hide evidence. For example, you may want to keep perfectly legal possessions private. Further, your refusal does not give law enforcement officials probable cause to search. If you do not consent to a search of your body or your property, the law enforcement officials need another basis for the search.

The most well-known reasonable search occurs under the authority of a search warrant, often called a *probable cause search*. The military calls its version of a search warrant a *search authorization*. The major difference between search warrants and search authorizations is who may issue them. Only civilian judges and magistrates may issue search warrants. But in the military, commanders, as well as judges and magistrates, may issue search authorizations. Three conditions must exist before any of them may issue a search authorization:

1. The official issuing the authorization must be neutral and detached. Being unbiased usually is not a problem with judges and magistrates because their jobs require them to be neutral and detached. Commanders, however, may not be unbiased. If, for example, the commander was the victim and wanted to see that the suspect was punished, the commander would have a personal interest in the case. The commander would also not be neutral and detached if he had too great an interest in the criminal investigation.

2. The person issuing the search authorization must have authority over the person or place to be searched. Military judges and magistrates can issue an authorization to search the body of any servicemember anywhere under military control or to search any property on military grounds. A commander may only authorize a search of the body of a servicemember of his command or of property within his unit area. A civilian judge must issue a warrant for off-post property.

3. The person authorizing the search must have probable cause. *Probable cause* requires the person authorizing the search to have a reasonable belief that what he is looking for is in the place in which he is searching. A reasonable belief means a 51 percent or greater probability. The person authorizing the search may have a reasonable belief for many reasons, but he must base his belief on facts, not rumors or guesses. A military judge would decide whether the belief was reasonable based on what the authorizing official knew at the time he authorized the search. The judge would not evaluate the reasonableness of the belief by what the searcher found.

If a law enforcement officer has a search authorization to search you or your property, you have the right to require the officer to tell you of the authorization and what he is searching for. He must also give you a receipt for any property that he takes.

In several situations, however, law enforcement officials may search without an authorization. Although the law enforcement officials must have probable cause, in the following situations they do not need a search authorization:

1. When they do not have enough time to get an authorization. If the delay necessary to get a search authorization would result in removal, destruction, or concealment of the evidence, law enforcement officers do not need an authorization.

2. When they have no communication means. When, because of the military mission or another good reason, they cannot communicate with a judge, a magistrate, or a commander, officials may search without an authorization if they have probable cause.

3. When they want to search an operable vehicle. An *operable vehicle* is a car, a truck, or any other vehicle that can be driven. Because of the ease with which someone may drive a car away and, hence, remove any evidence along with it, the law relaxes the requirement to have a search authorization when law enforcement officers have probable cause to search vehicles.

The law recognizes other reasonable searches besides probable cause searches. Although these searches are not based on probable cause or under the authority of a search authorization or warrant, they are reasonable because they do not invade an area in which the suspect has a reasonable expectation of privacy or because society's interest in preventing some harm, such as the spread of disease or the failure to accomplish a military mission, outweighs the individual's rights. Other than consent searches, the following searches do not require probable cause:

• *Searches of government property*. Officials may search some government property without a search authorization or probable cause. Whether, without probable cause, they may search government property you might put something in depends on whether your unit issued the property to you for your personal use. For example, your unit would normally issue a personal wall locker in your barracks room. A desk in your military office would generally not be for your personal use. A commander, supervisor, or law enforcement official may search government property not issued for personal use without probable cause or a search authorization.

• *Border searches*. Civilian courts have a rule that permits warrantless searches of persons crossing international boundaries, and it applies equally to the military. This exception to the probable cause requirement is based on the need to protect the security of the nation from those who enter the country illegally or bring in illegal items from other countries. You should not possess contraband, such as illegal drugs, at any time in the military, as discussed in chapter 7. But it is especially foolhardy to try to smuggle contraband across an international border. If, for example, border guards searched you and found contraband, even without probable cause or a warrant, it would be admissible as evidence against you in both courts-martial and civilian courts.

- *Searches upon entering or leaving overseas military bases, ships, or planes.* For much the same reason as for border searches, commanders overseas may authorize searches of persons and property entering or leaving overseas bases, ships, and planes, without probable cause and without a search authorization. Entering such military bases is legally the same as crossing an international border, from the country the base is in to a part of the United States. Although such a base is not actually a part of the United States, because the area is under U.S. military control, it is sufficiently U.S. territory to authorize this version of a border search to protect the facility from unauthorized persons or items.

- *Searches when a law enforcement officer stops you.* If a law enforcement official sees you doing something unusual that he considers wrong, he may question you. If he has a reasonable belief that you are armed and dangerous, he may frisk you for weapons. During this "pat-down" search, if the law enforcement official feels something in your pocket, for example, that might be a weapon, he can reach into the pocket to remove the weapon. If he discovers drugs or other contraband in your pocket when properly searching for a weapon, it would be admissible against you in a court-martial. If he does not feel anything like a weapon while searching, but he reaches in the pocket anyway, nothing he finds would be admissible.

- *Searches during arrest.* This type of search is called a *search incident to a lawful apprehension.* As further explained in chapter 7, the military calls taking a suspect into custody an "apprehension," whereas civilians call it an "arrest." When he takes you into custody, the apprehending official may search you and the area within your immediate control (where you could reach to grab a weapon or to destroy evidence) without a search authorization and without probable cause to search. In other words, the apprehending official may conduct this type of search if he properly arrests you, even if he doesn't suspect the presence of a weapon or evidence.

- *Searches in confinement facilities.* Commanders of military confinement facilities, such as brigs and stockades, may authorize searches of prisoners and confinement facilities, including cells, without probable cause. The law allows this type of search to protect guards and other prisoners and because prisoners do not have a reasonable expectation of privacy while in jail.

Military Inspections

Commanders and other supervisors will inspect most servicemembers sometime during their military service. And if an inspector finds contraband during an inspection, it may be admissible as evidence even without a search warrant. Because of the need to make certain that the military is ready to protect the country, such inspections do not violate the Fourth Amendment.

According to the Manual for Courts-Martial, an inspection is "an examination of the whole or part of a unit, organization, installation, vessel, air-craft, or vehicle, including an examination conducted at entrance and exit points, conducted as an incident of command the primary purpose of which is to determine and to ensure the security, military fitness, or good order and discipline of the unit, organization, installation, vessel, aircraft, or vehicle." The manual also states that inspections include examinations to find unlaw-ful weapons and other contraband, such as illegal drugs. An inspection may include urinalysis to test for illegal drugs.

A commander's authority to inspect would be meaningless without the authority to take corrective action if the inspection turned up something that could harm the unit's ability to perform its mission. Thus, if any inspection in your area turns up contraband, such as illegal weapons or drugs, the com-mander may seize it because you have no legal right to possession. As long as the commander did not use the inspection as a means to avoid getting a search authorization, he could also use the contraband as evidence against you in court-martial or at an administrative discharge board, which could dis-charge you from the military with an other-than-honorable discharge (see chapter 4). Because Military Rule of Evidence 313 in the Manual for Courts-Martial authorizes inspections specifically for contraband, a commander may use marijuana detection dogs or other aids to help him find contraband. Thus, it is sheer folly to possess drugs on military installations. See chapter 7 for a further discussion of the penalties for drug crimes in the military.

The commander's right to inspect his command includes testing his per-sonnel to ensure that they are fit to perform their mission. Mandatory urinal-ysis testing is another type of inspection. If your commander orders all or a part of his command to provide urine samples and your sample tests positive for drug use, he can use the test results against you at a court-martial or in an administrative proceeding, such as a discharge board. Thus, it is unwise as well as illegal to use drugs off duty, off base, and on leave.

YOUR RIGHT TO DUE PROCESS OF LAW

The Fifth Amendment to the U.S. Constitution provides that "no person shall . . . be deprived of life, liberty, or property without due process of law." This clause means that the government cannot take one's life, freedom, or property without giving him *due process*. Due process is a term that is hard to define. The simplest definition may be fairness. Any legal proceedings that can take life, liberty, or property must be fair. For such a proceeding to be fair, the person facing the action must receive notice of the action and an opportunity to explain why it should not occur.

Because the term "person" includes servicemembers, the military cannot deprive you of life, liberty, or property without affording you due process—notice and an opportunity to defend yourself. The Fifth Amendment applies to criminal proceedings, civil lawsuits, and administrative actions that could deprive persons of life, liberty, or property.

Servicemembers have the following due process protections when they face a criminal trial:

- Notice of the charges. The commander must give a servicemember facing court-martial a copy of the charge sheet and supporting paperwork.
- The presumption of innocence. The law presumes the accused at a court-martial to be innocent until proven guilty beyond a reasonable doubt. You do not have to prove your innocence. Rather, if the prosecution does not prove that you are guilty beyond a reasonable doubt, the court-martial must find you not guilty. The requirement for the government to prove you guilty means that if the prosecutor's evidence is not enough to convince the military judge or court members (jury) that you are guilty beyond a reasonable doubt, they must find you not guilty, even if you present no evidence on your own behalf.
- A speedy trial. The purpose of the speedy trial right is to keep criminal proceedings with all their uncertainties and adverse effects on the accused, from dragging on for extended periods.
- A public trial. This right protects those tried by court-martial by allowing the public to observe the proceedings to ensure fairness.
- A fair and unprejudiced court. Both the judge and the court members (jurors) must be fair and unbiased.
- The right to see, hear, and confront (cross-examine) prosecution witnesses.
- The right to present evidence and to call witnesses.
- The right to counsel. The law recognizes that the assistance of a lawyer is indispensable to the accused in a criminal trial.

See the discussion on courts-martial in chapter 7 for a more complete explanation of these due process rights in criminal actions as well as the due process rights in nonjudicial punishment actions under Article 15, Uniform Code of Military Justice. Similar due process rights apply in civil trials as well.

Although many people think of due process rights primarily in regard to criminal and civil trials, these rights also apply to adverse administrative actions that can affect one's life, liberty, or property. The law defines an *adverse administrative action* as a noncriminal proceeding to take an unfavorable action against an individual. Common administrative actions in the military include the following:

- Unfavorable efficiency report. If your efficiency report is not favorable, you get notice (a copy of the report) and an opportunity to explain why it is not accurate (an appeal).
- Letter of reprimand. Again, you get a copy of the letter and an opportunity to convince the commander that you should not receive it.

- Involuntary career field reclassification.
- Administrative reduction in rank.
- Security clearance suspension or revocation.
- Monetary liability for lost or damaged government property. See the discussion on property accountability in chapter 5.
- Administrative discharge.

Because administrative actions are not quite so serious as criminal ones, they do not provide the full range of due process rights found in criminal actions. But due process rights are important because you are more likely to be involved in an administrative action than in a criminal one.

You must do something illegal to become involved in a criminal action, but you may become involved in an administrative action through no fault of your own. For example, if you become disabled, the military may seek to discharge or to retire you for physical disability. You would then invoke your due process rights to prevent the loss of your military job without the chance to demonstrate why you should remain on active duty.

The amount of due process that the military must afford a servicemember when taking an administrative action against him depends on balancing the seriousness of the government's interest in taking the action against the seriousness of the harm to you. If the government's interest is more serious, as in, perhaps, a security clearance revocation, the interest in safeguarding classified information would outweigh your rights. In this case, the government would have to provide you only minimum due process—notice of the action and an opportunity to defend yourself. On the other hand, if the harm to you outweighs the government's interest and is very serious—if, say, the government discharges you from the service with an other-than-honorable discharge, thereby disqualifying you from military and VA benefits—the government must provide you more due process rights.

To exercise your due process rights intelligently, consult an attorney as soon as you receive notice of an administrative action that your service plans to take against you. Often, such as if you receive a letter of reprimand, you will not have an attorney to represent you before a board of officers because the governmental interest outweighs the harm to you. Consequently, the regulations do not authorize you to present your side of the situation to a board of officers. But you can usually consult a military lawyer who will help you prepare a response—your opportunity to explain. Although you may want the military to take the action against you, such as a discharge, you should still consult a military attorney, who would be aware of any harmful hidden effects. Make certain you take with you a copy of the proposed administrative action when you consult the attorney.

YOUR PROTECTION AGAINST CRUEL PUNISHMENT
The Eighth Amendment prohibits cruel and unusual punishment. Although servicemembers in the 1800s could be whipped or subjected to other cruel punishments, today servicemembers are protected from these types of punishments by the Eighth Amendment, as well as by Article 55 of the Uniform Code of Military Justice.

CONCLUSION
These and other constitutional protections safeguard your fundamental rights as a servicemember. Two keys to a successful military career are to understand your constitutional rights and to consult a lawyer to ensure that you exercise them intelligently.

3

Civil and Other Rights

The term *civil rights* refers to your rights to be free from discrimination based on race, color, religion, national origin, or sex. The U.S. Constitution guarantees these rights to all citizens, including servicemembers. For example, various amendments guarantee equality of voting rights for all citizens—the government may not discriminate against prospective voters because of their race or color.

Federal and state laws also protect your civil rights. The Civil Rights Act of 1964, for example, forbids discrimination because of race, color, religion, national origin, or sex in such areas as public housing, education, and employment. The law also prohibits retaliation for protesting discrimination, for exercising your rights under the Civil Rights Act, or for being a witness in an action brought under the Civil Rights Act. In addition, the Department of Defense and each service have policies to promote equal opportunity for all servicemembers and their families. Many Department of Defense directives and service regulations also protect servicemembers and their families from civil rights violations.

Civil rights problems that service families may encounter normally fall within the areas of housing, public accommodations, employment, and education.

HOUSING
Sometimes home sellers or landlords discriminate against service families when they try to find a place to live off post. If they discriminate against you, help is available both from the federal government under the Fair Housing

Act and from the military. The Fair Housing Act makes the following acts illegal if based on race, color, religion, national origin, or sex:

- To refuse to rent or sell to a person a place to live.
- To discriminate in the terms of a sale or rental agreement. For example, a landlord could not require a greater deposit from a Muslim than from a Christian.
- To pretend no dwelling is available to avoid offering it to a minority member.
- To use discriminatory advertising.
- To discriminate against children. Landlords may not refuse to rent to families with children.

The Fair Housing Act, however, has several exemptions. The act does not forbid the above practices when the offending party is one of the following:

1. A religious organization or a private club.
2. A multiple-unit dwelling of not more than four units when the owner lives in one of them.
3. A single-family house, so long as the owner does not own more than three houses.

The military may be able to help, however, when an owner who falls into one of these exempt categories discriminates against you.

If someone discriminates against you while you're seeking a place to live and the person or organization is not exempt from the Fair Housing Act, you have three ways to proceed under the act.

First, you can file a complaint with the Department of Housing and Urban Development (HUD). You must file the complaint within 180 days after the violation. HUD must investigate the complaint within 30 days. If HUD finds a violation, it will try to persuade the offender not to discriminate, but if it cannot, you have 30 days to sue the offender. This four-step procedure is called *conciliation*.

Second, you may sue the offender in federal district court for a violation of the Fair Housing Act or in a state or local court for a violation of state or local law. You do not necessarily have to file a complaint with HUD as explained above to file a lawsuit. If you sue under the Fair Housing Act, you must start the suit within 180 days after the violation or within 30 days after a HUD conciliation has failed. The federal court may even appoint an attorney to represent you in such a lawsuit and may permit the lawsuit to be filed without paying fees and court costs. If you win, the court can order the offender to stop discriminating and award you damages, court costs, and attorney's fees.

Third, if a person or group engaged in a pattern of resistance to fair housing denies you housing, or if a group you are a part of has been denied fair housing, the Attorney General of the United States may sue the offenders in federal court. If the Attorney General wins, the court may issue an injunction ordering the offender to stop the discrimination. The Fair Housing Act also provides for criminal penalties if discrimination involves the use, or threatened use, of force to prevent someone from getting housing.

What should you do if you are a victim of discrimination? First, you should consult a local housing referral officer or a legal assistance officer. You then have the choice of using the military's programs to end discrimination or using the federal government's programs as discussed above.

Often the military's programs to end discrimination in housing will be easier, quicker, and more effective than either working with Housing and Urban Development or suing the offender. A command fair housing program may also be able to help you if the discrimination is by a person or group that is exempt from the Fair Housing Act, such as the owner of a single-family house who does not own more than two other houses. Instead of filing a complaint with HUD or suing in civilian court, you may file a complaint with your command. The command will investigate the complaint, and if it is valid, the commander may forbid any servicemembers from moving into the offender's housing. In effect, the commander puts the property "off limits."

If the military's programs prove ineffective, you can try the federal government's antidiscrimination programs. A legal assistance officer may even help you prepare a complaint for HUD. If you sue the offender, however, you will probably have to hire a civilian attorney.

Fortunately, the military's antidiscrimination programs usually prevent you from being a housing discrimination victim. Military housing referral offices list only landlords and home sellers that show they will not discriminate, and servicemembers may only rent from landlords or buy from sellers listed by military housing referral.

PUBLIC ACCOMMODATIONS

Servicemembers and their families may also encounter discrimination in such public accommodations as hotels and motels, restaurants, places of entertainment (such as theaters, sports arenas, and concert halls), gas stations, and establishments inside or next to one of these public accommodations (such as a drug store in a hotel).

Title II of the Civil Rights Act of 1964 makes it illegal to discriminate in these, and similar, public accommodations. State or local laws may also prohibit discrimination. For example, North Carolina passed a law that makes it illegal to discriminate against servicemembers who want to enter public places. Title II does not cover private clubs and establishments that are closed to the public, but state or local laws may. If you experience discrimination at a motel, restaurant, or another public accommodation, you have several legal remedies:

Sue the offender. If a local law prohibits the discrimination, you may have to give the offender written notice of the violation. Then, if the offender does not stop discriminating, you may sue him in federal district court. If no state or local law covers the discrimination, you may immediately sue in federal court. The court may either decide the case or refer it to the Department of Justice's Community Relations Service. That agency would try to reach a voluntary settlement with the offender. If it could not, the case would go back to the federal district court, where the judge may allow you to file your lawsuit without payment of fees and costs. If you win, the court would order the offender to stop the discrimination. The court may also order the offender to pay your lawyer fees and court costs.

Let the U.S. Attorney sue the offender. The U.S. Attorney may also bring a civil suit in federal district court when a person or group is practicing resistance to nondiscriminatory public accommodation. If the offender uses force to harm, to intimidate, or to interfere with you when you are seeking nondiscriminatory public accommodations, his resistance is a federal crime, and the U.S. Attorney may prosecute the offender in a federal court.

Get military assistance. The military is against discrimination both on and off post. If an off-post public accommodation discriminates against you, your commander may place it off limits. Although the military permits private clubs on post, such as rod and gun clubs or wives' clubs, if they are open to the general public, they must not discriminate against minorities. If a club does discriminate against you, the military can cancel its permission to operate on post.

EDUCATION

Another area of potential discrimination is public education. If someone discriminates against you or your family members when you try to go to school, the law has a number of protections for you. For example, Title IV of the Civil Rights Act of 1964 prohibits discrimination in public schools. The act allows the U.S. Attorney General to sue in federal district court to stop discrimination in public schools based on race, color, religion, national origin, or sex. You may also be able to file such a lawsuit if an educator discriminates against you or one of your family members. In addition, a federal law, 18 U.S. Code Section 245, makes it a crime to use force or intimidation to prevent someone from attending public schools and colleges. Also, state and local laws may protect you from discrimination in education.

Similarly, Title VI of the Civil Rights Act prohibits discrimination by activities, including educational ones that receive federal funds. Activities that receive federal funds must have rules that comply with federal nondiscrimination laws. If federally funded activities do discriminate, the government will end their federal financial assistance. So, if you or a member of your family experiences discrimination in school, report it to your commander, to your installation's equal opportunity officer, or to a legal assistance officer.

EMPLOYMENT

Some of the most important of our civil rights concern our military service or our civilian careers. All of us want our employers to hire, to promote, and to treat us on the basis of our performance and not on the basis of race, sex, age, or other factors that have nothing to do with how well we do our jobs. The U.S. government agrees and has enacted laws to protect federal and civilian employees.

Your Right to Be Free from Job Discrimination

Title VII of the Civil Rights Act as amended protects workers that work in local, state, and federal government or for an industry or a business that has more than fifteen workers for at least twenty weeks of the year. The act could protect you, as a servicemember, if you have a part-time job. It also protects any family members who work. The act prohibits discrimination based on race, religion, sex, color, or national origin. This law also prohibits retaliation for making a discrimination complaint, for exercising your rights to be free from discrimination, or for being a witness in a civil rights case. Thus, if you were fired for making a discrimination complaint, you could sue under the Civil Rights Act.

Employers covered by this act may not refuse to hire, may not fire, and may not deprive a person of an employment opportunity, such as a promotion, for a discriminatory reason. If religion, sex, or national origin is a necessary qualification for the job, however, it is not illegal discrimination to use such criteria in employment decisions. For example, it would not be illegal discrimination for a church to refuse to hire a person who is not a member of the clergy to be a minister. Very few jobs, however, cannot be filled by a member of either sex.

The federal government established the Equal Employment Opportunity Commission (EEOC) to help prevent discrimination in employment. If you are a victim of such discrimination, the EEOC can investigate your complaint and, if the complaint is valid, try to correct the situation by conferring with the offender. If the EEOC cannot resolve the complaint, it may sue on your behalf, unless the offender is a state or local government. In those cases, the U.S. Attorney General must bring the lawsuit.

If an employer discriminates when you try to get a job or to get a promotion, you may also sue in federal court. Again, the court may waive fees and court costs and appoint an attorney for you. If your complaint is valid, the court may order the offender to comply with Title VII of the act or order the employer to reinstate you in a job, pay you back pay, or take similar actions.

The act also protects you in another way. Forcible injury, intimidation, or interference in seeking employment or employment benefits because of race, color, religion, or national origin is also a federal crime, so the U.S. Attorney could prosecute such an offender in federal court and send him to jail for violating your civil rights.

If the military discriminates against you, your spouse, or your child when seeking a job or obtaining the benefits of employment, you should use the chain of command to try to resolve the problem. If the command cannot solve the problem, you should next go to a legal assistance officer or to the equal opportunity office for help.

An example of the federal government's policy prohibiting illegal sexual discrimination on the job is the Equal Pay Act of 1963. It forbids sex-based pay differences when the work performed is of equal skill, effort, and responsibility. It does not, however, prohibit pay differences based on other factors, such as seniority or merit.

Some people feel that it is discriminatory that women cannot enlist when they are single parents, cannot be drafted, or cannot serve in combat. These policies rest on a court ruling that says that if the employer has a valid occupational qualification for a job, hiring only people with that qualification is not illegal discrimination. The courts, including the Supreme Court of the United States, have found that these practices by the military are not discriminatory because of the military's need for a fighting force that can deploy immediately in a national crisis. This legal principle is also the logic behind the military's regulations that require single parents who are on active duty to have plans to take care of family members if the parent must deploy (see chapter 9). Because of the excellent performance of women servicemembers in Operations Desert Shield and Desert Storm, however, the role of women in combat is expanding. The Navy now permits women to fly combat aircraft, for example.

Sometimes employers discriminate against people because of age or physical condition. The government's antidiscrimination policy, however, also protects older people and those who are disabled. The federal Age Discrimination in Employment Act protects federal civilian job applicants and employees who are at least forty years old from discrimination in hiring, pay, job conditions, and discharge from employment because of age. Similarly, the federal Rehabilitation Act and the federal Americans with Disabilities Act protect disabled or handicapped employees from discrimination, as may state and local laws. Procedures for getting relief from illegal discrimination based on age or handicap are similar to those for complaints based on other discriminatory practices. The military services also have policies that try to give full consideration to hiring and to fully employing the disabled. If disabled applicants are qualified for the job, the employer must consider them equally with able applicants. Further, working places must have accommodations, such as wheelchair ramps, for the disabled.

Your Right to Be Free from Sexual Harassment at Work

Although some jobs are closed to female servicemembers, the policy of the Department of Defense is that all servicemembers and civilian employees be free from illegal discrimination and sexual harassment. The so-called "Tail-hook" incident demonstrated that, notwithstanding the policy, the services have certainly not eradicated sexual harassment. Nevertheless, the increased attention the incident focused on sexual harassment may help to eradicate it in the long run. The 1984 Manual for Courts-Martial added a passage to Article 93, Cruelty and Maltreatment of a Subordinate, to ensure that military law made sexual harassment illegal.

The Federal Personnel Guide defines sexual harassment as deliberate or repeated unsolicited and unwelcomed verbal comments, gestures, or physical contact of a sexual nature. A supervisor who uses coercive sexual behavior to control, influence, or affect the career or compensation of a subordinate is violating DOD policy. Likewise, if the subordinate performs similar acts that interfere with job performance, it is a form of sexual harassment.

If a superior, a subordinate, or a coworker commits sexual harassment, don't put up with it. Report it to your commander, an equal opportunity officer, or even the military police.

Other Employment Rights

State or local law may provide additional employment protections of special interest to servicemembers and their families. Some states prohibit discrimination on account of an unfavorable discharge, although typically they do not prohibit discrimination against a person with a dishonorable discharge. Some states prohibit discrimination based on sexual orientation.

Other laws that protect workers include minimum wage and overtime pay laws, protection for whistleblowers (those who report unsafe conditions or illegal acts), and workers compensation.

VOTING

As long as you are at least eighteen years old, you can vote whether you are a servicemember or a civilian. Under federal law, no official may deny a citizen the right to vote based on race or color. Nor is it legal to intimidate or to coerce people to keep them from voting.

Generally, the states may not deny new residents the right to vote, so long as they have resided in the state for some minimum period (often thirty days). Those who have not lived in the state for such a period may vote by absentee ballot in the state they left. Title 42 of the U.S. Code requires the states to permit members of the military and their families who are stationed away from their legal residence to vote by absentee ballot. It also allows citizens living outside the United States to vote by absentee ballot in the state they lived in before going overseas.

If the state you are stationed in won't let you register to vote, or if you have any other problems voting, see your commander, your voting assistance officer, or a legal assistance officer.

OTHER RIGHTS

Federal law gives servicemembers other important rights. Two acts that are especially important are the Freedom of Information Act and the Privacy Act. Both acts limit the government's ability to manage information.

Freedom of Information Act

Because of citizens' concern that the federal government was getting too secretive, Congress passed the Freedom of Information Act (FOIA) to guarantee the public more access to government information. Military departments must make documents available to members of the public if they make a proper request, unless the documents fall within one of nine exemptions to the FOIA and releasing the documents would hurt the government. Of course, the military services give you many of your records, such as your personnel record, without requiring you to file a request under the FOIA.

A proper FOIA request for a document reasonably describes the record and complies with the agency's (here the agency is the branch of service) rules. Although each service has somewhat different rules, the services generally require a written request describing the record. The agency may also require the payment of reasonable fees for duplicating the record. A legal assistance officer, a civilian attorney, or a records custodian could help you find out the requirements for requesting the particular record you want.

The military or other agency must release the requested record unless the law exempts the record from release and its release would be harmful to the government. Of the nine exemptions, only seven may apply to the military:

• *Exemption one, classified records.* If information is properly classified, it is exempt from release. If you do not believe the information you want is properly classified, you could sue in federal court to have the court review the documents.

• *Exemption two, internal personnel rules and practices.* This exemption covers operating rules, guidelines, manuals, procedures, and schedules when disclosure would hurt the effective performance of the military department.

• *Exemption three, other federal withholding statutes.* If another federal law restricts public access to government information, such as the law prohibiting the release of alcohol and drug abuse patients' records, the agency may withhold this information under this exemption.

• *Exemption four, business information.* This exemption refers to "trade secrets and other commercial or financial information" that is privileged or confidential. The purpose of this exemption is to protect those who submit information to the government in such matters as bidding for government contracts.

•   *Exemption five, certain agency memoranda.* This exemption protects certain confidential communications that the law protects from disclosure in trials. Examples include memoranda of decision-making and matters privileged by the attorney-client relationship (see chapter 7).

•   *Exemption six, personnel, medical, and similar files.* This exemption protects the privacy of individuals by preventing unwarranted disclosure of such information as their medical condition.

•   *Exemption seven, investigatory records compiled for law enforcement purposes.* This exemption protects such records as those about confidential informants, those whose release would deprive a criminal defendant of a fair trial, and those whose release would hurt law enforcement by disclosing investigative techniques or endangering law enforcement personnel.

From this list of exemptions it may seem as though most records are exempt from release. But just because a record may be within an exempt category does not mean that it cannot be released. If you ask for an exempt record, the government agency must give it to you unless its release would harm the agency. The agency has the burden of showing this harm. The agency must also disclose portions of otherwise exempt records that are releasable. The Freedom of Information Act provides a workable method of getting government records that you cannot get otherwise.

Privacy Act

The Privacy Act is related to the Freedom of Information Act because Congress passed it to protect people from unwarranted disclosure of information about them by the government. For example, you might not want the government to release your efficiency reports or your medical files to anyone who asks for them.

The Privacy Act applies to records kept within a system of records. Such a system is one in which the government keeps information about an individual by means of the person's name or an identifying number, a code, or a symbol. The act both restricts the government's ability to maintain such records and gives individuals rights to maintain their privacy.

The act places the following requirements on the government:

•   *Public notice.* To prevent government agencies from keeping secret systems of records, the government must announce in the *Federal Register* whenever it establishes a system of records.

•   *Collection of information from the subject.* The act requires the government to collect information about you from you as much as possible. This requirement reflects the ideas that you are the most accurate source of information about yourself and that having you provide the information would ensure that you knew the government was collecting the information.

- *Privacy Act advisement.* The government must advise the person from whom it is collecting information of the authority to collect the information, the principal use for collecting the information, the routine uses that the government will make of the information, whether disclosure is mandatory or voluntary, and the effect of not providing the requested information.

- *Relevancy requirement.* The act allows a government agency to maintain in its records only information that is necessary to the purpose for which the record is collected. For example, a military hospital may keep your medical records to treat you properly if you need medical care, but it could not keep your financial records because that information has nothing to do with giving you good medical care.

- *Accuracy requirement.* The act requires agencies to make certain that the information they keep is accurate and complete.

- *Prohibition on information about First Amendment rights.* In chapter 2 we discussed your First Amendment rights of freedom of speech, association, and religion. The act enforces the First Amendment by forbidding the government from keeping records about how an individual exercises those rights. The only exceptions are if the individual consents to the government keeping such a record, if a law authorizes the keeping of such a record, or if the record is a law enforcement record.

Your rights under the Privacy Act include the following:

- *Access rights.* The act provides a right for you to get access to your records and to make a copy. If the agency involved denies your request to see your records, the agency must provide an administrative appeal in which the agency will have to justify denying such access. The Privacy Act, however, has some of the same exemptions as the Freedom of Information Act. For example, the Central Intelligence Agency and federal law enforcement agencies are exempt from providing you access to their records. Also exempt is defense information if its disclosure could hurt national security.

- *Amendment rights.* The right to gain access to one's records is meaningless without the right to correct them. Thus the act provides that you may request that an agency correct an inaccurate record about you. If the agency does not correct the record, you may appeal. If the agency denies the appeal, you can file a statement saying why the record is wrong. If you do, your statement must be attached to the record if the agency gives it to anyone.

- *Disclosure prohibition.* Perhaps the most important rule of the Privacy Act prevents agencies from disclosing information on you, unless either you consent or one of the following exemptions applies:

1. Disclosure within an agency where letting others have the record is necessary if the agency is to perform its functions. For example, a military hospital could transfer your records from one clinic to another so that the right doctor could treat you.

2.   Disclosures that the Freedom of Information Act requires. Even under this exception, however, an agency cannot release records that involve a "clearly unwarranted invasion of personal privacy," such as an efficiency report.

3.   Routine use. This exception involves using records for the purpose for which the agency collected them, such as using an immunization record to see whether your shots were current.

4.   Law enforcement. An agency may disclose records to other federal or state agencies for purposes of law enforcement. For example, if a state law enforcement official arrested you, the military could tell the state whether you had a military criminal record.

5.   Court orders. This exception permits disclosure when required by a court order. For example, in a divorce case, a court might order the military to provide information about your income, so that it could decide how much alimony and child support would be proper.

6.   Debt collection. This exemption permits the government to notify a consumer reporting agency (see chapter 15) that an individual has not repaid a debt, such as a student loan, to the United States.

The Privacy Act provides for criminal penalties for people who violate some of its provisions. For example, it is a crime for an agency employee to disclose information he knows the act prohibits him from disclosing. If an agency violates your rights under the act, you may bring a lawsuit against the agency in a federal court. You could seek an injunction (a kind of court order) to prevent the agency from disclosing information about you. You could also sue for damages if the agency had already released the information.

AIDS TESTING

The military may legally test you for AIDS when you have a physical. If you test positive, your commander may lawfully issue a "safe sex order." Such an order may include the following:

•   A requirement for the infected servicemember to inform his or her partner of the presence of AIDS or the AIDS-causing virus.

•   A requirement for the infected servicemember to use barrier protection—a condom—any time he or she has sexual relations. The infected servicemember must not pass any body fluids such as semen, saliva, blood, and so on.

•   A requirement that the infected servicemember refrain from certain sexual practices, regardless of whether the partner consents and regardless of the partner's sex, specifically oral-genital sex and anal intercourse.

Violation of any of these orders can result in a court-martial, imprisonment, and a dishonorable discharge.

CONCLUSION

If you feel that someone has violated your rights, you should, as with any other complaint, discuss the problem first with your superior and then with your immediate commander. If the chain of command cannot solve the problem, each service has agencies, such as family housing officers and equal opportunity officers, to help you. You may also need to see a military attorney or the inspector general in some cases. Whatever your rank or position, you can help promote the military's policy to stop discrimination.

4

Discharge from the Service

The military discharges servicemembers for several reasons—both good and bad—and with several consequences—both good and bad. A good reason with good consequences would be the honorable completion of a term of service with an honorable discharge and veterans benefits. A bad reason with bad consequences would be committing a crime with a dishonorable discharge and the loss of veterans benefits.

Being discharged from the military is different from quitting a civilian job or being fired. As discussed in chapter 1, the difference is that your military service is more than just an employment contract. It is also a status. And the duties and responsibilities of that status mean you must qualify for a discharge by completing your service obligation or qualify for an early release for either a good or a bad reason.

Discharges fall into two broad categories: administrative and punitive. Administrative discharges are most common. An administrative discharge is one that the military gives for a variety of good and bad reasons without having a court-martial. The military gives a punitive discharge only with a court-martial sentence as punishment for criminal misconduct. The administrative and punitive categories include a number of types of discharges.

ADMINISTRATIVE DISCHARGES
The military has three types of administrative discharges: honorable, general under honorable conditions, and other-than-honorable. Honorable and general discharges are reserved for servicemembers who have served honorably and thus qualify for veterans and military benefits to which they are entitled. Most Department of Veterans Affairs (VA) benefits require two years of honorable service.

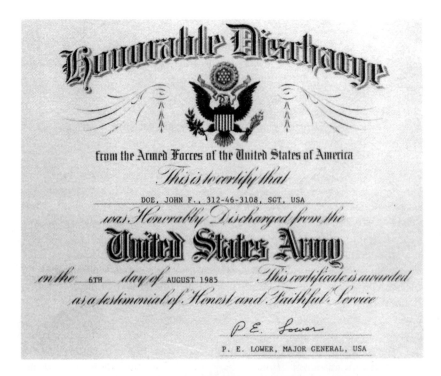

An honorable discharge certificate

Although both honorable and general discharges are under honorable conditions, the best type of discharge—and the only type you should settle for—is an honorable discharge. An *honorable discharge* means that you have served your period of service honorably. It does not mean that you did everything perfectly or never made a mistake. You can get an honorable discharge even with a court-martial conviction on your record if it was for a minor crime and you served honorably before and after the conviction.

A *general discharge,* under honorable conditions, is for those who have served honorably but not as well as those who receive an honorable discharge. For example, a servicemember who had a court-martial conviction on his record and was discharged for alcohol abuse might get a general discharge. If you received a general discharge, you would qualify for the same benefits as a servicemember who got an honorable discharge, but you might suffer some prejudice. Some employers, for example, will not hire servicemembers who do not have fully honorable discharges.

An honorable or general discharge makes you eligible for VA benefits, although the VA might not give you all of them if you have a general discharge. These are some of them:

- *Disability compensation.* In addition to military disability retirement pay or severance pay, the VA pays disability pay to those who become disabled because of their military service. If you retired or separated for physical disability, you should file a VA claim. Although you cannot get both the full amount of your military disability pay and VA disability pay, the VA may also pay monthly payments to your family members. If you lose an arm or a leg or have other severe disabilities, the VA may pay extra disability compensation.

- *Medical benefits.* Disabled veterans who are entitled to VA disability compensation also may receive VA medical care, such as hospitalization and outpatient care.

- *VA insurance.* If you are discharged or retired with a service-connected disability, the VA makes life insurance available to you.

- *Educational assistance.* Several programs exist that encourage servicemembers to make voluntary contributions to an educational fund. Some of these programs include matching funds by the federal government. The noncontributory GI Bill terminated on December 31, 1989.

- *VA guaranteed home loans.* (see chapter 13).

- *Burial rights* (see chapter 9).

Obviously, an important part of your discharge is getting a job once you are out. If your service was honorable, you qualify for the following assistance in finding employment:

- Reemployment rights. A federal law requires your employer to give you your job back if you meet the following conditions:

    1. You served for four years or less or you served for five years because the military required you to do so.
    2. You received a discharge under honorable conditions.
    3. You are qualified to perform the job you're applying for.
    4. You applied within ninety days after separation from service.

If you meed these qualifications and your employer won't rehire you, contact the nearest Veterans Reemployment Rights office of the Department of Labor. If this office can't solve the problem, you or the U.S. Justice Department may sue the employer.

- Federal employment preference. The federal government gives several advantages to veterans who apply for federal jobs. For example, you may qualify for extra points on a federal civil service examination. If you are a Vietnam-era veteran, you may not have to take an examination; instead, you agree to enter a training program. You may also get special consideration to allow you to remain working when others are laid off.

- State and local employment preferences. Many state and local governments also give honorably discharged veterans job preferences similar to the federal ones.

• Federal laws require government contractors to take affirmative action to hire Vietnam veterans and disabled veterans.

Grounds for Good Administrative Discharges

Your service can discharge you under honorable conditions in several ways. Although the specific grounds for discharge may differ among the services, generally your service may discharge you for one of the following reasons:

• *You have finished your enlistment or period of obligated service.* Your service would provide you an honorable or general discharge certificate for such a separation.

• *As a result of a reduction in force,* even though you had not finished your enlistment or period of obligated service.

• *You are a conscientious objector* (see chapter 2). A conscientious objector discharge would be an honorable or a general one because there is nothing wrong with being a conscientious objector if you have followed the proper procedures. If, however, you disobey orders or otherwise get into trouble, your service could give you a less-than-honorable discharge.

• *You have a medical problem.* A medical discharge may be awarded if your condition is serious enough that you cannot perform your duties. You may be medically retired if you meet the following criteria:

1. The condition did not result from your willful misconduct or neglect.

2. The condition did not happen during a period of AWOL.

3. You have twenty years of service or a required shorter period if the military is currently offering early retirements.

4. Your disability is at least 30 percent and is service connected. Service connected means that it occurred because of your military service.

If you haven't served in the military long enough to retire, you would be discharged with severance pay instead of retirement pay. If you did not incur the injury in the line of duty, you would not receive the severance pay (see chapter 5).

Because the military often discharges servicemembers involuntarily for medical reasons, it must provide due process so that you have the opportunity to contest the discharge. Your service would permit you to present your explanation at a medical board at which you could show why you should not be discharged or that the percentage of your disability is greater than the doctors say (important for VA disability compensation). Because the rules concerning disability are very complicated, you must see an attorney when contesting a medical discharge.

Usually, the medical board, called the Physical Evaluation Board (PEB), meets informally and makes an initial recommendation based on your medical and personnel records. You would not be present at this initial meeting. If you agreed with the board's findings, the board would send a report to an official designated by your service secretary for his review. If you didn't agree with the board's findings, you could request a formal hearing, which you could attend with an attorney. Your service would appoint military counsel for you, or you could hire a civilian attorney. If, after the formal hearing, you were satisfied with the recommendations of the board, your case would be sent to your service secretary's designate for review. If you were not satisfied with the board's recommendations, you could submit a rebuttal, which would be included with the board's findings that would go to the official who would review the case. If, after this step, you were still not satisfied, each service has a physical disability review board in Washington that may hear your case. After a physical disability review board heard your case and reviewing officers approved the board's findings and recommendations, your service secretary would make the final decision whether you should receive a medical discharge. Even after that decision, however, you could appeal to your service's board of correction of military records (see chapter 5).

• *You may qualify for a hardship or dependency discharge.* If a condition has arisen during your military service that causes extreme, permanent hardship to your family, you may qualify for this type of discharge. Such hardship is usually based on financial or medical problems. It would result in an honorable or general discharge certificate. To receive this type of discharge, you would have to show, through statements by people such as doctors or ministers, the seriousness of the problem and that a discharge is the only way to correct it. A military chaplain is often the best person to talk to about such a discharge. If the condition is temporary, however, the military may instead grant a compassionate reassignment, so you would be stationed close to your family.

• *You are pregnant.* You may request that your service discharge you for pregnancy.

• *You have a problem with drugs or alcohol.* The grounds for an honorable or general discharge under these circumstances generally involve your failure to be rehabilitated by a drug and alcohol abuse program. If someone catches you in possession of or using drugs, however, your commander could discharge you with an other-than-honorable discharge or even court-martial you (see chapter 7).

• *You are unsuitable for the service.* If you cannot or will not adapt to military life, are untrainable, or have some other problem that makes it unlikely that you will become a satisfactory servicemember, the military may discharge you.

• *You are underage.* If you enlisted before you were old enough (less than age seventeen or less than age eighteen without parental consent), you are eligible for discharge for minority. In these cases, you were never really in the service, so the military would not give you a discharge certificate. Instead, your service would simply release you from active duty.

• *You retire for length of service.* If you have served honorably for at least twenty years or such lesser period as required when the military is seeking early retirements, you may retire. To retire as a commissioned officer, you must have served at least ten of the twenty years as an officer. You would normally retire in the grade you were serving in when you retire. Retiring servicemembers receive additional benefits, such as retirement pay, medical care, and such privileges as use of the commissary. Retirement, however, is not as complete a severance of military status as is a discharge. The military may recall you to active duty if you are a retired regular officer, and retired regulars are subject to court-martial jurisdiction. Federal laws also place restrictions on the jobs retirees may hold and prohibit them from engaging in transactions that may be in conflict with the federal government (see chapter 16).

Grounds for Bad Administrative Discharges

The worst type of administrative discharge is a discharge under other-than-honorable conditions. *Other-than-honorable discharges* are roughly equivalent to bad-conduct discharges and result in the loss of many military and veterans benefits.

When the military seeks to take an adverse action against you, such as discharging you and taking away any benefits you have earned, it must provide you due process (see chapter 2). If the military tries to discharge you with an other-than-honorable discharge, it must give you administrative due process by holding an administrative board, which would let you present your case to the board with the assistance of a lawyer. The board procedure would also allow you to have your lawyer cross-examine witnesses testifying against you and present evidence on your behalf, including witnesses to testify on your behalf.

The grounds for receiving an other-than-honorable discharge all involve some type of misconduct, such as the following:

• *Fraudulent enlistment.* If you concealed something in your past that would have disqualified you from entering the service, such as a civilian felony conviction, your service could discharge you for fraudulent entry. Because fraudulent enlistment is also a criminal offense under the Uniform Code of Military Justice, your commander would decide whether to get you an administrative discharge or to try you by court-martial.

• *Conviction by a civilian court.* If a civilian court convicts you for a serious offense, your service may discharge you. Accordingly, you should consult with a military attorney about the military consequences of a civilian conviction before deciding how to proceed in civilian court (see chapter 8).

• *Commission of a serious offense.* Generally, a serious offense is a felony offense in civilian court or one punishable by a punitive discharge if tried by court-martial. Common felonies include murder, robbery, rape, assault with a dangerous weapon, and serious drug offenses. If you commit a serious offense, the command has the option of trying you by court-martial or discharging you administratively. Your commander may try to use an administrative discharge board for misconduct in a case that may be difficult to try by court-martial, such as spouse or child abuse when the victim cannot or will not testify in court.

• A *pattern of misconduct*. A pattern of misconduct involves a number of minor offenses, such as short absences without leave, disrespect to superiors, disobedience of orders, and so on.

• *Homosexuality*. With the adoption of the new "Don't Ask—Don't Tell" policy concerning homosexuals in the military, the law is a lot more complicated than it was under the previous policy, under which gays could not serve in the military. In the past, gays could be discharged fairly easily regardless of whether they actually engaged in homosexual conduct and also faced court-martial for engaging in any homosexual conduct that violated the Uniform Code of Military Justice. In other words, under the former policy, homosexual orientation alone was disqualifying. Now, under the current policy, so long as one does not "tell" that he or she is gay and does not engage in homosexual activity, he or she should be able to continue service in the military. Several gay servicemembers have challenged the new policy in the courts, however, based on arguments such as that the policy violates their rights to freedom of speech. Thus, the future of the policy is unclear. A gay servicemember should consult with a military attorney before divulging his or her sexual orientation and refrain from engaging in any homosexual activity that violates the Uniform Code of Military Justice or harms good order and discipline at least until the law clears up.

PUNITIVE DISCHARGES

Of the four types of bad discharges a servicemember can receive, three are punitive, given by a sentence of a court-martial for criminal misconduct. Punitive discharges include bad-conduct discharges, dishonorable discharges, and dismissals. (The fourth type of bad discharge, the discharge under other-than-honorable conditions, is an administrative discharge.)

The most severe punitive discharge is a *dishonorable discharge*. A court-martial may sentence a servicemember to a dishonorable discharge when his crime warrants a discharge under conditions of dishonor. Such crimes as murder, rape, robbery, and drug sales often result in dishonorable discharges. The officer version of a dishonorable discharge is called a *dismissal*.

The other type of punitive discharge is a *bad-conduct discharge*. It also is for serious crimes, although less serious than those a dishonorable discharge covers. Often, long AWOLs, stealing, and military crimes, such as disobeying an order or assault of an officer, result in bad-conduct discharges.

Punitive discharges result in the loss of substantially all military and veterans benefits. In addition, servicemembers with punitive discharges may encounter prejudice in civilian life because of the stigma of a bad discharge certificate. For example, some employers may not hire them. For more about the military criminal justice system that handles punitive discharges, see chapter 7.

The grounds for punitive discharges involve committing a crime that has a maximum penalty under the Uniform Code of Military Justice that includes a dismissal or a dishonorable or bad-conduct discharge. Not all crimes under the UCMJ authorize a punitive discharge, but all serious crimes, such as murder, rape, robbery, larceny of valuable property, disobedience of a superior commissioned officer, and long AWOLs, authorize a court-martial to sentence the accused to a punitive discharge.

CONCLUSION

Regardless of which discharge your service may consider giving you, unless it is an honorable discharge, you should see a military attorney to ensure that you understand your rights and the consequences of the particular discharge involved. Many servicemembers say they "just want out," regardless of which discharge they will get. I have talked to many of them who "got out" with some lesser form of discharge who later encountered prejudice and wanted to upgrade their discharges. Each service has a discharge review board that may upgrade a discharge (see chapter 5), but all in all, the military rarely upgrades discharges. Get an honorable one the first time!

As you can see after reading part 1, although the particular requirements of military service change your rights somewhat, the Constitution, federal laws, and service regulations adequately protect you. And if you fulfill your obligations to the military, not only will you have the satisfaction of having served your country well, but also you will qualify for military and veterans benefits as the holder of an honorable discharge.

PART II

Your Legal Remedies

Even if you follow all the rules for having a good period of military service, something may still go wrong. You may be in an accident, your property may be damaged in a move, or you may be sued. The military wants you to be able to help defend our country without undue worry about family and personal affairs, so it has a number of legal procedures and protections to help you if you suffer a loss while on active duty. These remedies, however, cannot help you unless you know what they are and know how to use them intelligently. Chapter 5 explains the military's claims system and other military remedies, and chapter 6 explains lawsuits you may file and those someone may file against you.

5

Claims and Remedies

Unfortunately, servicemembers and their families sometimes suffer losses or experience adverse actions because of their military connection. The federal government has provided a system to compensate service families for these losses and to correct wrongs done to them. Of course, the government also has a system to compensate it when someone harms the service. An example is the medical care recovery system, in which the government seeks reimbursement for the medical expenses of servicemembers or family members when the care was necessary because another person injured the victim.

The system created to protect you consists of many remedies, including seeing your commander, the claims system, and discharge review boards. These remedies are all administrative because they do not involve going to court.

When administrative remedies fail, however, you may need to go to court (see chapter 6). First, though, you must usually try to exhaust the administrative remedies or to have an improper action corrected. For example, if a military doctor commits medical malpractice and harms your spouse, you cannot sue the government without first having filed a claim that the government denied. If you tried to sue the government without first trying the claims system, the judge could dismiss your lawsuit (see chapter 6).

Several situations could cause you to use these administrative remedies: a moving company could damage your household goods in a move; your commander could refuse to recommend you for promotion for an improper reason, such as discrimination; you could be injured in a car accident that was the fault of a military driver; or a servicemember could steal your stereo. Each of these situations would have a different remedy. As a general rule, however,

you should always go through your chain of command because many remedies require you to try to solve the problem in this way first. Even when they
don't, you should go through the chain of command to get excused from your
duties to pursue the matter. Also, using the chain of command is often the
easiest, most effective remedy.

You need to know about the military's claims system because you may
need to make a claim yourself, or the military may make one against you. A
claim is a written demand for money due to the person making the claim. The
money may pay for property loss or damage, death, personal injury, medical
expenses, or burial costs. If you suffer injury as the result of something another
person, a business, or a government organization does, you may file a claim
against the other person or activity. Under some circumstances, the federal
government may file a claim against you. Also, although it is beyond the
scope of this book, you may be able to file a claim against a state government.

CLAIMS AGAINST THE U.S. GOVERNMENT

You can file a claim against the government when you have suffered loss or
damage connected with your military service if the government has enacted a
law that authorizes paying you for that loss or damage. For example, the government may pay you for damage to your household goods caused by a move
from one duty station to another on government orders by paying a claim
under the Military Personnel and Civilian Employees' Claims Act. A different act, the Federal Tort Claims Act, would cover a different loss, such as an
injury caused by an accident to a servicemember's spouse that was the fault of
a military driver. Each act has different rules. Consequently, unless it is a very
simple claim, such as for damaged household goods caused by a move, you
should consult an attorney.

The government set up the claims system to pay what it rightfully owes
you, so don't hesitate to file claims for what you think the government owes
you and your family because of your military service. On the other hand, be
careful not to misuse the claims system because Article 132 of the Uniform
Code of Military Justice, which deals with frauds against the United States,
makes it a crime to file a false claim against the United States. When in
doubt, check it out; go ask your legal assistance or claims officer.

The Military Personnel and Civilian Employees' Claims Act

The most important claims act for you to know about is the Military Personnel and Civilian Employees' Claims Act because it will pay you for damages
to or loss of personal property, such as a car or a stereo. You can file this kind
of claim if, for example, a military move damaged your household goods. You
must meet three conditions before the military will pay a claim under this
act: the loss or damage must be incident to service; the property must be reasonable for you to have; and the loss or damage must not be your fault.

CLAIM FOR LOSS OF OR DAMAGE TO PERSONAL PROPERTY INCIDENT TO SERVICE

PART I - TO BE COMPLETED BY CLAIMANT (See reverse side for Privacy Act Statement and Instructions.)

1. NAME OF CLAIMANT (Last, First, Middle Initial)	2. BRANCH OF SERVICE	3. RANK OR GRADE	4. SOCIAL SECURITY NUMBER

5. HOME ADDRESS (Street, City, State and Zip Code)	6. CURRENT MILITARY DUTY ADDRESS (If applicable) (Street, City, State and Zip Code)

7. HOME TELEPHONE NO. (Include area code)	8. DUTY TELEPHONE NO. (Include area code)	9. AMOUNT CLAIMED

10. CIRCUMSTANCES OF LOSS OR DAMAGE (Explain in detail. Include date, place, and all relevant facts. Use additional sheets if necessary.)

	YES	NO
11. DID YOU HAVE PRIVATE INSURANCE COVERING YOUR PROPERTY? (E.g., say "Yes" on a shipment or quarters claim if you had transit, renter's or homeowner's insurance; say "Yes" on a vehicle claim if you had vehicle insurance. Attach a copy of your policy.)		
12. HAVE YOU MADE A CLAIM AGAINST YOUR PRIVATE INSURER? (If "Yes," attach a copy of your correspondence. If you have insurance covering your loss, you must submit a demand before you submit a claim against the Government.)		
13. HAS A CARRIER OR WAREHOUSE FIRM INVOLVED PAID YOU OR REPAIRED ANY OF YOUR PROPERTY? (If "Yes," attach a copy of your correspondence with the carrier or warehouse firm.)		
14. DID ANY OF THE CLAIMED ITEMS BELONG TO THE GOVERNMENT OR TO SOMEONE OTHER THAN YOU OR YOUR FAMILY MEMBER? (If "Yes," indicate this on your "List of Property and Claims Analysis Chart," DD Form 1844.)		
15. WERE ANY OF THE CLAIMED ITEMS ACQUIRED OR HELD FOR SALE, OR ACQUIRED OR USED IN A PRIVATE PROFESSION OR BUSINESS? (If "Yes," indicate this on your "List of Property and Claims Analysis Chart," DD Form 1844.)		

16. UNDER PENALTY OF LAW, I DECLARE THE FOLLOWING AS PART OF SUBMITTING MY CLAIM:

If any missing items for which I am claiming are recovered, I will notify the office paying this claim. (For shipment claims.) Missing items were packed by the carrier; they were owned prior to shipment but not delivered at destination; after my property was packed, I/my agent checked all rooms in my dwelling to make sure nothing was left behind.

I assign to the United States any right or interest I have against a carrier, insurer, or other person for the incident for which I am claiming; I authorize my insurance company to release information concerning my insurance coverage.

I authorize the United States to withhold from my pay or accounts for any payments made to me by a carrier, insurer, or other person to the extent I am paid on this claim, and for any payment made on this claim in reliance on information which is determined to be incorrect or untrue. I have not made any other claim against the United States for the incident for which I am claiming. I understand that if any information I provide as part of my claim is false, I can be prosecuted.

17. SIGNATURE OF CLAIMANT (or designated agent)	18. DATE SIGNED (MMDDYY)

PART II - CLAIMS APPROVAL (To be completed by Claims Office)

19. PROCEDURE (X one)	20. AMOUNT AWARDED. The claim is cognizable and meritorious under 31 U.S.C. 3721; the claimant is a proper claimant; the property is reasonable and useful; the loss has been verified in accordance with applicable procedures as prescribed by the controlling departmental regulation; and the following award is substantiated:	
a. SMALL CLAIMS		$
b. REGULAR CLAIMS		

21. SIGNATURES (Signatures at a and c not required if small claims procedure is utilized.)

a. CLAIMS EXAMINER	b. DATE SIGNED (MMDDYY)	c. REVIEWING AUTHORITY	d. DATE SIGNED (MMDDYY)
e. TYPED NAME AND GRADE OF APPROVING AUTHORITY	f. SIGNATURE OF APPROVING AUTHORITY		g. DATE SIGNED (MMDDYY)

DD Form 1842, DEC 88   *Previous editions may be used until exhausted.*   119 I/3

You may use this Department of Defense form to put in a claim for property damage under the Military Personnel and Civilian Employees' Claims Act.

The most important of these three conditions is that the loss or damage must be "incident to service." *Incident to service* means that the loss or damage must have occurred within the boundaries of normal military service, such as during permanent changes of station, when household goods are in storage, or when living in quarters.

The second condition is that the government will pay you for loss of or damage to property under this act only when your possession of the property is "reasonable, useful, or proper under the circumstances." This clause means that the property must be the normal type of property a member of your service and rank would have. If it is not, it is not protected by this act. For example, if you had a $50,000 painting in your quarters, the government might well refuse to pay a claim if it were damaged, because it is not reasonable for a servicemember to have such a valuable item in his quarters. If you have such property, you need private personal property insurance. The regulations about what property this act covers and the maximum dollar amount of the coverage vary from service to service. Thus, if you have either a great deal of property or some that is very valuable, you should contact a claims officer to see whether you need personal property insurance.

The third condition that you must satisfy before the military will pay a claim under this act is that the loss or damage must not have been your fault. The military will not pay a claim if the damage or loss resulted from either your negligence or something you did wrong. For example, if you left a diamond ring on the kitchen table and left your quarters unlocked, so that anyone could walk in and take the ring, the government would not compensate you for the loss because of your failure to safeguard the ring.

Even if you have satisfied these three conditions, however, the military will not automatically pay any claim you make. The Military Personnel and Civilian Employees' Claims Act covers losses of or damage to personal property only in the following situations:

- *In quarters*. The circumstances under which you may claim compensation for loss of or damage to your property in your quarters vary depending on your service and location. For example, overseas the military may pay you for losses due to floods, fires, hurricanes, and so on, whether you live on or off post. Within the United States, however, the military will pay for such losses only if you live in government quarters. If you don't, you need personal property insurance, renter's insurance, or a homeowner's policy that covers personal property.
- *In storage*. If a servicemember's personal property is in storage because of official orders, or if the property is in a government facility where it is normal to leave such property temporarily and leaving it there is incident to service, the military will pay a claim for its loss or damage.
- *During transportation*. Transporting household goods causes more claims for damage or losses than any other situation under the act. A "during

transportation" claim applies when the government moves your property at government expense, even if a private company is actually moving the personal property.

*   *During aircraft or ship disasters.* This ground for a valid claim covers your losses during travel only when your losses are incident to service, not when you lose your luggage when you are flying on a commercial airline on leave.

*   *As a result of enemy action.* This ground for payment of a claim does not require that the loss or damage happen during a declared war. A guerrilla action in a country in which we have a military mission, for example, would qualify as enemy action.

*   *Other circumstances.* You may file claims under certain other situations, so if your personal property is lost or damaged, you should go to a claims office and find out whether you can file a claim.

If you have a claim under the Military Personnel and Civilian Employees' Claims Act, you must file it within two years from the date the loss or damage happened or from the time you should have discovered it. The government may extend this two-year period during time of war.

To make a claim, you must file a written claim with a claims officer. You will have to *substantiate the claim.* This legal term means that you must describe the property, show you had possession of it, give details of how the property was lost or damaged, provide receipts (especially for video equipment, tapes, and cassettes), and establish the replacement or repair cost. Then the claims service will investigate your claim. Make sure you don't fudge when you fill out the form because filing a false claim is a serious offense under the Uniform Code of Military Justice. It is punishable by a dishonorable discharge and confinement for five years.

The government will not pay a claim that should be paid by someone else, such as an insurance company or whoever caused the loss or damage. If a commercial carrier or warehouse, for example, caused the loss or damage, or if you have an insurance policy that may cover the claim, you may have to make a demand for payment for the loss or damage by the carrier, the warehouse, or the insurance company as part of the claims procedure. In that event, you will receive the claim money from the government, and the government will get the money back from the carrier or insurer. The amount of money the government pays you will also reflect depreciation of your property. *Depreciation* is the decrease in the value of property because of age and wear and tear. For example, your sofa will decrease in value after several years of your children spilling drinks and climbing on it.

When you submit a claim, the claims officer will decide whether to pay it, if it is within the dollar amount he can approve. If he approves some or all of the claim, your acceptance of that amount is a full and final settlement of the claim. You cannot later ask for more money for that loss. If the claims officer does not have authority to settle the claim, he will send it to a higher-level claims office for decision. If the claim is denied or paid in an amount less than you think you should receive, you may ask for reconsideration of the claim and submit additional substantiation of the claim.

The Federal Tort Claims Act
Congress passed Federal Tort Claims Act (FTCA) to compensate victims of *torts* (wrongs) committed by the government (see chapter 6 for a more detailed discussion of torts). The FTCA provides for monetary compensation to victims for damage to or loss of property or for personal injury or death caused by a wrongful or negligent act of a U.S. employee who was acting within the scope of his employment. Unlike other claims acts, this act sets no dollar limit on the amount of the claim.

Not everyone may file a claim under the Federal Tort Claims Act. Civilian employees or their surviving family may not, for example, if they are injured or killed while performing their duties. Of more importance to servicemembers, however, is the rule that they cannot be compensated under the FTCA for injuries or death that happens "incident to service" (the *Feres* doctrine). The phrase *incident to service* means more than performing duties. The following situations are among those that are incident to service:

• The harm happened on military property.

• The harm happened when the victim was on duty.

• A command relationship between the government employee and the victim caused the harm to the victim. *Command relationship*, as used here, is broader than merely within the same chain of command. The phrase refers to any relationship that might disrupt command authority. Medical malpractice is one example of the breadth of the phrase command relationship. Although your doctor may not be in your chain of command, under the *Feres* rule you cannot sue the government for harm you receive because of negligent or wrongful medical care; to allow such claims would threaten a disruption of medical care for all servicemembers and their families.

• The harm happened while the servicemember was using a military benefit, such as space-available transportation or commissary privileges.

Thus, if you are a servicemember, you cannot file a claim under the FTCA unless the harm happened while you were both off duty and off post, and the harm must have been unrelated to command relationships or special military privileges or benefits. The U.S. Supreme Court recently refused to throw out the *Feres* rule, so it remains the law. Congress has considered amending the FTCA to permit claims and lawsuits by servicemembers who are the victims of medical malpractice in military medical facilities but has not, as yet, done so. So if you are a servicemember and are injured by your military service, it would be wise to consult a lawyer to see whether you can file a claim under the Federal Tort Claims Act in case Congress changes the law or your situation is one of the rare ones that are not barred by the *Feres* rule.

As a military member, you normally cannot use the FTCA to file claims for your injuries, but it is still important to understand the act because your spouse and other family members could receive compensation for their injuries under the FTCA—even if they were receiving military benefits, such as hospital care. For example, if you and your spouse were injured on post in a car accident caused by the driver of a military vehicle, your spouse would have a valid claim against the government under the FTCA. As a servicemember, however, you would not; because your injury occurred on military property, it would be incident to service. For your spouse to have a proper claim, the FTCA requires that the government employee must have been acting within the scope of his employment. This means that the driver in this example must have been driving on duty and not have deviated from his route for some personal reason. If he was not on duty, your spouse would have to sue the driver as an individual rather than put in a claim against the government under the FTCA.

This act has several exceptions. The government will not pay a claim, nor could you sue the government, if a government employee harmed you under the following conditions:

• The harm happened overseas.

• The harm was the result of combat activities.

• The government employee did the harm by committing assault, battery, false imprisonment, false arrest, malicious prosecution, abuse of process, libel, slander, misrepresentation, deceit, or interference with contract rights. Again, check with a claims officer or an attorney, because other ways to receive compensation may exist.

Recent cases have allowed service family members to sue the U.S. government for tort actions arising out of complying with regulations. For example, the court permitted a lawsuit against the government for damages arising from an accident involving a lawn mower that was being used to comply with a base order to mow housing area grass. And, you could certainly sue a government employee as an individual if he assaulted you.

The law of the state where the harm happened determines whether the government is liable. State law controls what acts are wrongful or negligent and what defenses the government may have. Thus, you must consult a legal assistance officer or civilian lawyer who knows the state's law to determine whether you should file a claim under this or some other act.

Under the Federal Tort Claims Act, you must file a claim within two years after the date the harm happened or the date you knew or should have known of the harm. If the government denies the claim, you have six months to sue in federal court. You may make a claim under the act at any military claims office. Your claim must consist of a written, signed demand on the government for a specific dollar amount of damages. The claims office will investigate your claim, and the government will approve your claim, negotiate a compromise with you, or deny your claim. If the government does not pay or settle the claim, you may sue the government in federal district court (see chapter 6). Because of the complexity of the FTCA, you should consult an attorney if your claim may involve a large sum of money.

The Military Claims Act

The Military Claims Act is another act under which you may be able to file a claim. This act covers personal injury or death and property damage on two grounds. First, as under the Federal Tort Claims Act, the government may pay a claim for harm caused by governmental employees acting within the scope of their employment. The other ground concerns "noncombat activities." This term does not include every military activity other than actual combat. Under this act, noncombat activities are those that do not have any civilian equivalent, such as field training exercises, weapons drills, and movement of combat vehicles, such as tanks, fighter planes, or destroyers. If noncombat activity causes damage or injury, it is unnecessary to prove negligence or a wrongful act as it is under the Federal Tort Claims Act. It is generally enough to prove that the noncombat activity caused the loss.

Just as under the Federal Tort Claims Act, you, as a servicemember, cannot claim damages for personal injury or death if your injury was incident to service (see the discussion above about the Federal Tort Claims Act). In addition, the military will normally pay for your property damage under the Military Personnel and Civilian Employees' Claims Act instead of this claims act. If, however, your lawyer or a claims officer tells you to use this act, you must submit a written claim within two years of the harm or when you learned of it. No provision under this act allows you to file a lawsuit against the government if the military does not pay or settle the claim.

Article 139, Uniform Code of Military Justice

Article 139 of the Uniform Code of Military Justice compensates victims of certain crimes committed by servicemembers for loss of or damage to their property caused by the crime. If another servicemember steals or willfully damages your property, for example, you can complain to your commander under Article 139. The commander will usually investigate the claim by appointing a board of officers to conduct the investigation. If the board finds that a servicemember wrongfully took or willfully damaged your property, your finance office will collect the amount of money due from the wrongdoer's pay and pay it to you. You may consult a victim assistance officer (see chapter 7) to find out whether an Article 139 complaint is proper and to get help in making one if it is.

YOUR OTHER REMEDIES

Sometimes money cannot compensate for the wrong done to you. Thus, the claims system cannot solve every problem by providing money as restitution. The military provides further remedies, however, to correct other problems, such as an improper discharge or passover for promotion based on an improper reason.

Discharge Review Boards

Part of the system Congress created to solve servicemembers' problems is the discharge review board. A discharge review board consists of five members, usually high-ranking officers. It can review a discharge to upgrade it, if appropriate, as from other-than-honorable to honorable or general (see chapter 4). These review boards can only reconsider administrative discharges; they cannot upgrade punitive discharges given by courts-martial, such as bad-conduct or dishonorable discharges.

If you feel that your type of discharge is unfair, you can seek to have a discharge review board upgrade it. You must ask the board to do so within fifteen years of the issuance of the discharge. You may present evidence to the board, either on your own or with the help of a lawyer. The board will also consider your military records. It is not easy to get a discharge upgraded. You would have to show that your discharge was given you improperly or unfairly.

You can contact the discharge review board for your service at one of the following addresses: Air Force Discharge Review Board, Air Force Personnel Council, 1745 Jefferson Davis Highway, Washington, DC 20330; Army Discharge Review Board, Army Council of Review Boards, 1941 Jefferson Davis Highway, Washington, DC 20310; and Navy (includes Marine Corps) Discharge Review Board, Naval Council of Review Boards, 801 N. Randolph Street, Arlington, VA 22203.

To upgrade your discharge, you must first fill out Department of Defense (DD) Form 293, *Application for Review of Discharge or Dismissal from the Armed Forces of the United States.* You can get this form from a military personnel officer or a VA center. You may want the assistance of an attorney in preparing the application and the supporting materials. You will need to submit evidence, either with the application or later, to show how and why the discharge was unfair or improper. You can do this entirely by submitting documents, such as your military records, or you can have a hearing either in Washington or at a more convenient location.

If the board denies your application to upgrade your discharge, you may either ask the board to reconsider or appeal to the secretary of your service. You can also try to get your service's board of correction of military records to upgrade your discharge. Finally, in rare circumstances, you could sue to have your discharge upgraded.

Boards of Correction of Military Records

Boards of correction of military records are not limited to correcting improper discharges. Although they can consider such cases, they can also consider other matters, such as an improper denial of a promotion or a missing notation that you had received a medal. These boards also can consider cases involving punitive discharges, which are beyond the jurisdiction of discharge review boards.

Unlike discharge review boards, boards of correction of military records comprise civilians, not military officers. Each service has a board of correction of military records, which can correct an error in a military record if you bring it to the board's attention within three years of the time you learned of the error. The board may grant an exception, however, and consider a case involving an error that is more than three years old.

You may contact your service's board of correction of military records at one of the following addresses: Air Force Board for Correction of Military Records, The Pentagon, Washington, DC 20330; Army Board for Correction of Military Records, The Pentagon, Washington, DC 20310; and Navy (includes Marine Corps) Board for Correction of Military Records, The Pentagon, Washington, DC 20370.

You should use DD Form 149, *Application for Correction of Military or Naval Record*, to ask your service's board to correct your records. You will have to submit proof to show that your military record is incorrect. The requirement that you prove the record to be incorrect illustrates the importance of reviewing your records and making sure that they are complete and accurate.

A legal assistance officer or civilian attorney can help you ask the board to correct your records. Keep in mind that a military attorney would know more about military discharges than would his civilian counterpart.

Although a board of correction of military records may sometimes permit a personal appearance, you have no right to appear before such a board. If the board rules against you, you may request reconsideration and perhaps sue in a federal district court.

Article 138, Uniform Code of Military Justice

Article 138 of the Uniform Code of Military Justice is a powerful remedy for wrongs done by commanders. If you believe that your commander has done you a wrong and you want to make an Article 138 complaint, you must first ask him to correct the wrong. The best way is to write your request and say that it is a "request for redress under Article 138, Uniform Code of Military Justice." The complaint should clearly state what you think your commander did wrong and how he or she should correct it. If the commander does not satisfy you by taking appropriate action to correct the situation or does not answer your request, you should then complain to his or her superior under Article 138. The superior must send the complaint to the General Court-Martial Convening Authority (GCMCA).

DATA REQUIRED BY THE PRIVACY ACT OF 1974

AUTHORITY:	Title 10, U.S. Code 1552, Executive Order 9397, 22 Nov 43 (SSN)
PRINCIPAL PURPOSE:	To apply for correction of a military or naval record.
ROUTINE USES:	To docket a case. Reviewed by board members to determine relief sought. To determine qualification to apply to board. To compare facts present with evidence in the record.
DISCLOSURE:	Voluntary. If information is not furnished, applicant may not secure benefits from the Board.

BRANCH OF SERVICE

☐ ARMY ☐ NAVY ☐ AIR FORCE ☐ MARINE CORPS ☐ COAST GUARD

1. NAME (Last, first, middle initial) (Please print)	2. PRESENT RATE, GRADE	3. SERVICE NUMBER	4. SOCIAL SECURITY NUMBER

5. TYPE OF DISCHARGE (If by court-martial, state type of court.)	6. PRESENT STATUS, IF ANY, WITH RESPECT TO THE ARMED SERVICES (Active duty, retired, Reserve, etc.)	7. DATE OF DISCHARGE OR RELEASE FROM ACTIVE DUTY

8. ORGANIZATION AT TIME OF ALLEGED ERROR IN RECORD	9. I DESIRE TO APPEAR BEFORE THE BOARD IN WASHINGTON, D.C. (No expense to the Government) ☐ YES ☐ NO

10. NAME AND ADDRESS OF COUNSEL (If any)

11. I REQUEST THE FOLLOWING CORRECTION OF ERROR OR INJUSTICE:

12. I BELIEVE THE RECORD TO BE IN ERROR OR UNJUST IN THE FOLLOWING PARTICULARS:

13. IN SUPPORT OF THIS APPLICATION I SUBMIT AS EVIDENCE THE FOLLOWING: (If Veterans Administration records are pertinent to your case, give Regional Office location and Claim Number.)

14. a. THE DATE OF THE DISCOVERY OF THE ALLEGED ERROR OR INJUSTICE WAS _____. b. IF MORE THAN THREE YEARS SINCE THE ALLEGED ERROR OR INJUSTICE WAS DISCOVERED, STATE WHY THE BOARD SHOULD FIND IT IN THE INTEREST OF JUSTICE TO CONSIDER THIS APPLICATION.

15. APPLICANT MUST SIGN IN THE SPACE PROVIDED. IF THE RECORD IN QUESTION IS THAT OF A PERSON WHO IS DECEASED OR INCOMPETENT, LEGAL PROOF OF DEATH OR INCOMPETENCY MUST ACCOMPANY APPLICATION. IF APPLICATION IS SIGNED BY SPOUSE, WIDOW OR WIDOWER, NEXT OF KIN OR LEGAL REPRESENTATIVE, INDICATE RELATIONSHIP OR STATUS IN APPRO-PRIATE BOX. ☐ SPOUSE ☐ WIDOW ☐ WIDOWER ☐ NEXT OF KIN ☐ LEGAL REP. ☐ OTHER (Specify) _____

16. I MAKE THE FOREGOING STATEMENTS, AS PART OF MY CLAIM, WITH FULL KNOWLEDGE OF THE PENALTIES INVOLVED FOR WILFULLY MAKING A FALSE STATEMENT OR CLAIM. (U.S. Code, Title 18, Sec. 287, 1001, provides a penalty of not more than $10,000 fine or not more than 5 years imprisonment or both.)

17. COMPLETE ADDRESS, INCLUDING ZIP CODE (Applicant should forward notification of all changes of address.)	DOCUMENT NUMBER (Do not write in this space.)

18. DATE	19. SIGNATURE (Applicant must sign here.)	

DD FORM 1 FEB 78 **149**

EDITION OF 1 APR 69 IS OBSOLETE AND REPLACES DD FORM 149, PRIVACY ACT STATEMENT, 26 SEP 75, WHICH IS OBSOLETE.

You may use this Department of Defense form to ask a board of correction of military records to correct your service records.

GCMCAs are officers, usually general or flag officers, who are authorized to create general courts-martial. They must investigate the complaint and correct it if it is valid. The GCMCA must forward a report of the complaint, and any action taken on it, to the service secretary and tell you what, if anything, the command did about the complaint. The service secretary normally has his Judge Advocate General act on the complaint.

Article 138 complaints are very powerful because the complaint goes to such high officials. You cannot use Article 138, however, to complain about disciplinary actions under the Uniform Code of Military Justice because they have their own appeal system (see chapter 7). The command will process an Article 138 complaint only if you have requested your commander to correct the wrong and if your commander or someone acting in his or her stead committed the wrong.

The right to complain under Article 138 is guaranteed by federal law. As with other remedies, however, it is better to first work through the chain of command to resolve the problem. Because you have to submit an Article 138 complaint to the commander anyway, you are less likely to alienate him or her by using the chain of command to correct a problem informally. If that approach does not work, then you may resort to an Article 138 complaint.

Inspectors General

Federal law states that inspectors general are responsible for investigating and reporting to commanders on mission performance and discipline, efficiency, economy, and morale of the armed force to which they belong. In addition to inspecting military organizations, they investigate servicemembers' complaints. When inspectors general receive a complaint from a servicemember, they conduct an investigation and report the results to the commander. Although inspectors general have no authority to correct improper situations, they can make recommendations to the commander who does have the authority to take the proper corrective action.

While inspectors general do not require you to see your commander before seeing them, it is usually the best course. First, you will have done the proper thing and tried to resolve the problem within the chain of command. Second, the commander will eventually become involved when the inspector general talks with him during the investigation and later when he makes his recommendations. If you do go to the inspector general, however, and are not satisfied with the results, you can pursue other remedies, such as an Article 138 complaint.

CLAIMS BY THE GOVERNMENT AGAINST INDIVIDUALS

In chapter 1 you learned that military status imposes certain responsibilities on servicemembers that civilians who are not government employees do not ordinarily have. One such responsibility is the requirement to take care of government property and money that the government entrusts to you. For example, if you mishandle government property and damage it, the government may file a claim against you for the amount of the damage. The remainder of this chapter will discuss how the government may seek to recover money from you in such situations and what you should do about it.

Liability for Government Property
Congress has authorized the service secretaries to write regulations to account for the military property of their services and to fix responsibility for lost or damaged property. Each of the service secretaries has used this authority to set up report-of-survey systems. *Reports of survey* are the usual method for the military to recover the cost of, loss of, or damage to military property entrusted to you or others by the government. The government may file a property damage claim against you in those situations in which it cannot get compensation for the loss or damage through the report-of-survey system. If you don't pay the sum claimed, or some compromise amount, the government may simply take the amount owed out of your pay or may sue you in federal court (see chapter 8).

When the military entrusts you with military property, you are responsible for keeping it in safe custody, for caring for it properly, and for returning it on time to the proper authorities. If you lose or damage property the military entrusts you with because you were negligent or misused it willfully, the military can make you pay for it. In addition, the Uniform Code of Military Justice covers a number of crimes concerned with the abuse of military property (see chapter 7):

• Article 108, sale, loss, damage, destruction, or wrongful disposition of military property. This article makes it illegal to sell, damage, destroy, or wrongfully allow another to take possession of military property.

• Article 109, waste, spoilage, or destruction of nonmilitary property of the United States. This article forbids voluntary destruction of or damage to real property of the United States, such as buildings, trees, and so on.

• Article 121, larceny and wrongful appropriation. This article covers stealing and illegal borrowing (without the owner's permission) of all property, including government property.

Most cases involving responsibility for government property do not involve criminal charges. The military uses the report-of-survey system to determine whether servicemembers must pay for lost or damaged government property with which the military entrusted them. Although the procedures vary according to which service you are in, the report-of-survey system would have to provide you due process before the military could hold you liable. As discussed in chapter 2, before the government may take property (such as your money) from you, it has to give you notice of the action and an opportunity to explain why it should not do so.

In the report-of-survey system, the commander appoints a report-of-survey officer who will tell you what property loss or damage he is investigating and allow you to tell him why you are not liable. You can consult a military attorney or a civilian attorney. Usually no formal board meets, and if the commander upholds the survey officer's recommendation finding you liable, you can appeal. An attorney could help you prepare the appeal. The local staff judge advocate also reviews reports of survey to make certain the surveying officer does them properly.

How much you would have to pay for lost or damaged property depends on how the military entrusted you with it and the kind of property it is. If you are an accountable officer, you are liable for the full amount of the loss or damage. Accountable officers are those whose jobs carry an obligation to keep an accurate record of property imposed by law or regulation. A property book officer is a good example of an accountable officer, although commanders and other supervisors may also be accountable officers. They do not have to be commissioned or warrant officers. Noncommissioned officers and civilian employees may, in some circumstances, be accountable officers.

If you are not an accountable officer, the amount you would have to pay for lost or damaged government property depends on what kind of property it is. If the government property is your personal issue equipment or a weapon, you are liable for the full amount. Personal equipment includes such things as gas masks and binoculars. If the government property is not personal equipment or weapons, your liability is limited to one month's basic pay unless you willfully lost or damaged the property. In such cases, you would be liable for the full amount of the loss or damage. Finally, you would be liable for the full amount of government funds entrusted to you.

Another example of your liability for government property is the requirement to pay for damages to government quarters you inhabit. A federal law, Title 10 U.S. Code, section 2775, states that you must pay the United States for damage you or your family members cause to government housing you live in if the damage resulted from your or a family member's negligence. You do not have to pay for damage caused by fair wear and tear.

Medical Care Recovery Act

Another area in which the military can make a claim against you is for the cost of medical care you cause the military to provide either to you and your family or to someone else. Congress decided that taxpayers should not have to bear the costs of the medical care of servicemembers when someone other than the U.S. government itself injures them. Consequently, it enacted the Medical Care Recovery Act. If, for example, a civilian is negligent and causes an off-post accident that injures you and the military treats you in a military hospital, the government could use this act to recover the cost of your treatment from the civilian.

The Medical Care Recovery Act is for the government's benefit. You cannot make a claim under this act against the U.S. government or any of its agencies. The act also does not allow claims against servicemembers or their family members unless an insurance policy would pay the claim or unless the servicemember or dependent is guilty of gross negligence or willful misconduct. Because the law defines negligence as not taking due care, then gross negligence is a great absence of due care.

If you harm someone by your negligence or wrongful act and the military must provide medical care, the military may look to you to pay for the care. If you do not either pay the claim or reach a compromise with the military, the Department of Justice may sue you in federal court to recover the costs. If the government makes such a claim against you, you should consult a legal assistance attorney.

Line-of-Duty Determinations

Line-of-duty determinations can be very important to you because they may determine which military and veterans benefits you qualify for. The line-of-duty system is a means for the government to avoid paying for medical care or other benefits, such as Department of Veterans Affairs benefits, when you suffer an illness or injury that you did not incur "in the line of duty."

An illness or injury happens in the line of duty when it occurs while you were conducting yourself properly in your role as a servicemember. The term means more than performing military duties, however. You can be in the line of duty while on a proper leave or pass. You are not in the line of duty, however, while AWOL or if the injury or sickness is a result of your own misconduct or willful negligence.

When you are injured or become ill while on active duty, your unit makes a line-of-duty determination. Usually, it finds no evidence of misconduct, negligence, or absence without leave, and your commander determines that the injury or illness was in the line of duty. If you suffer serious injury or death, or if the command suspects negligence, misconduct, or unauthorized absence, the command will conduct an investigation. Because a nonline-of-duty determination may adversely affect your property rights, the investigating officer must provide you due process, including notice of the action, an opportunity to present evidence to show why the finding should be "in line of duty," and an appeal. If you ever face the possibility of a nonline-of-duty determination, consult a legal assistance officer or other military attorney.

CONCLUSION

If you understand and properly use the system of claims and remedies, you can ensure that the military will correct or compensate you as much as possible for any harm you suffer during your military career. Because the claims system and other remedies are so complicated, you should feel free to consult an attorney about these matters. No system of compensation, military or civilian, can repay a person entirely for all harms that happen, but the military does provide a fair and reasonable system to compensate members of its military family for wrongs done them.

6

Lawsuits

Lawsuits have become increasingly more common in today's society. You and your family should be as concerned about the possibility of becoming parties to a lawsuit as are civilians. In fact, if the claims and military remedies discussed in chapter 5 do not correct a wrong, you may start a lawsuit yourself. Therefore, you need to be aware of the legal aspects of suing and of being sued.

A *lawsuit* is a legal proceeding to get a remedy for a wrong done you. Lawsuits are civil proceedings, as opposed to criminal proceedings, which can only determine whether a person is guilty of a crime and, if so, what punishment is appropriate. Civil proceedings determine things other than criminal matters.

A civil lawsuit can determine who has injured you and how the wrongdoer should compensate you for the injury. If, for example, someone breaks your arm, you could have the wrongdoer pay your doctor bills. Civil suits can also grant other remedies, such as an *injunction*, which orders the wrongdoer to stop doing the wrong.

Every lawsuit obviously has two sides. The party that is filing the suit is called the *plaintiff*. The person whom the plaintiff sues is the *defendant*. The plaintiff and the defendant may be a person, a business, or a governmental agency. A single lawsuit may have many plaintiffs and many defendants.

GROUNDS FOR LAWSUITS

You cannot sue someone on a whim: you must have grounds for the suit. Lawyers call these grounds a cause of action. A *cause of action* is a factual situation that would cause a court to give relief to the plaintiff and, thus, entitle him to bring a lawsuit. Generally, the situation must fall within a recognized ground for a lawsuit. If, for example, someone you hire to fix your car fails to do so, this cause of action is a breach of contract—the agreement to fix your car for money.

Many lawsuits come under the cause of action of a tort. A *tort* is a civil wrong done to another. A tort could also be a crime, but it does not have to be. The concept underlying tort cases is that if one person injures another, that person should compensate the injured one. The law recognizes three general types of torts:

- *Intentional torts.* Intentional torts happen when the defendant purposely harms another. This does not mean that the defendant either is criminal or even wanted to hurt the plaintiff. It does mean that he intentionally did the act that harmed the plaintiff, as opposed to doing it by accident.

- *Carelessness.* The legal term for carelessness is negligence. In negligent torts, the defendant had a duty to use care toward the defendant and did not do so. If, for example, you can see that others could be in danger if you do not use ordinary care and skill, you owe them the duty to use that care and skill. If you do not, you are negligent. For example, if you drive knowing that you have bald tires or bad brakes, you are negligent. If you have an accident because of that negligence and harm another person or his property, a court can find you liable for the damages you caused.

- *Strict liability.* When the defendant does some dangerous act and it causes injury to another, society requires him to compensate the victim, because by doing such a dangerous act he assumed the risk of hurting someone. For example, a person who keeps a lion as a pet does so at his peril. If it escapes and hurts someone, he is liable for the damages caused by it, even if it was not his negligence that caused the escape.

Generally, each person or each corporation is responsible for its torts. Children are generally liable for their torts, and sometimes their parents may be liable for their children's torts. For example, if the parent were negligent in allowing a child access to a firearm and the child shot someone, the parent, as well as the child, would be guilty of negligence.

Torts are not the only grounds for lawsuits. If the dispute involves a contract between the plaintiff and the defendant, the proper ground for a lawsuit may be a *breach of contract.* Such a suit is proper when the defendant did not live up the contract's promises. For example, if someone agreed to landscape your home in return for $500, which was paid in advance, and then he did not do the work but kept the money, you could sue for breach of contract. In the suit you would seek to get the $500 back plus any other damages resulting from the broken contract.

Another ground for a lawsuit related to breach of contract is a *breach of warranty.* If a seller warrants that what he sold you works properly and it does not, a lawsuit for breach of warranty would be proper if he does not replace or fix the item.

The law recognizes many other possible grounds for a lawsuit. Violations of constitutional or other rights, for example, may also be grounds for lawsuits (see chapters 2 and 3). Again, it is your lawyer's job to figure out which avenue is best to use to protect your rights and to resolve the conflict in your favor. Your attorney cannot choose the proper grounds for a lawsuit unless he knows the whole truth about what happened. Remember, too, that it is folly to sue someone based on a situation that did not happen as you told the attorney it did. In fact, a person you sued could sue you back for suing him maliciously when he did not really harm you by a wrongful act. So be sure you tell your attorney everything.

STARTING A LAWSUIT

A lawsuit starts when the plaintiff files a complaint (or pleading) with the clerk of the court that will hear the case. A *complaint*, or *pleading*, is a paper that tells the judge who is suing whom, what the suit is about, and what the plaintiff wants from the suit. If the defendant does not agree with the pleading and does not want to do what the plaintiff wants, he will file an answer denying those parts of the complaint that he does not agree with. A denial may also contain counterclaims for damages that the defendant contends the plaintiff owes him. In other words, both sides could say that the other side is wrong and should pay.

If the pleadings agree on the case's facts, the judge can enter a summary judgment about which side should win. A *summary judgment* means that the judge decides who wins without hearing any evidence; he decides the case based on the papers the plaintiff and the defendant have submitted.

If the defendant does not file an answer with the court, the plaintiff may get a *default judgment*, in which he wins the case without the defendant defending himself. A court can enter a default judgment because the law says that if the defendant does not bother to answer the complaint, he must be liable for the damages or other relief.

This rule illustrates the importance of the complaint and the answer. An attorney must prepare the pleadings so that they are in proper form and have all the magic words that you'll need to stand an equal chance in court. If the pleadings are not in proper form, the judge could dismiss the lawsuit. Normally, although a legal assistance officer may tell you whether a lawsuit would be advisable, a civilian attorney would have to represent you in the civilian court.

One of the reasons you must consult an attorney when you are thinking about filing a lawsuit is that the decision about which court should hear the case is critical. Both federal and state civilian courts can hear civil lawsuits. No military court can hear a lawsuit, because its jurisdiction is restricted to criminal cases. No court, however, can hear a lawsuit unless the court has *jurisdiction*—the power to hear and decide a case—over the particular case before the court.

To hear a case, the court must have two different types of jurisdiction: jurisdiction over the subject of the lawsuit and jurisdiction over the plaintiff and the defendant. Jurisdiction over the subject means that the case is about a subject that the court is allowed to hear, such as a divorce case in a divorce court. Jurisdiction over the plaintiff and the defendant means that they have satisfied any residence and notification requirements of the court. For example, the plaintiff may have to satisfy residency requirements in some cases; jurisdiction over the defendant exists when the plaintiff properly notifies him about the case.

An attorney must determine which court would have jurisdiction over your possible case. If you file a lawsuit in a court that does not have jurisdiction, the court must dismiss it. Therefore, go to an attorney for help from the beginning, so that you won't waste any more time in court and money for lawyers than you need to for your lawsuit.

When a plaintiff files a lawsuit, someone must notify the defendant for the court to have jurisdiction. The plaintiff or his representative notifies the defendant by a proceeding called service of process. *Service of process* is the act of bringing a lawsuit to the attention of the defendant by giving him a copy of the pleadings, which is sometimes called a *summons*. It will notify the defendant of what the lawsuit is about, when he must appear in court to defend himself, and when he must file any written answers to the plaintiff's complaint.

The plaintiff has two general ways to notify a defendant of a lawsuit. One is *personal service of process*. This happens when an official, usually a sheriff, personally hands a copy of the summons to the defendant or an adult member of his family. In some cases, he may notify the defendant by mailing the notice to the defendant's address. Another way for the plaintiff to give the required notice is constructive service. *Constructive service* involves the plaintiff's publishing a notice of the lawsuit in the newspaper for, say, three consecutive Tuesdays. The plaintiff may use constructive service in certain cases, normally involving real estate or sometimes divorce.

If you receive notice that you are a defendant in a lawsuit, see a legal assistance attorney immediately! Remember, you may need to file an answer so that the judge does not enter a default judgment against you. The lawyer can tell whether you need to file an answer and whether you need a civilian attorney. Although you may ultimately need a civilian attorney to defend you, it's a good idea to see a legal assistance officer first. A civilian attorney may not be aware of the provisions of the Soldiers' and Sailors' Civil Relief Act, which can help servicemembers who are facing a lawsuit while on active duty. The legal assistance lawyer, however, will, and he also can help you understand the legal proceedings so that you can cooperate more fully with the civilian lawyer who will try to help you win your case.

If you are named as a defendant in a lawsuit, another reason to see a lawyer quickly is that he may find grounds to dismiss the case. The judge could dismiss the case against you for several reasons, such as that the court does not have jurisdiction or that the *statute of limitations* (the time during which a plaintiff may start a lawsuit) has expired.

PAYING FOR A LAWSUIT

Two ways exist to pay a lawyer to represent you when you sue someone. One way is to pay the attorney his hourly rate and the costs of the lawsuit, such as court costs, costs of serving notice on the other party, photocopying costs, and so on. A good attorney's hourly rates can easily be from $50 to $250, and a good attorney can spends hundreds of hours on a big case.

Because few people can afford those rates, attorneys have developed the contingent-fee system. In it, the attorney agrees to take the plaintiff's case for a percentage of the damages if the plaintiff wins. The percentage is often one third if the losing party does not appeal and up to one half if he does. If the plaintiff loses, the attorney does not get any payment except maybe the costs of the case. While one third to one half of the damage award may seem excessive, the contingent-fee system allows many plaintiffs to take their cases to court when they don't have the money to pay hourly fees. The attorney whose client pays him by the hour gets the money whether the plaintiff wins or loses.

The contingent-fee option is generally not available to a defendant unless the defendant countersues for a large sum. Defendants normally pay their lawyers by the hour. In many cases, however, the losing party must pay attorney's fees for both sides. If you are suing in federal court, the Equal Access to Justice Act may put you in the enviable position of having the government pay your attorney's fees. In any case, you need to make certain that you fully understand how and when you must pay your lawyer. The lawyer should have you sign a written employment contract that specifies what he will do for you and how you will pay the attorney. He should give you a copy of the contract.

IF SOMEONE SUES YOU

The best way to avoid getting sued is to avoid doing anything that may get you sued. In today's society where lawsuits are more and more common, this may be difficult. But even if you can't avoid doing something that may cause a lawsuit, you can do something to minimize the potential harm of such a suit. Unless you live in the barracks or on a ship's berthing quarters, you should consider having liability insurance. *Liability insurance* is protection against having to pay damages in a lawsuit because you injured another person or his property. The other major thing you can do to protect yourself from losing a lawsuit is to do the right things when an accident happens:

- Notify the police.
- Get any necessary help, such as an ambulance. You always want to try to minimize the damage.
- Make notes and sketches of what happened.
- *Do not* admit you were at fault—even if you were or think you were.
- Do not tell the injured party how much insurance you have.
- Notify your insurance company promptly.
- Get names, addresses, and phone numbers of all witnesses.

If someone sues you, you will probably find out about it when you receive notice of the lawsuit, usually by personal service of process as discussed previously. You must take it to an attorney immediately. When you see your attorney, make certain you tell him everything. A civilian or military attorney's advice is only as good as what he knows about your case. Facts that you might want to hide because they don't seem favorable to you might actually be a good defense to a lawsuit. Only your lawyer can evaluate your case properly, and he can do so only if he knows what really happened. If you tell him everything, he may also be able to find grounds for a *counterclaim* in which you can seek damages from the plaintiff.

The Soldiers' and Sailors' Civil Relief Act

The Soldiers' and Sailors' Civil Relief Act protects you as a servicemember involved in a lawsuit in several ways. First, before the plaintiff—the person who is suing you—can get a default judgment, he must file a sworn statement showing that you are not in the military service. If the plaintiff does not provide such an affidavit, the court cannot enter a default judgment against you without appointing an attorney to represent you. The court may also require the plaintiff to post a bond to repay you if he wins in court but loses on appeal. The act also provides that if you do not appear in court or if you don't have an attorney represent you, the court may appoint an attorney to protect your rights.

If the court enters a *default judgment*—a win for the plaintiff based only on what he said in the pleadings because the defendant did not answer—against you, the act allows the court to reopen the case if military service hurt your case. For example, if the military orders you overseas and you cannot appear in court, your military service has hurt your ability to defend yourself.

Perhaps the most important protection of the Soldiers' and Sailors' Civil Relief Act regarding lawsuits is that section 201 authorizes a *stay* (a suspension or delay) in the case for a military plaintiff or defendant whose military service hurts his ability to proceed with his case. For example, if you are suing a civilian who wrecked your car, and the military sends you overseas for three months, you can apply under section 201 for a stay to keep the defendant from getting the judge to dismiss the case when you don't appear in court for your lawsuit. A legal assistance attorney can tell you how the Soldiers' and Sailors' Civil Relief Act applies to your particular situation. He can also help you fill in the blanks in the accompanying sample letter requesting a delay in a lawsuit.

LETTER REQUESTING A DELAY IN A LAWSUIT

                                        (Servicemember's Unit)
                                        (Date)
SUBJECT: Civil Action No. _____

            _____ v.   _____

Clerk of the Court
(court's address)

Dear (Sir) (Madam):

    I am the (defendant) (respondent) in the above-titled case, now scheduled for trial on _____ 19 ____ .

    I hereby respectfully request a stay of that action under the Soldiers' and Sailors' Civil Relief Act, 50 U.S.C., App. §521, until _____ . I am now on active military duty with the United States Army, and currently assigned to _____(unit, location)_____. My military service will materially affect my ability to appear and defend the matter on that date for the following reasons: (I will not be permitted to leave at that time because of a scheduled unit inspection/field exercises/temporary duty at _____/other) (I will not be able to return to _____ in sufficient time to obtain legal counsel to assist me in defending the action) (other).

    Please notify me if my request has been granted.

    I certify that I have mailed a copy of this request to opposing counsel on this date; I further certify that I will keep the court advised of any changes in my status or obligations which will permit an earlier resolution of this matter.

                                        Sincerely,

                        _____
                                        (Signature)
                                        (Typed name)

Are You Liable, or Is the Government?

A person can sue you in two capacities. One is your personal capacity. The plaintiff would sue you in your personal capacity if he accused you as a private individual of doing the harm to him. Your other capacity is that of a federal employee if the plaintiff accused you of harming him while doing your military duties.

The importance of which capacity the plaintiff sues you in is that if he sues you for an act you did as a federal employee, the U.S. government may defend you. The government will substitute itself for you as the defendant, and if the plaintiff wins, the government will pay the damages, not you. A U.S. attorney also will defend the case, saving you attorney's fees.

For the government to defend you, you must have done the act that is the basis for the lawsuit within the scope of your employment and in good faith. In other words, you must have done the act as a proper part of your duties when you were trying to do the right thing. For example, if you were driving a military vehicle on an authorized route to pick up supplies and had an accident, the accident would have occurred within the scope of your employment.

An example of an act occurring outside the scope of your employment would be if you had an accident after you had detoured fifty miles from the normal military duties route to visit a friend. Besides having to face a civil suit for such an accident that happened outside the scope of your employment, you might also face military criminal charges because using a military vehicle for an unauthorized purpose is a violation of Article 121, larceny (stealing) or wrongful appropriation (illegal borrowing).

REMEDIES

Because people sue others to remedy wrongs done to them, the normal remedy they seek from the court is money, called *damages*, to pay for the harm. Damages are the money paid by the defendant in a lawsuit to compensate the plaintiff. Courts can award several kinds of damages:

- *Compensatory damages.* The court may order damages for many different harms suffered by the plaintiff. For example, if someone injures you in a car accident, the damages could include repair costs for your car, your medical expenses, lost earnings for job time you missed, and money to compensate you for the pain and suffering the injury caused.

- *Punitive damages.* A court may add punitive damages to compensatory damages to punish the defendant when the wrong he did the plaintiff was wanton or malicious.

- *Liquidated damages.* These damages are sums of money that the parties to a contract agree to in advance for a breach of the contract. For example, a contract to paint a building might state that if the painting is not finished within two weeks, the painter will receive $100 less than if he finished on time.

It is important for you to know that, just because the defendant does something wrong to you, it does not mean you are entitled to damages. The defendant must have harmed you by the wrong. It is almost like the "no harm, no foul" rule in basketball: if you are dribbling and the person guarding you slaps your wrist but you don't lose the ball, the referee may ignore the foul because it did not damage you. Usually, the plaintiff must show that the defendant harmed him in a way that a court may compensate by monetary damages before the court will also consider awarding punitive damages.

Sometimes the plaintiff does not sue for damages. Instead, he wants a situation corrected or wants to prevent someone from taking some action that will be harmful to him. Therefore, the law has several additional remedies:

• *Mandamus.* Mandamus is a legal term that means "we command." It is a command from a judge to an officer or an employee of the government to do something he should do for the plaintiff, such as to promote the plaintiff when he is qualified for promotion.

• *Injunction.* An injunction is the opposite of mandamus. It is a judge's order not to take a particular action. For example, if the military tried to discharge you for an improper reason or without due process (see chapter 4), you could seek an injunction barring the military from discharging you.

• *Habeas corpus.* This legal phrase translates into "you have the body." It is an order to a government official to bring the body (the plaintiff) before the court to determine whether the government is properly holding him in custody. Habeas corpus may be an appropriate lawsuit to determine whether the government has properly confined a person convicted by court-martial or to determine whether the military's refusal to discharge a person is proper.

DISCOVERY

Sometime during the pretrial preparations, the discovery procedure will happen. *Discovery* is a method for the parties to the lawsuit to learn the facts about the situation that is the basis of the suit. Its purpose is to get all the facts into the open, so that the trial can focus on what is genuinely in dispute between the two sides. Either side can force the other to disclose relevant facts about the case before trial. Often, when both sides know all the facts about the case, they can reach an out-of-court settlement.

Discovery may include taking depositions (one party questions the other under oath) and furnishing evidence, such as photographs, written statements, and so on. Obviously, the help of one's attorney is critical during discovery procedures.

SETTLEMENT

Many lawsuits never get to court because the parties settle out of court. A settlement could be advantageous to both you and the other party. Even if you have a good case, it could be wise to accept a settlement for a lesser amount than you are suing for. For example, if you sued the defendant for $5,000, and you and the other side agreed that your actual damages were only $3,000, the defendant could agree to pay this lesser sum to avoid losing the whole $5,000 in court and having to pay court costs besides.

Any good attorney will tell you that one never knows what will happen at a trial. Often, a lesser amount of damages in the plaintiff's hand is worth a possible greater amount that depends solely on the way a judge or jury views his case. Also, it may be better for the defendant to pay a lesser amount than the plaintiff is suing for to avoid paying the greater amount if he loses the case, plus paying court costs and attorney's fees.

You need to remember two things about settlements. First, never talk to the other party about a settlement yourself; have your lawyer do it. (Your attorney cannot settle your case without your consent.) Second, because you may still need to go to court to get a court order to make the defendant pay you the settlement, you should ask the judge not to dismiss the case until after the defendant has paid you.

THE TRIAL

A case must go to trial if the parties do not settle the case out of court, if the plaintiff does not drop it, or if the judge does not dismiss it. If the parties dispute what happened, the judge or jury will determine what happened. Sometimes, the parties will have a right to a jury trial. In other cases, the judge will decide the case without a jury trial. Even when you have a right to a jury trial, it may be advantageous to waive this right and have the judge decide the case. Again, an attorney must advise you on this decision because he will have much more knowledge than you do about how the judge or the jury will likely view your case.

In a civil trial, the plaintiff has the burden of proving, by a preponderance of the evidence, that the defendant harmed him and damaged him by that harm. A preponderance of the evidence means that more proof supports the plaintiff's version of what happened than supports the defendant's version. If the plaintiff does not prove his case, the defendant wins. Of course, preponderance of the evidence is a lesser standard than that used in criminal proceedings, which is beyond a reasonable doubt (see chapter 7). In some civil lawsuits the plaintiff has to prove his case by a higher standard, such as clear and convincing evidence.

THE JUDGMENT

After the judge or jury reaches a verdict, the court enters its decision, which is called a *judgment*. If, in a case, the plaintiff sued the defendant for $5,000 for damages caused by the defendant's negligence in not having his car's defective brakes repaired—causing him to hit the plaintiff's car, thereby causing $5,000 worth of damages—and won, the judgment would be an order for the defendant to pay the plaintiff $5,000 and perhaps court costs and attorney's fees.

The losing party may move (ask) the judge for a new trial, appeal the case to a higher court, or both. The law has strict time limits for such motions or appeals. The party who appeals is called the *appellant*, and the person whom the appeal is against is called the *appellee*. Although the plaintiff started the case, he can end up as a defendant on the appeal. The appellant usually will have to post an *appeal bond*—a guarantee that he will pay the costs of the appeal.

Although television has popularized the phrase "I'll appeal all the way to the Supreme Court," the appellate court must have jurisdiction to hear the appeal, and the U.S. Supreme Court has limited jurisdiction over appeals and hears very few of those it has jurisdiction over. The lowest level of state or federal appeals court will normally decide the appeal.

Appellate courts decide appeals on the basis of a transcript of the evidence heard at the trial and briefs (written legal arguments) of the parties. The appellate court may deny the appeal, leaving the decision of the trial court intact, or grant the appeal. Often, when the court grants an appeal, it sends the case back to the trial court for a new trial, which is supposed to be free from the error that happened in the first trial and that caused the appellate court to grant the appeal. For example, in our $5,000 defective brake case, if the judge incorrectly told the jury that the plaintiff had to prove the case beyond a reasonable doubt and, consequently, the plaintiff lost and appealed, the appellate court would grant an appeal and return the case for a new trial, instructing the judge to inform the jury that the plaintiff had to prove the case by a preponderance of the evidence.

A court's decision becomes final after the time allowed for an appeal has expired. After the judgment becomes final, the winning party may have to go back to court to enforce the decision if the losing party does not pay the damages or otherwise satisfy the judgment.

If the losing party does not pay the damages, the winner may ask the court for a *writ of execution*. This written order tells the sheriff to take the loser's personal property (see chapter 14) and sell enough of it to pay the judgment and expenses. If the defendant does not have enough personal property to satisfy the judgment, the winning party may be able to put a *lien* on the loser's real property and get a judge to order a sheriff to sell it to get the money. Another way for the winner to get his money is to get a *garnishment order*—an order for anyone, such as an employer, who owes money to the loser to pay it to the court, which will pay it to the winner.

Not all personal property or all one's earnings are subject to writs of execution and garnishment. For example, your home and one car are not subject to writs of execution in most states. And only a certain percentage of your income is subject to garnishment because the law recognizes that you must have enough earnings to support yourself and your family.

Sometimes the defendant is what is known as *judgment proof*. This term means he does not have enough assets to satisfy the judgment. If you get a million-dollar judgment against an airman basic who only owns some clothing and a stereo and has a couple hundred dollars in the bank, you are not going to collect more than a fraction, if any, of this judgment, unless he has liability insurance for a large enough sum.

Liability insurance is a contract between you and the insurance company in which the insurance company agrees to pay the damages you have to pay if someone sues you for injury to him or to his property. The contract may also provide that the insurance company will defend you in court. If the judgment is for more than the policy's coverage, you will have to pay the difference. Remember that liability insurance is a contract and that if you do not live up to your part of the contract, such as by not promptly notifying the insurer of an accident you were involved in, the insurance company will not have to live up to its obligations. If you are involved in an incident that causes injury to another person or his property, check your liability insurance policy immediately and see what you have to do. If you are in doubt, visit a legal assistance officer and take the policy with you.

SUING THE GOVERNMENT

The law has an old doctrine called sovereign immunity. A sovereign is the chief authority of a nation, formerly the king. Long ago, people could not sue the king unless he allowed them to sue him. According to sovereign immunity, therefore, no one may sue the government without its consent. The rule applies to our federal and state governments as well.

By the Federal Tort Claims Act (FTCA), the United States has waived a part of its governmental immunity. The act gives consent to people harmed by certain torts committed by U.S. officers and employees to sue the federal government for damage to or loss of property, personal injury, and wrongful death. (A next of kin may bring a wrongful death suit to get damages when a wrongful act of a government employee killed the victim.)

Before you may sue the United States under the FTCA, you must file a claim (see chapter 5) within two years of the time you were injured or learned of the injury. If you and the U.S. government cannot agree on a settlement or if the government refuses to pay the claim, then you may sue in the federal district court in the area where the injury happened. You must file the lawsuit within six months of the time the claim is denied, or the court will not accept your case.

The U.S. government is liable, under the FTCA, for damages caused by the wrongful or negligent acts of its officers and employees acting within the scope of their authority, just as though the government were a private person.

The federal court uses the law of the state in which the tort happened to determine whether the government employees were negligent and other issues in the case.

You may not sue the government for certain torts under the act:

• Intentional torts, such as assault and battery. An *assault* is an attempt to do violence to a person, such as by taking a punch and missing. A *battery* is a completed assault, such as by taking a punch and connecting.

• Injuries caused by combat activities during wartime. If a U.S. bomber drops a bomb on your quarters, you could not sue the U.S. government for damages under the FTCA.

• Torts committed by a government employee, using due care, while doing a discretionary function. A *discretionary function* is an act that is based on the personal judgment of a federal employee. For example, the decision whether to repair a road or to resurface it is a discretionary one because the engineer would have to use his professional judgment to decide which was appropriate. But if the engineer failed to inspect the work, and it was done improperly, resulting in an accident, that failure would not be a discretionary act. One helpful way to look at whether an act is discretionary is to think about whether it is a preliminary or planning step or the execution of the act. If it is a preliminary action, it is a discretionary one.

• Injuries happening outside the United States. Other laws may permit a suit for an injury caused by a government employee overseas, such as the Military Claims Act (see chapter 5). For example, if a column of tanks moving to a maneuver area damages your property, you could put in a claim under the noncombat activity provision of the Military Claims Act.

Military members also may not sue the government under the FTCA for injuries they receive when they are engaged in activities that are "incident to their service." In other words, if a government employee acting within the scope of his employment injures you, you cannot sue under either of the following conditions:

• You were on active duty at the time of the injury.

• Even if you were not on active duty, a significant connection existed between your status as a military member and the injuries. For example, an off-duty sailor who enters a military base to use the commissary and is injured there cannot sue under this act, because commissary use depends on military service, and, thus, a significant connection exists between the sailor's injury and his military status.

This prohibition against suits by military members for injuries done them is known as the *Feres* doctrine, for the name of the Supreme Court case that established the rule (see chapter 5). The reasons for the court's decision were that it thought allowing servicemembers to sue their superior officers would hurt military discipline and that the military provided medical care, disability retirement, and veterans benefits to compensate servicemembers for the damage their injuries caused. Currently, if medical malpractice in a military hospital injures your nonmilitary spouse, your spouse could sue. But a military spouse could not sue for a similar injury because of the *Feres* doctrine.

Before you can sue the government, you have to exhaust your administrative remedies. In other words, if you have grounds for a lawsuit against the government, you must first try to resolve the problem out of court through government-established procedures, such as the claims system, Article 138 complaints, boards of corrections of military records, and discharge review boards (see chapter 5). If you do not exhaust your administrative remedies, the court may dismiss the lawsuit or, while not dismissing it, require you to go back and try your administrative remedies. The court may not, however, require you to exhaust administrative remedies when doing so would be futile.

SUITS AGAINST OTHERS

Not only the government commits torts. Individuals sometimes commit wrongful acts for which a lawsuit is a proper remedy. Often, whom to sue is one of the more important questions in a lawsuit. For example, if the negligence of a military doctor in a military hospital harms your child, do you sue the doctor or do you sue the government? If you sue the doctor, he will win, because the Military Malpractice Act, often called the Gonzales Act, says that you cannot sue military medical personnel for medical malpractice they commit as government employees. Instead, you have to file a claim against the U.S. government under the Federal Tort Claims Act.

Another Supreme Court case, *Chappel v. Wallace*, says that servicemembers cannot sue their commanders for monetary damages for constitutional wrongs committed against them. If your commander does not promote you solely because you are a minority member, for example, which would violate your constitutional rights, you may not sue him to get money to repay you for this damage. It does not mean that you cannot sue; you just cannot sue for money to compensate you for the wrong. You could sue to get a court order telling the Army to promote you if you are qualified and maybe get back pay at the higher grade that you would have had if promoted properly on time. But you cannot get your commander to pay money from his pocket for the damage he did.

The reason the court ruled this way was that if servicemembers could sue their commanders for monetary damages, commanders would be afraid to make decisions about such things as their subordinates' promotions, assignments, and jobs. If your commander or other supervisor injures you in a way unrelated to his duties, however, such as in an off-duty car accident, you can sue him for damages just as you can any other private individual.

Not only might you have to decide whether to sue another servicemember or the government, but also you might have to decide which family member to sue. If a child injures you, for example, you may be able to sue the child's parents. Suing the child would normally be futile, because the child is unlikely to have the money or the insurance to be able to pay a judgment. Whether you can sue the parent for the child's action depends on the law of the state you are in and the nature of the wrong. For example, some states permit the victim of a child's act to sue the parents if the child's action was intentional and the parents encouraged the improper act.

SMALL CLAIMS COURT

All states have established some form of small claims court. The purpose of such courts is to hear minor lawsuits, those that are not complicated and do not involve much money. The maximum amount that you can sue for in a small claims court varies from state to state, but is usually $1,000 to $5,000. Although most small claims courts permit the use of lawyers, hiring one is usually not cost effective because the lawyer's fees would wipe out your gain if you won or cost you more than you would have to pay if you lost.

Not only do small claims courts hear cases without lawyers, but also the legal procedure is streamlined, so that nonlawyers can represent themselves. In addition, the court costs (fees for filing the lawsuit, service of process, and calling witnesses) are very reasonable. Typically, small claims courts don't involve juries. Rather, the judge will hear and decide the case.

A legal assistance attorney can tell you whether taking your case to small claims court is proper and what the procedure is. He can also tell you what to do if someone sues you in small claims court. Your library may have books about how to win a case in small claims court, too.

CONCLUSION

The thought of a lawsuit can be frightening. If, however, you are careful when you do things that could hurt others, you can minimize the chance of harming another and being sued. A good insurance policy can also protect you from having to make a large damage payment in a lawsuit. If someone harms you or you harm someone else and he sues you, the best thing you can do is to see a legal assistance officer immediately. Remember to take with you any papers you have, such as notice of the suit, police reports, your insurance policy, and so on, when you see the lawyer.

With the military's remedies and the court system, you, as a servicemember, can usually correct or receive damages for any wrongs you suffer. But military remedies, such as the claims system, and judicial remedies are complicated and require you to consult an attorney early and often. Preventative law, however, such as you will learn about in the rest of this book, can prevent your having to correct a bad situation after it happens.

PART III

What You Need to Know about Criminal Law

When you are in the service, you are subject to more laws than are civilians. Not only do you have to obey military laws, but also you must obey civilian laws. Your rights when accused of a crime also change because of your military status. Although family members are not subject to the Uniform Code of Military Justice as servicemembers are, their status as military dependents may affect how law enforcement officials treat them if they get in trouble with the law. Thus, all servicemembers and their families need to understand what may happen if one of them becomes involved with the criminal justice system. Chapter 7 will tell you about the military justice system, and chapter 8 will tell you about the civilian justice system.

7

Military Justice and You

Any servicemember could run afoul of the military criminal justice system because the military defines more actions as crimes than does the civilian justice system. So, the more you know about military crimes and the military criminal justice system, the better your chances are of keeping yourself out of trouble. This chapter first explains military crimes and the military justice system and then discusses what could happen if you got into trouble with the military justice system.

MILITARY CRIMES

Although both military and civilian courts call some of the same actions crimes, such as murder, rape, and robbery, other actions are crimes only in the military. Absence without leave (AWOL), for example, is a crime in the military but not in civilian life. If you do not go to your civilian job, you may be fired, but you will not have committed a crime. In the military, however, if you do not go to your job or place of duty, you will have violated Article 86 of the Uniform Code of Military Justice and may receive nonjudicial punishment under Article 15, UCMJ, or you may be tried by court-martial. Because absence without leave is the most well-known military crime, you may already know about it. You also need to know about some of the other actions the military calls crimes so that you won't commit them out of ignorance. Here are some of the military laws that you ought to know (from the Uniform Code of Military Justice, the federal law that says what actions are crimes in the military):

- *Article 86, absence without leave and failure to repair.* AWOL means leaving your unit without authority. *Failure to repair* means not going to your job at the proper time or leaving your job without permission. This article also covers desertion, which is leaving your unit with the intent never to return to the military.

- *Article 87, missing movement.* This crime involves missing the movement of your unit, aircraft, or ship, either on purpose or through neglect.
- *Article 89, disrespect to a superior commissioned officer.* As discussed in chapter 2, one restriction on your freedom of speech is that you cannot use disrespectful language or gestures to superior commissioned officers. And truth is no defense!
- *Article 90, assaulting or willfully disobeying a superior commissioned officer.* Although Article 128 makes it a crime to assault any person, this article provides a more severe punishment for assaulting an officer than for assaulting other people. Disobeying the lawful order of an officer is also a criminal offense. (See the discussion of lawful orders in chapter 1.)
- *Article 91, insubordinate conduct toward warrant, noncommissioned, or petty officers.* This article is similar to Article 90, but it covers disrespect to noncommissioned and warrant officers.
- *Article 92, failure to obey an order or a regulation.* Disobeying the order of someone other than an officer or a warrant, a noncommissioned, or a petty officer is a crime under this article. Of course, the person you are disobeying must have the authority to give you an order (such as a military policeman). *Dereliction of duty,* which is performing your duties in a criminally inefficient manner, and disobeying a regulation are also crimes under this article.
- *Article 93, cruelty and maltreatment.* Under this article, it is illegal to be cruel toward or to mistreat someone who is subject to your orders. This article also makes *sexual harassment* (influencing or threatening the career of another in exchange for sexual favors, or offensive sexual language or gestures) a crime.
- *Article 94, mutiny and sedition.* These crimes are very serious. *Mutiny* involves a group of servicemembers who refuse to obey orders, who refuse to do their duty, or who do violence. A revolt or violence directed by one person against lawful civil authority with the intent to overthrow that authority is *sedition.*
- *Article 99, misbehavior before the enemy.* Also very serious, this crime includes such acts as running away from the enemy, throwing down weapons, cowardly conduct, and failing to try to fight the enemy.
- *Article 104, aiding the enemy.* This crime involves giving weapons, supplies, or information to the enemy.
- *Article 112, drunk on duty.* According to military law, you are drunk on duty if you are intoxicated—from drugs or alcohol—enough so that you cannot perform at 100 percent of your physical or mental ability.
- *Article 112a, drugs.* The following acts are crimes under Article 112a:

1. Possession of drugs.
2. Use of drugs.
3. Distribution of drugs (selling or giving them to another person).
4. Manufacture of drugs.
5. Bringing drugs onto a military base.

Penalties for drug crimes range from a dishonorable discharge and confinement for two years for possession of small amounts of marijuana to a dishonorable discharge and confinement for fifteen years for the sale of cocaine. Although possession of marijuana may not be a crime in the state in which you are stationed, it is still a crime under the Uniform Code of Military Justice. Although court-martialing servicemembers who took drugs off post used to be difficult, it has become quite easy and common. In fact, courts-martial have convicted and given dishonorable discharges and jail sentences to servicemembers who had used small amounts of marijuana or other drugs while on leave, but whose drug use had shown up in a urinalysis upon their return to duty. Further, you could forfeit any property, such as your car, that you used in a drug transaction. Therefore, my best legal advice to you is to stay away from drugs while you are in the military, because not only are they dangerous to use, but also they can easily ruin your career.

• *Article 115, malingering.* This article makes it a crime to pretend you are ill or injured or to injure yourself to avoid duty.

• *Article 132, frauds against the United States.* Making a false claim is illegal. Sometimes a new servicemember commits this crime after temporary duty with senior personnel who tell the junior that it is common practice to do something like share rooms but claim separate rooms so that they can get more money. Such false claims against the United States are illegal and can result in a dishonorable discharge and confinement for five years.

• *Article 133, conduct unbecoming an officer and a gentleman/gentlewoman.* Officers are not supposed to dishonor or disgrace themselves. For example, the military calls cheating on a test, being drunk and disorderly in public, and failing to support one's family conduct unbecoming an officer.

• *Article 134, the general article.* Under this article, engaging in conduct that harms good order and discipline or that may bring discredit upon the armed forces is criminal. If, for example, you do something wrong that another UCMJ article does not cover, this article may cover it if what you did hurts good order and discipline or tends to hurt the service's reputation. Among the many crimes listed under Article 134 are adultery, indecent assault, bad check offenses, dishonorably failing to pay debts, drunk and disorderly conduct, indecent exposure, indecent language, and wearing unauthorized insignia.

Don't let all these laws scare you, however. Common sense usually will help you know what is legal in the military and what is not. If you are in doubt, however, check with the chain of command or with a military lawyer.

Don't rely on the advice of "barracks lawyers"—other servicemembers who probably know less about military law than you do.

CIVILIAN CRIMES

As a result of a Supreme Court decision, the military may court-martial you for a civilian-type crime even if committed off post and off duty. Civilian-type crimes include murder, rape, robbery, assault, and drug crimes, as opposed to military crimes such as going AWOL or disobeying a lawful order. In fact, both the military and civilian authorities could prosecute you for an off-post civilian-type crime. Doing so would not be double jeopardy because the prohibition against trying a person more than once for the same offense means that a single sovereign can try a defendant only once; the military and the state or local authorities represent different sovereigns—federal and state. In practice, however, the military and the civilian authorities will get together and decide which will prosecute the case. The defendant does not have the right to decide which system will prosecute him.

WHAT TO DO IF ARRESTED

The military uses the term *apprehend* instead of the word *arrest*. Both terms mean to take a suspect into custody. Any officer or noncommissioned officer or the military police may apprehend service personnel. They would apprehend you, for example, by telling you that they were taking you into custody. They would not have to use any special words, so long as you knew that they were taking you into custody.

If an officer, a policeman, or a noncommissioned officer apprehends you, do not resist. Even if you are not guilty of anything and someone is arresting you improperly, resisting apprehension is a crime under the Uniform Code of Military Justice. The punishment for resisting apprehension includes a bad-conduct discharge and confinement for one year. Therefore, cooperation is best, because it is stupid to give law enforcement personnel a charge that they could prove—resisting apprehension—when they may not be able to prove the one they arrested you for.

After the arrest, the officials who apprehended you may search you and the area within your reach. Do not interfere with the search even if it is unlawful, because any evidence found in an illegal search cannot be used against you.

The person who apprehends you will probably read you your rights shortly after the apprehension. A proper rights warning will include these elements: what crime the officer suspects you of, your right to remain silent, the statement that anything you say may be used as evidence against you at a trial by court-martial, and your rights to a lawyer. You have the right to a military lawyer free of charge. You may also hire a civilian attorney, but the military will not pay for a civilian attorney.

After the commander or policeperson reads you your rights, he will ask you to waive them. When you waive your rights, you give them up. The best practice is to refuse to waive your rights until after you have talked with an attorney. Even if you are not guilty, you could say something that law enforcement officials could use against you because you may not know military criminal law. A statement that seems to show that you are innocent may instead be a vital piece of evidence that the prosecutor could use to prove your guilt.

For example, I once defended a soldier accused of rape. When he was apprehended, he waived his rights and told the criminal investigator that he had had voluntary sexual intercourse with the woman who said he had forced her to have sex with him. His statement certainly was not a confession to rape, but it turned out to be very damaging to him. The woman who said she had been raped could not identify him, so only his admission to voluntary sexual intercourse identified him as the alleged rapist. Without his admission, no evidence tied him to the alleged crime, so he would not have had to face a general court-martial and a possible life sentence. Although the court-martial did not convict him, he had to undergo the fear and uncertainty of being tried by court-martial because of his seemingly innocent statement. Remember that the best thing to do is to refuse to discuss any suspected offense with anyone until after you have talked with a lawyer.

Contrary to popular belief, to make a legal apprehension, the military police don't need to read you your rights. A rights warning is necessary only before the military police question you. To take you into custody, even civilian police do not need to read you your rights. So, even though no one has read you your rights, do not blurt out any statements. Some servicemembers believe that if they confess before being read their rights, no one can prosecute them. Nothing could be further from the truth. Not only could your commander prosecute you, but also your statement could be used as evidence against you if you volunteered it without any attempt on the part of the military police to question you.

Investigators rely on the interaction of two types of pressures to get arrested persons to confess: the fear and uncertainty of being arrested and effective interrogation techniques. No one is free of these pressures to confess.

For example, a military policeman read my wife her rights once for "failure to control pet." Our dog had broken loose and run straight to the military police station. When my wife arrived to claim the dog, the policeman read her rights to her. She promptly waived them and confessed to failure to control her pet. She did not ask to see a lawyer, even though I was the chief of criminal law on the post and even though she had no idea what the punishment for failure to control a pet was. Under the pressure of the situation, she did what most people do: she talked. Fortunately for her, the penalty for failure to control pet was for me to get a lecture from my commander on making sure our dog was on a leash. Not all penalties are so lenient, however, so you must keep quiet and resist the pressure to waive your rights, especially the right to remain silent and the right to have an attorney.

Some servicemembers are afraid that a military lawyer works for the commander and not for them, but this is not so. For one thing, the Canons of Ethics of the American Bar Association require lawyers to defend their clients zealously within the limits of the law. Military defense lawyers also belong to separate defense units, so local commanders do not write their efficiency reports. Rather, senior defense counsel do. Finally, the Uniform Code of Military Justice makes it illegal to give a less favorable efficiency report to a defense counsel because of the zeal with which he defended an accused servicemember.

You should also be aware that military attorneys must be qualified as civilian lawyers before they can become military ones. They have to graduate from a law school and pass a bar examination just as civilian attorneys do. Thus, you should have confidence that the military attorney detailed for you to consult is qualified to help you and has your best interests at heart. If you don't, you may, of course, obtain a civilian lawyer. Remember, however, that a civilian lawyer may know nothing about the military justice system.

Regardless of whether you consult a military or a civilian defense lawyer, you must tell him the truth about your involvement with the incident being investigated; your lawyer's advice is only as good as his knowledge of what you really did or did not do. You may be frank with your lawyer because the law prevents him from revealing anything you tell him to anyone, unless you give him permission to do so. The only exception to this rule is that he must reveal any statement you make about your intent to commit a future crime. Thus, because you do not have to worry about his telling anyone what you tell him and because he cannot advise you properly unless he knows what you actually did, you must tell your attorney the whole truth.

If someone apprehends you for a serious offense, he may require you to provide other evidence—by participating in a lineup, by providing a handwriting sample, or by being fingerprinted. If the criminal investigator asks you to consent, the best practice is to consult your attorney before doing so. If the investigator does not ask for consent, but rather orders you to do something, you should comply. If the order is illegal, your attorney will be able to prevent the prosecutor from using such illegally obtained evidence in court. On the other hand, if the order is legal, you can use your cooperation to show the court that you should get a lighter sentence if you are convicted.

Sometimes investigators ask suspects who say that they are innocent to take a polygraph, a lie detector test. Lie detector is not a totally accurate name. The polygraph shows deception. In other words, the person taking the test does not have to actually lie to flunk. If he is hiding something, he may react to a question about it and thus "indicate deception." I have some doubts about the reliability of a lie detector test, because I have had clients pass the exam given by one examiner and flunk one given by another examiner.

The polygraph is, however, a great way for the police to obtain confessions. If the suspect appears to be lying, a skilled polygraph examiner simply uses the test results to obtain a confession. Therefore, you should never take a lie detector test without first consulting your lawyer. Further, you should not take a military polygraph without getting an independent civilian test first, if possible. Most large cities have a number of civilian polygraph operators who do not work for police departments.

Even if you pass the polygraph test, the results of the test are probably inadmissible in court. Courts have been reluctant to use polygraph evidence because they are not sure of its validity and are afraid the jury would automatically find the accused guilty if the polygraph showed he had been deceptive.

After the military police have completed their processing, they will turn you over to your commander. The commander, not the military police, determines what will happen to you and to any charges against you. He will decide whether he will place you in pretrial confinement, in arrest in quarters (a type of restriction in which you cannot leave your quarters), or on restriction until the case is concluded.

If your commander places you in pretrial confinement, a defense counsel will visit you. This lawyer can seek your release as well as advise you on what is happening in your case. A military magistrate, typically either a military judge or an officer appointed by the commander, also must review your confinement within seven days of the date you begin confinement to make certain it is legal. If it isn't, he will order your release. If you are in pretrial confinement, you will receive credit for any time already served if you receive a jail sentence at your court-martial.

WHAT HAPPENS TO THE CHARGES

Just because someone has apprehended you or the military police have told you that they have charged you with a crime does not necessarily mean that your commander will take disciplinary action against you. At some point, your immediate commander will conduct a preliminary inquiry to determine the facts and circumstances of the alleged offense; then he will decide what to do about it.

Your commander may dispose of the offense in a number of ways. He may take no action, or he may take an administrative action rather than a criminal one, such as a counseling statement, a letter of reprimand, or even an administrative discharge for misconduct. Military law considers administrative actions as ways to correct problems rather than as punishments. If, for example, your conduct shows you cannot behave as a noncommissioned officer should, your commander could try to reduce your grade administratively instead of punishing you by a court-martial.

Administrative actions give you certain due process rights (see chapter 2). At a minimum, the command must notify you of the proposed action and give you an opportunity to explain why the command should not take the action against you. For more serious administrative actions, such as a discharge, your opportunity to explain may include representation by an attorney in front of a board of officers. The key to dealing with administrative procedures is to consult an attorney so that you can understand your rights and exercise them effectively.

If the commander decides that the offense is serious enough to warrant punishment rather than handling it by administrative action, he may impose nonjudicial punishment under Article 15 or prefer court-martial charges.

Nonjudicial Punishment

Authorized by Article 15 of the Uniform Code of Military Justice, nonjudicial punishment gives commanders a way to punish servicemembers for minor offenses without going through the complicated procedure of a court-martial and without putting a criminal conviction on their records. Thus, nonjudicial punishment is less serious than a court-martial. Unless you are on a ship, you may refuse to let your commander use Article 15 to punish you by demanding trial by court-martial. Because a court-martial, however, may result in a record of conviction and more serious punishments, such as confinement, it is seldom wise to demand trial by court-martial. Certainly, you should talk to a lawyer before refusing to accept nonjudicial punishment.

A common misconception about nonjudicial punishment is that by accepting the Article 15 procedure you are pleading guilty. Such is not the case. You are agreeing only to let the commander decide whether you are guilty or innocent rather than to have a military judge or a jury at a court-martial make that decision.

If your commander offers you nonjudicial punishment, you may accept it, plead not guilty, and present matters in defense and in extenuation and mitigation. *Extenuation* refers to facts that make the offense less serious than it might be otherwise. For example, if you struck a noncommissioned officer, an extenuating circumstance might be that he had provoked you by calling you a name. The punishment for a provoked assault should be less than that for an unprovoked one. Factors in *mitigation* are any other considerations unrelated to the crime that would indicate that punishment should be light, such as no previous disciplinary problems, good duty performance, good combat service, and so on.

RECORD OF RECOMMENDED NONJUDICIAL PUNISHMENT PROCEEDINGS

TO: *(Name, Rank, Organization, SSAN, and Major Command of Service Member)* | THRU:

1. I am considering whether to recommend to[1] Uniform Code of Military Justice *(UCMJ)* for the following alleged misconduct in violation of Article(s) — that you be punished under Article 15, , UCMJ:[2]

2. You have the rights listed on the reverse side. A military lawyer is available to further explain these rights to you and help you decide what to do. You may contact:

3. If you accept nonjudicial punishment proceedings, and if I find you committed one or more of the offenses alleged, the maximum punishment I could impose upon you is listed on the reverse side in paragraph_____ under maximum permissible punishments.

4. You will notify me of your decision by _____ , _____ *(3 duty days)*, unless I grant you an extension.
   (time)   *(date)*

DATE | NAME, RANK, AND ORGANIZATION OF COMMANDER | SIGNATURE

DATE/TIME SERVED ON MEMBER | SIGNATURE OF PERSON SERVING MEMBER *(If not Commander*

5. I understand the rights listed on the reverse side:[3]
   I [ ] have [ ] have not consulted a lawyer. My decisions are:
   a. [ ] I demand trial by court-martial.
   b. [ ] I waive my right to demand trial by court-martial and accept nonjudicial punishment proceedings under Article 15, UCMJ.
   (1) I [ ] do [ ] do not request to make a personal appearance before you. I [ ] do [ ] do not desire that it be public.
   (2) I [ ] have [ ] have not attached a written presentation.[4]

DATE | NAME AND RANK OF SERVICE MEMBER | SIGNATURE

6. I have considered any matters you presented in defense, mitigation, or extenuation, and find that:
   a. [ ] Nonjudicial punishment is not appropriate.
   b. [ ] You did not commit the offense(s) alleged. I hereby terminate these proceedings.
   c. [ ] You did commit one or more of the offenses alleged.[5] I hereby impose the following punishment:[6]

7. This punishment is effective immediately unless otherwise stated. If you decide not to appeal at this time, you still have the right to appeal this punishment within 5 days. An appeal made after that time may be rejected as untimely.[7]

DATE | NAME, RANK, AND ORGANIZATION OF COMMANDER | SIGNATURE

8. [ ] I do not appeal
   [ ] I appeal and [ ] will [ ] will not submit additional matters in writing within 3 duty days. *(72 hours)*

DATE | NAME AND RANK OF SERVICE MEMBER | SIGNATURE

[ ] I hereby withdraw my appeal.
[ ] I withdraw my decision not to appeal and hereby appeal. | DATE | MEMBER'S SIGNATURE

9. After consideration of all matters presented in your appeal and after referral to a judge advocate, I have decided that your appeal is:
   [ ] Denied [ ] Granted as follows:

DATE | NAME, RANK, AND ORGANIZATION OF APPELLATE AUTHORITY | SIGNATURE

10. Article 15 [ ] will [ ] will not be filed in member's UIF.

DATE | NAME, RANK, AND ORGANIZATION OF COMMANDER | SIGNATURE

11. I have seen the action taken on my appeal and/or was informed of my commander's decision to [ ] file [ ] not file this record in a UIF. | DATE | MEMBER'S SIGNATURE

12. This record was examined and found legally sufficient on _____ , A copy was received by CBPO on _____ and AFO on _____ The record is being forwarded per AFR 111-9.

DATE | NAME, RANK, AND ORGANIZATION OF JUDGE ADVOCATE | SIGNATURE

AF FORM 3071
JUN 85 | PREVIOUS EDITIONS ARE OBSOLETE

An Air Force nonjudicial punishment form.

An Article 15 proceeding against you would start when the commander or his representative (in the grade of E-7 or above) notified you of his intent to impose nonjudicial punishment. This notice would include the following elements:

- What crimes you are suspected of committing.
- A summary of the evidence against you or the opportunity, if you ask, to see this evidence.
- Your right to demand trial by court-martial, unless you are on a ship.
- The maximum punishment that you may receive from an Article 15. The commander should not tell you what punishment he would give you because he should not have decided on the case yet.
- The right to appear in person before the commander to present matters in defense, extenuation, or mitigation. If you exercised this right, the commander or his representative would tell you what you'd need to know:

1. You have the right to remain silent and any statement you make may be used as evidence against you in a trial by court-martial.

2. You have the right to have a spokesman with you unless the punishment will not be more than fourteen days' extra duty, fourteen days' restriction, and an oral reprimand. The spokesman may speak for you but may not question witnesses unless the commander permits. The right to a spokesman, however, does not entitle you to have a military lawyer act as your spokesman. If you have trouble expressing yourself, you may want to have a trusted officer or noncommissioned officer act as your spokesman.

3. You have the right to have witnesses present if their testimony would help in deciding the case and if they are reasonably available. A witness is reasonably available if the military would not have to pay for his appearance, if he can appear without unduly delaying the proceedings, and if his commander can excuse him from his duties.

4. You have the right to request an open hearing unless the punishment is limited to fourteen days' extra duty, fourteen days' restriction, and an oral reprimand. Remember that the commander would have already told you the maximum punishment you could receive. So if he does not tell you of your right to request an open hearing, you do not have this right because the punishment would be so limited.

When you have the right to request an open hearing and you do so, the public may be present unless the commander determines that good cause exists to close the hearing. Good causes, for example, would be to prevent the release of classified information. Few legal considerations are involved in the decision whether to request an open hearing. Few servicemembers request an open hearing, perhaps to avoid embarrassment. Another reason not to have an open hearing is the fear that, if the commander has an audience, it may make him want to appear "tough" in enforcing discipline and that he will give you more severe punishment than he would otherwise.

5. Depending on the possible punishment and on the military justice regulations of your service, you may consult a military lawyer before deciding whether to accept nonjudicial punishment. Again, if you have any questions or doubts, see an attorney. Of course, you could also see a civilian attorney, but the military would not provide him free of charge as it would the military attorney. If you see an attorney, tell him the truth. Otherwise, his advice is worthless.

If you do not demand trial by court-martial, the commander will continue with the nonjudicial punishment procedure. You do not have to sign the Article 15 form for the commander to proceed with nonjudicial punishment. He may impose punishment unless you demand trial by court-martial. Silence or refusal to sign to accept nonjudicial punishment is not the same as demanding trial by court-martial.

After hearing anything you and any witnesses have to say in the Article 15 proceeding, the commander will decide whether you are guilty. He will not impose punishment unless he is convinced that you committed the offense and believes that he should punish you. If he does not believe you need punishment, he will notify you and end the proceedings. If he thinks he should punish you, he will tell you the punishment and of your right to appeal.

If you feel the punishment was not fair or was too severe for the offense, you may appeal to the next higher commander. You appeal should be in writing and explain why the punishment was unfair or too severe. You must appeal within five days of the day the commander tells you the punishment unless you have a good reason for needing extra time. You will have to serve any punishment you receive even though you have appealed. If, however, the next higher commander does not decide on the appeal within five days after you submit it and if you so request, the commander must stop the punishment until the next higher commander acts on the appeal.

If your commander has punished you by Article 15, you should try to perform your duties as well as possible and to avoid further disciplinary problems. Your commander or his replacement may suspend, remit, or set aside an Article 15 punishment at any time within four months after imposing it—a good reason to perform in an outstanding manner.

Courts-Martial

The worst action your commander could take against you would be to prefer court-martial charges against you. Any servicemember may prefer (swear out) charges against any other servicemember, but only the commander may decide whether the charges should go to a court-martial. If your commander decided a court-martial was appropriate, he would call you in and read you the charges. You should not discuss the offenses with him. In fact, you should not talk about the case with anyone until after you have seen your defense counsel. At this point, your commander could restrict you or place you in arrest in quarters or pretrial confinement.

The military has three types of courts-martial: summary, special, and general. The least serious court-martial is a *summary court-martial*. Its punishment is limited to confinement for thirty days, hard labor without confinement for forty-five days, forfeiture of two thirds of your pay for one month, and reduction to the lowest enlisted grade. A summary court-martial may not sentence servicemembers in pay grades E-4 and above to confinement, hard labor without confinement, or a reduction of more than one grade.

You have the right to object to trial by summary court-martial. If you did object, the commander would send the case to a special court-martial, which could impose more severe punishments. Why would you object to trial by summary court only to face the possibly more severe punishments of a special court-martial? The main reason is that you would have no right to an attorney at a summary court-martial. You would have that right, however, at special and general courts. A summary court-martial also has no judge or court panel (military jury). The summary court officer, who is seldom an attorney, acts as prosecutor, defense counsel, judge, and jury. Thus, in a complex case or in one that involves a technical legal defense, such as entrapment, the advantage of having a defense counsel and a qualified military judge may offset the risk of a stiffer sentence.

Another important consideration in the decision of whether to object to trial by summary court-martial is that the U.S. Supreme Court has ruled that a summary court-martial is not a real court. Thus, if someone, such as a prospective employer, asked you whether you had ever been convicted and your only "conviction" was from a summary court, you could legitimately answer no. Obviously, you should make the decision of whether to object to trial by summary court-martial only after consultation with a lawyer.

The commander who is authorized to send your case to a summary court is called the summary court-martial convening authority. He will often be one step higher than your immediate commander. If the convening authority sent your case to a summary court, your commander would give you a charge sheet and tell you the following information at a preliminary proceeding:

- What he is charging you with.
- The names of witnesses whom the summary court officer will call to testify and what other evidence (objects, documents, and so on) he will consider.
- Your right to plead guilty or not guilty.
- Your right to cross-examine witnesses or to have the summary court-martial officer cross-examine them on your behalf.
- Your right to call witnesses and to present evidence on your behalf.

• Your right to testify or to remain silent, in which case the summary court-martial officer will not assume that your silence means that you are guilty.

• Your right to present evidence in extenuation or mitigation if you are found guilty. To show why you should receive a light sentence, you may testify under oath or make an unsworn statement, either spoken or written, or both. You may also call witnesses and introduce documentary evidence, such as good efficiency reports and commendations, to show why the court-martial should not punish you severely.

• The maximum sentence you could receive.

• Your right to object to trial by summary court-martial.

If the summary court officer found you guilty and sentenced you to confinement at hard labor, that officer would have to tell you of your right to request that the convening authority defer (put off) the confinement. Regardless of the sentence, after a legal clerk or court reporter had prepared the record of trial, you would receive a copy that you and your lawyer could use to help you appeal or request clemency.

You could petition the convening authority for clemency, which he could grant by reducing the sentence. He could not, however, increase the sentence. You could also petition the Judge Advocate General of your branch of service for relief if the summary court officer conducted the trial improperly or on certain other grounds. You should consult defense counsel to help you prepare such petitions. A military attorney would provide this help free of charge.

Another type of court-martial you could face is a *special court-martial*. It is more serious than a summary court, but it also offers you more protections: a defense counsel, a judge, and a military jury. The Staff Judge Advocate would appoint a military lawyer to prosecute the case. The maximum punishment a special court may impose is confinement for six months, forfeiture of two thirds pay per month for six months, and, in the case of enlisted members only, reduction to the lowest enlisted grade. In some circumstances, a special court may sentence an enlisted servicemember to a bad-conduct discharge.

The third type of court-martial—the *general court-martial*—is the most serious. Depending on the maximum punishment for the offenses the accused is facing, a general court-martial may sentence the accused to the death penalty, confinement for life, a dishonorable or a bad-conduct discharge, total forfeiture of all pay and allowances, and reduction to the lowest enlisted grade (enlisted members only). Officers may be dismissed—the officer version of a dishonorable discharge.

If the charges against you were sent to a general or a special court-martial, a supervising defense counsel would appoint a military lawyer for you at no charge. You could also request military counsel of your own choice at no expense to you. The defense office would provide this counsel, known as individual military counsel, if he is reasonably available, and the military judge or the detailed counsel's supervisor would normally excuse the detailed counsel from the case.

Another option you would have is to obtain a civilian attorney at no expense to the U.S. government. Normally, it is not a good idea to hire a civilian attorney to represent you at a court-martial, however, because most civilian attorneys are not familiar with the court-martial system. They also may lack the ability to relate to a military jury. If your lawyer alienates or angers the jury, you may receive a more severe sentence if they find you guilty. The disadvantages of a civilian attorney are particularly great in cases involving military offenses that are not crimes in civilian life. You may, however, want to hire a civilian attorney if you are charged with a serious civilian-type crime, such as murder or rape, and if you know that he is a very experienced criminal lawyer or is experienced with the military justice system, or if you do not trust your detailed military attorney. It is very important that you have an attorney you trust to represent you.

You may also defend yourself before special and general courts-martial by convincing the military judge that you are knowingly and intelligently waiving your right to counsel. But remember the old legal saying: Only a fool has himself for a client. Even lawyers should not defend themselves, because they are likely to be so emotionally involved with their own cases that they would not make good decisions. It would be even harder to defend yourself if you did not know military law and procedure. In the only case I saw in which a servicemember defended himself, he brought out more evidence to hurt his case than did the prosecutor. So don't waive your right to counsel.

You must trust your attorney because, as discussed earlier, you must confide in him. He cannot represent you effectively unless you tell him the truth. Remember, the attorney-client privilege prevents him from telling anyone else what you have told him without your permission. He may miss a good way to defend you if you lie and tell him you were not involved in the offense at all. For example, a servicemember who tells his lawyer he was not present at a drug sale and makes up an alibi might have a perfectly good defense that he was entrapped into the sale. But if he says he was not there at the sale, he cannot say that he was entrapped; and prosecutors are good at proving that made-up alibis are untrue.

While the best thing to do is to talk truthfully to your lawyer, it is extremely unwise to discuss your case with anyone else. Courts-martial have convicted many servicemembers, despite a good effort by their defense counsel, because they talked about their cases with friends. Many such friends end up being witnesses for the trial counsel (prosecutor).

In one case in which I defended a soldier, I had prepared an excellent defense, using aerial photography and engineer surveys, to show that the crime could not have happened the way the victim said it had. My client, however, bragged to his friends, "I did it, but my lawyer is going to get me off." His friends told the prosecutor, who notified me that these friends would be witnesses against my client. With this additional evidence against him, he had to plead guilty in exchange for a plea bargain.

Discussing your case with anyone other than your defense counsel can only hurt your case. The only possible exception is your spouse, unless your spouse is the victim of the crime. Your spouse cannot testify against you unless he or she was the crime victim. Even so, don't talk to your spouse unless your attorney says it is okay to do so. Don't talk to anyone else about your case! It is especially important not to talk to the prosecution's witnesses. Trying to get them to change their stories could, in addition to making you look guilty, result in more charges, such as obstruction of justice.

During an early meeting with your defense counsel, he would advise you of some of your options. One would be to submit through your defense counsel a request for discharge for the good of the service, sometimes known as a discharge in lieu of a court-martial. If you qualified for such a discharge, you would normally receive an other-than-honorable discharge. Accordingly, you would lose substantially all military and veterans benefits, but you would also avoid getting a court-martial conviction and a possible jail sentence. The chain of command would approve or disapprove such a request for discharge, not the military lawyers. This option is another reason for you to stay out of trouble while pending charges, because every additional offense you committed would make it less likely that the command would be satisfied with a discharge instead of a court-martial.

If your case went to court, you would have some other decisions to make. Your attorney would advise you which would be best, but the decisions must be yours. One is whether to plead guilty or not guilty. You have an absolute right to plead not guilty and to require the government to prove your guilt beyond a reasonable doubt, even if you did what you are charged with doing. If you are guilty, however, you should consider pleading guilty because you may plea bargain. A plea bargain—called a *pretrial agreement* in the military—is an agreement in which you plead guilty in return for some benefit. The following are among the benefits you could receive in return for your plea of guilty:

• Limitation on the sentence. An example of this benefit would be suspension of any confinement or disapproval of any confinement in excess of six months.

• Dismissal of some of the charges against you.

• Agreement that the court cannot impose the death penalty when you are charged with an offense carrying a possible death sentence.

After consulting your defense counsel, you could submit a pretrial agreement through the Staff Judge Advocate to the convening authority (the officer who created the court-martial and sent your case to it). The convening authority would decide whether to accept any pretrial agreement you offered. Of course, some accused servicemembers plead guilty without a plea bargain. If the government has a very good case, for example, it may not be willing to plea bargain. But pleading guilty may still be wise because sometimes a guilty plea results in a lesser sentence by showing the court that the accused accepts responsibility for his crimes.

If you do plead guilty, you will have to answer questions from the judge to convince him that you are guilty. If he is not sure that you are guilty, he will enter a not guilty plea on your behalf. You have no constitutional right to plead guilty, and the judge does not want you to plead guilty if he believes you may be innocent.

Another decision you must make is who will decide your case: a military judge or a military jury. If you give up your right to a military jury, the judge will decide your guilt or innocence. If he finds you guilty, he will also decide on your sentence.

In the military justice system, the jurors are called *court members*. Court members are normally officers, but if you are enlisted, you have a right to have not less than one third of the court members be enlisted members. The enlisted members will normally be senior noncommissioned officers. A special court-martial must have at least three court members; a general court must have at least five. If a jury tries you, two thirds of the members of the jury must vote that you are guilty before the jury can convict you.

This system is different from civilian courts, which require that all jurors agree on the verdict. The military jury system, however, is not necessarily worse for you. The need for two thirds to agree avoids a "hung jury"—one that cannot decide guilt or innocence.

The same two thirds requirement is necessary to reach a sentence. To sentence anyone to ten years' confinement or more, however, three fourths of the jurors must agree. A death sentence requires all jurors to agree.

Military judges appear, on the average, to convict in a slightly higher percentage of cases and to impose slightly more severe sentences. Most accused servicemembers, however, choose to be tried by judge alone. One reason accused servicemembers often waive their right to a military jury is that judges are more predictable than court members because judges develop track records, which make gauging the outcome of the trial easier. Many military lawyers also believe that judges are softer on some military offenses, such as AWOL and disrespect, than are court panels.

But military attorneys often also perceive court members as being softer on some civilian-type offenses, such as assault. Court panels with senior enlisted members may be sympathetic with a senior NCO accused of an offense that does not strike at the core of noncommissioned officer values. For example, such a court panel might sympathize with an NCO charged with a minor trainee abuse offense after the trainee had provoked him.

The key point in selecting who will decide the case, however, is not to rely on generalizations. Your military defense counsel will know the track record of the judges and court panels at your installation. You should not decide what type of court should hear your case without both your lawyer's advice and this information.

Another decision you will have to make is whether to testify. I cannot give you any hard and fast rules on what to do. You must make that decision according to the circumstances of your particular case and the recommendation of your defense counsel. If you testified on the merits of the case—on the question of your guilt or innocence—you would be subject to cross-examination by the prosecutor. If cross-examination would hurt your case more than your testimony would help it, you may be better off not testifying. If you testified, the prosecutor could also introduce evidence that you were not a truthful person, because by testifying you would be asking the court-martial to believe you, and the prosecutor could try to convince the court that it should not believe you. If you chose not to testify, the court should not assume that you are guilty just because you did not testify.

You would also have to decide whether to testify in the sentencing phase of the trial if the court convicted you. If you decided to testify, you would again be subject to cross-examination. Another option during the sentencing phase would be to make an unsworn statement: you could make an unsworn statement, your lawyer could make it for you, or you could write it and give it to the court to read. The prosecutor could not cross-examine you on an unsworn statement. He could, however, attempt to show that your statement was untrue by offering evidence to prove it was false.

Regardless of whether you testify or make an unsworn statement, the keys to testifying successfully are these:

- Be truthful.
- Answer the questions asked without volunteering additional information.
- Direct your answers to the judge in a judge-alone case or to the court in a jury case.
- Be calm and respectful even during a difficult cross-examination.

If the court convicted you, your defense attorney would explain your rights to appeal. Some cases include an automatic appeal to your service's Court of Military Criminal Appeals. If that court decided the appeal against you, you could ask the U.S. Court of Appeals for the Armed Forces to review your case. The U.S. Court of Appeals for the Armed Forces comprises five civilian justices appointed by the president. A new law permits appeals to the U.S. Supreme Court from final decisions of the Court of Appeals for the Armed Forces. Your defense counsel would also assist you in petitioning the convening authority to lessen your sentence. He would also ask for deferral of any confinement you received if you requested it.

Because your attorney would not necessarily be stationed in Washington, D.C., where these appellate courts are, your service would appoint a military attorney who specialized in appeals to help you with yours and to work with your defense counsel. Of course, you could have a civilian lawyer to help you with any appeals, too, but the government would not pay for a civilian attorney's help in an appeal, just as it wouldn't pay for one at your trial.

If you were facing trial by court-martial, you would have some other important rights. One is the right to a speedy trial. The Manual for Courts-Martial requires the prosecution to try servicemembers waiting for a court-martial within 120 days. Delays that you or your lawyer requested or caused, however, would not count in the 120 days. If you were in pretrial confinement, the prosecution would have to bring you to trial within 90 days. If a military judge found that the government violated your right to a speedy trial, he could dismiss the charges, or an appellate court could dismiss the charges on appeal.

Another important right is that of a public trial. This right is designed to protect you, because having a trial open to the public should reduce improper or unfair results. A military judge, however, may close a court-martial for a proper reason, such as to prevent the disclosure of classified information. But the judge may exclude the public only as a last resort.

If you were awaiting trial by general court-martial, the government could not try you unless it had completed an Article 32 investigation. An Article 32 investigation is the military version of a grand jury hearing, but it offers far more rights than does a grand jury. The Article 32 investigating officer would thoroughly and impartially investigate the accusations against you and recommend whether the charges should go to a general court-martial. You would have the right to have a military lawyer represent you at the Article 32 hearing, either one appointed for you or one of your own choice if reasonably available. You could also get a civilian lawyer at no expense to the United States. Unlike grand jury proceedings, you could be present throughout the investigation, could cross-examine witnesses, and could present evidence in your behalf.

Two more important rights at courts-martial are the right to confront—see and cross-examine—witnesses against you and the right to have witnesses for you at the court-martial. Normally, your defense counsel would handle these matters for you.

CONCLUSION

I hope you will never need the advice I've given you in this chapter. But if you do, the key points to remember are to stay out of more trouble, to keep quiet about the case except with your lawyer and perhaps with your spouse if your lawyer has approved your discussing it with your spouse, and to follow your lawyer's advice.

8

Civilian Criminal Justice

If you break the law while you are in the service, you could face prosecution not only in the military justice system but also in the civilian court system. Therefore, you need to know how your military status could affect you and your family in civilian criminal proceedings both in the United States and overseas.

IN THE UNITED STATES
If you are serving within the United States and you break the law, you could be breaking several laws at the same time. For example, if you sold drugs off post, you would be committing a crime under the Uniform Code of Military Justice, which applies worldwide, on or off post. The act of selling drugs off post would also break federal and state drug laws. Thus, both state and federal courts could try you for the same crime.

The federal court could be either a military court-martial or a civilian court. It would not be double jeopardy for both courts to try you because the double jeopardy rule means only that the same government system cannot try you twice for the same crime. Usually, though, the state and federal prosecutors involved would decide who should try the case. The prosecutor who had the greater interest in trying your case would prosecute it. You would not have the right to decide which system would try you.

If civilian police arrest you, you should neither resist nor say anything— the same as if the police were military. Unless civilian police arrest you for a very serious offense, they will turn you over to your commander after processing (fingerprinting and so forth). If civilian police arrest you for a serious crime and put you in jail, you must immediately report back to your unit after you have posted bail and have been released. Otherwise, you will be absent without leave.

If you are arrested, immediately get an attorney to help you. As a general rule, if civilian police arrest you, the military will not provide you an attorney. You will have to get a civilian attorney. Nevertheless, the advice in chapter 7 about what to do if arrested applies equally to arrests by civilian police: do not resist, do cooperate, and do not say anything until after you have talked with a lawyer.

If you are not in the custody of the civilian police or in jail, you may consult a military lawyer. Even though you may be innocent (and legally you are innocent until proven guilty), you need to know the worst possible consequences of a civilian arrest. A military lawyer can advise you of the effect of a civilian conviction on your military service. For example, if a civilian court convicted you of a serious offense, your commander could try to discharge you from the military with an unfavorable discharge certificate. (See chapter 4.)

It would be unusual for a federal prosecutor to try a servicemember in a federal court because federal prosecutors would usually prefer to let the military prosecute military offenders. In two situations, however, the federal government would try a servicemember in a federal civilian court rather than by a court-martial. One exception is minor crimes, such as traffic offenses, which federal prosecutors would usually try in a U.S. magistrate court. The other exception is major crimes, such as spying, that the FBI, rather than the military, would have investigated. A U.S. attorney would probably prosecute these serious crimes in a federal district court rather than let the military try the case by court-martial.

U.S. Magistrate Court

Many installations have a U.S. magistrate court to handle minor offenses, such as traffic violations, committed on post by either civilians or servicemembers. Normally, the military does not allow its military attorneys to defend servicemembers (or family members) in magistrate court. Because the magistrate court on post is a part of the local federal district court, it can try misdemeanors (minor crimes) that happen on post. One example of a common crime tried in magistrate court is a speeding violation on post.

The maximum punishment you could receive in magistrate court is one year in jail and a $5,000 fine. Because most crimes tried in magistrate court are traffic offenses, however, the usual punishment is a small fine.

Often when you receive a traffic ticket, the military policeperson who gives you the ticket will tell you how to mail in the fine if you want to plead guilty and not appear in court. You may, however, want to go to court and plead not guilty. Normally, you would not have a right to a jury trial in magistrate court, and the magistrate would decide the case.

Sometimes, however, the law will not allow you to plead guilty by mailing in your fine. The law enforcement official will give you a summons to appear in magistrate court on a certain date, usually within several weeks. If you are told to appear, you must go to court at the time and day you are told. Otherwise, the magistrate will issue a warrant for your arrest, and a U.S. marshal will arrest you and put you in jail. So, either go to court when told or have your lawyer get a delay. If your military duties prevent your going to court, see your commander and ask him to call the staff judge advocate's office to get you a delay.

Magistrate court is a consent court. This legal term means that the magistrate could not hear the case unless you agreed to let him. But if you did not agree, then a U.S. attorney would prosecute you in federal district court. It is seldom wise to refuse trial in the magistrate court. The federal district court can give much stiffer sentences and would require you to travel to wherever that court was, which could be fifty miles or more away from your duty station. Do not refuse a trial in magistrate court unless advised to do so by a competent lawyer.

OVERSEAS

If you are serving overseas and break the law, you could be breaking not only U.S. military laws but also the laws of the country you are in at the time. The Uniform Code of Military Justice applies worldwide, so even if you are in, say, Germany or Korea, your command may try you by court-martial. If you commit a crime, either the courts of the country you are in may try you or the U.S. military may try you, depending on the treaty between that country and the United States. Such treaties are called Status of Forces Agreements.

Under the North Atlantic Treaty Organization Status of Forces Agreement (NATO SOFA), for example, the United States can court-martial you for crimes that violate the Uniform Code of Military Justice but do not violate the laws of the country you are serving in. Let's take Germany, for example. If you went AWOL while stationed there, you would violate Article 86 of the Uniform Code, and the military could try you by court-martial. AWOL from the American forces does not violate German law, however, so the Germans could not prosecute you.

If your crime violated German law, but not ours, the Germans could try you and the American military could not. For example, the Germans have a law that you can't hitchhike on the autobahn, but that is not a crime under the Uniform Code of Military Justice. So, if the German police arrested you for hitchhiking on the autobahn, the Germans could prosecute you, but your commander could not have you tried by court-martial.

The situation is more complicated, however, if your crime violates both our law and that of the country you are in. For example, murder violates both Article 118 of the Uniform Code of Military Justice and German law. In such a case, both court systems could prosecute you because both would have jurisdiction. The NATO SOFA and some other agreements have a rule to help determine which country's court system would actually try the case. Under the NATO SOFA, if your crime was against an American citizen, against an American citizen's property, or against the security of the U.S. government or its property, then the United States would have the primary right to try you. In all other cases, the country you are in would have the primary right to try you. So, if you committed a crime against a German or his property, the Germans would have the right to try you.

If you committed the crime while you were on official duty, the United States would have the right to try you. For example, if you were driving a military vehicle on official business and hit a German, a German court would not try your case even though the victim was German. But if you were off duty, driving your own car, and hit a German, a German court could try you.

The SOFA provides, however, that the country that has the right to try you is supposed to give "sympathetic consideration" to a request for it to turn your case over to the other country to try you. If you were off duty and hit a German while driving your own car, the Germans would often let our military court-martial you rather than trying the case in a German court. Letting the U.S. military try the case would save the Germans money and the difficulty of trying someone who may not speak the language.

Although the German system is fair, the United States almost always asks for Germany, or any other country you are in, to let the United States prosecute you to ensure that you receive the special rights and protections of our legal system. You do not have the right to decide who will try you.

If foreign police arrest you, the same advice about not resisting and not saying anything applies as it does in the United States. As a general rule, if foreign police arrest you, they will turn you over to our military. If the foreign nation decides to try you, your commander will turn you back over to the foreign authorities for trial. If the foreign country puts you into one of its jails, you are still under the protection of the American military. You would, for example, still receive such benefits as medical and dental care and legal assistance. In addition, your commander or his representative would have to visit you at least once a month to make certain that your confinement met certain standards. These protections would continue during your stay in a foreign jail. In fact, it is U.S. military practice that even if you qualify for a discharge for having a civilian conviction, you could expect to remain in the military and thus continue receiving certain military benefits until you completed your sentence and returned to the United States.

If a NATO country or another one that has signed a similar status of forces agreement tried you in one of its courts, you would have the following rights:

- To receive a speedy trial.
- To have an official notify you of the charges against you before the trial.
- To see and cross-examine the witnesses against you.
- To have the country trying you produce witnesses to testify for you.
- To have a lawyer of your own choice.
- To have an interpreter.
- To have a U.S. observer watch the trial to make certain that no one violates your rights and that your trial is fair.

Agreements with Japan, Korea, and Australia are similar to the NATO SOFA. The treaty with Panama is also similar, but it lets the United States try servicemembers for any crime committed within U.S. defense sites.

Although you can receive advice from a military attorney, if you face trial in a foreign court, you must obtain the services of a civilian attorney who practices in that country to defend you. Under some circumstances, the United States would pay for your foreign attorney and certain other trial expenses.

Remember, while you are overseas you must obey not only the Uniform Code of Military Justice but also the laws of whatever country you are in. If you break these laws, you may be tried by court-martial or in the foreign court. Regardless of what court you are tried in, you will have certain rights. You will want a good attorney to make certain that you exercise your rights wisely, and the United States will ensure that a foreign court does not violate your rights.

FAMILY MEMBERS IN CRIMINAL COURTS

Not only may law enforcement officials arrest and prosecute servicemembers but they may arrest service family members. Although the military cannot court-martial family members who are not in the service, family members must obey the civilian laws of the country where they live or visit.

If a member of your family is arrested, the advice in chapter 7 about not resisting, about keeping quiet, and about consulting an attorney applies. The military will not provide a military attorney to defend a family member, so you will have to get a civilian attorney.

In the United States, family members who broke the law off post would face prosecution in a federal, state, or county court. If they violated the law on a military installation, the federal government would try them in magistrate court unless the case involved a serious offense. A U.S. attorney would prosecute a serious crime in a federal district court. You could consult a legal assistance attorney for advice, but you would have to get a civilian attorney to defend the family member in any of these courts.

Although staying out of trouble overseas can be more difficult because of language barriers and unfamiliarity with other countries' laws, if your family goes overseas with you, they are also subject to the laws of whatever country you are in. Very few American laws apply outside of the United States. Spying and income tax laws apply worldwide, but prosecutors may try other offenses only if they are crimes under the laws of the country where they are committed. So if a German policeman, for example, caught family members with drugs, the United States could not try them by court-martial or by a civilian U.S. court, but the Germans could try them in a German court.

If a foreign court does try service family members, status of forces agreements give them the same rights servicemembers have when tried in foreign courts. Although not required to do so by law, the military usually provides family members in foreign jails the same support it gives servicemembers.

If the crime a family member commits is not too serious, the U.S. forces may be able to convince the foreign government not to prosecute the crime if the military takes some administrative action against the family member. An example of such action would be to revoke such privileges as the commissary and the PX or BX. If a family member commits a crime, the military may also revoke command sponsorship, so the family member would no longer be eligible for transportation, housing, and so on.

Therefore, you need to make certain that your family members know about the laws of the country all of you are stationed in, and you need to help your family adapt to being away from home in a strange culture. If you do so, chances are your overseas tour will be free of any legal problems with the host nation's criminal justice system.

LOSS OF PRIVILEGES

What often hurts family members most when they commit a crime is the loss of privileges. Not only may the command take privileges away from family members, but it may also take privileges away from servicemembers who do something illegal in addition to punishing them under the Uniform Code of Military Justice. The command may take some of the following administrative actions and revoke privileges instead of, or in addition to, taking legal action against a wrongdoer:

• *Bar letters.* These letters order an offender to stay away from the military installation. Often these letters are conditional and allow the barred person to come on post for certain reasons, such as to receive hospital care.

• *Denial of privileges.* Senior commanders may deny commissary and exchange privileges to servicemembers or family members who abuse those privileges, such as by writing bad checks or shoplifting in the commissary or exchange. The command usually revokes the privilege by overstamping the offender's identification card.

• *Denial of driving privileges.* The command may suspend or revoke your driving privileges if, for example, your repeated traffic violations show that you are unfit to drive.

• *Quarters termination.* If, for example, you use your quarters for an illegal purpose, the command may order you to get out of them. In such a case, you would have to find a place to live off post. The command may also order you to vacate your quarters for a family member's misconduct. For example, if a law enforcement official or a post engineer found marijuana in your child's room, the command could terminate your quarters, thus requiring you to move off post. In this situation, however, the military would have to move you and pay you quarters allowance.

If the command notifies you that it is going to deny you privileges, the command also must give you a chance to explain why you should not lose the privilege. You should consult a military attorney who can help you prepare your explanation.

JUVENILE JUSTICE

Unfortunately, juvenile service-family members sometimes commit crimes on military installations. The juvenile justice system on military posts, however, does not function nearly as effectively as does the adult system. On an installation that has exclusive federal jurisdiction, a federal prosecutor could bring a juvenile before only the federal district court or the magistrate court. How old is a juvenile? In both these federal courts, a juvenile is a person less than eighteen years old at the time of the crime and less than twenty-one at the time of trial.

Federal law provides very limited punishments for juveniles. The maximum sentence for a misdemeanor, such as shoplifting, is custody of the attorney general (placement in a juvenile home), probation, or a suspended sentence for not more than one year. For a petty offense, which is a lesser crime than a misdemeanor, the federal courts may sentence the juvenile to the same punishments, but for not more than six months. If the crime was the juvenile's first offense and if he did not get into any more trouble, the court usually would put the juvenile on probation with his consent but without a formal trial, so that he would not have a federal conviction on his record.

Before a magistrate court can hear a case, the juvenile must file a written consent to trial by the U.S. magistrate. If he does not, the trial will move to federal district court. Because the punishments are limited in magistrate court, however, a juvenile should seldom refuse to consent to have the case decided in magistrate court.

If the installation has concurrent federal-state jurisdiction, so both systems can prosecute crimes that take place on post, then the state may be willing to handle the matter under its juvenile court procedure. In such situations, however, the juvenile or his sponsor has no say in deciding which court will try the case. If one of your juvenile family members gets in trouble and faces a court appearance, see a lawyer.

Often, the most effective sanction the military can take against a juvenile is the loss of privileges. If a juvenile fights in a post theater, for example, the command may deny him the privilege of using it and other similar post facilities. The command can even evict the sponsor and his whole family from government quarters because of the misconduct of a juvenile family member. Because of the potential harm to a service family when one family member gets in trouble, it is even more important than in civilian life to know something about the law.

IF YOU ARE A CRIME VICTIM

Servicemembers can become involved with the military justice system by doing something wrong or by being the victim of a crime. Victims also have certain rights. In 1982, Congress passed the Victim and Witness Protection Act to help crime victims. The Department of Defense (DOD) has applied this act to the military. DOD has directed that the services establish programs to provide witnesses and victims the following help:

• Information about available assistance and about what will happen in their case throughout the criminal justice process.

• Referral to assistance agencies. For example, if you suffered emotional distress as a result of a crime, the victim assistance officer would refer you to a doctor, a mental health center, or a social worker who could assist you. If the military cannot provide free of charge a service you need, such as a civilian psychiatrist, CHAMPUS, the military medical insurance, may pay for it.

• Consultation. If you were the victim of a serious crime, for example, a witness assistance officer would consult you concerning the pretrial confinement of the accused, plea bargaining, and other parts of the case. Although the commander would not have to take your advice on whether to accept a plea bargain, at least you would have the chance to express your opinion as to whether it was too lenient. For example, if you were the victim of an indecent assault, and the accused was facing a maximum sentence of a dishonorable discharge and five years' confinement, the accused might agree to plead guilty if the convening authority agreed to suspend confinement in excess of two years. In such a case, the victim assistance officer would consult you and both tell you his opinion of the plea bargain and ask you how you felt about it. Your recommendation would become part of the information the convening authority would consider in deciding whether to accept the plea bargain.

The Victim and Witness Protection Act should make certain that, if you are a crime victim, the military will tell you not only what you must do to help the system punish the criminal but also what support you may receive for any problems you have as a result of the crime. Also, you will have a voice in what happens to the criminal.

Another protection available to victims of sex crimes is the Rape Shield Law. In the past, a common defense tactic when defending a rapist or other sex criminal was essentially to put the victim on trial. Defense counsel did so by cross-examining the victim or by introducing other evidence of the victim's past sex life. This defense tactic could be very degrading to the victim and probably stopped many victims from reporting sex crimes or from testifying in court.

Under the Rape Shield Law, however, evidence of the victim's reputation for sexual behavior or an opinion about the victim's sexual behavior is inadmissible in a court-martial. Civilian federal courts and some state courts also have rape shield laws. Evidence of a specific past sexual activity is admissible only in certain instances:

•   If the U.S. Constitution requires the court to admit it. Evidence that the victim had sexual intercourse with some person is admissible under this ground only if by not allowing this evidence the government violates the accused's right to due process and to confront and cross-examine witnesses against him. Military judges and appellate courts have limited this exception to those few cases in which past sexual activity has some real connection with the case. One example might be that the victim is a prostitute and the accused's defense is that her claim of rape was a result of a payment dispute.

•   If, when the evidence is of past sexual behavior with persons other than the accused, it may prove that the accused did not provide the semen or cause the injury to the victim.

•   If the evidence is of past sexual behavior with the accused to show that the victim consented to the act charged as a crime.

Although the Rape Shield Law does not totally prevent the use of evidence of past sexual behavior, it is a significant protection for sex crime victims. If the defense wants to introduce evidence of past sexual behavior by using one of the three exceptions stated above, the defense has to provide notice to the court of its intent to do so. The judge will then conduct a hearing to determine whether the evidence would be admissible. Often, evidence of past sexual behavior would not be admissible because the facts of the crime would not fall within the exceptions permitting the introduction of such evidence.

The majority of crime victims are not victims of sex crimes, however. More often a criminal act involves property.

If another servicemember has taken or damaged some of your property, for example, Article 139 of the Uniform Code of Military Justice provides you a good way to get paid for its loss or damage. Under Article 139, your commander may convene a board of one to three officers to investigate the matter. If the board finds that another servicemember has taken or willfully damaged the property, it determines the amount of money that the wrongdoer should pay for this loss or damage. If the commander approves the board's findings, the finance office will deduct the money from the wrongdoer's pay, and then you will receive that money from the government. This procedure does not even require that a court-martial find the wrongdoer guilty, although he has the right to present evidence to the Article 139 board to show that the board should not find him liable for the loss or damage to your property.

Another possible method of getting someone to compensate you for your losses is to make a claim against the government (see chapter 5). Finally, you could sue the wrongdoer in a civilian court.

If you are a victim, report the crime immediately. Although any servicemember may charge another servicemember with a crime, remember that only the commander decides whether the case goes to court. You cannot decide to drop the charges later; only a commander can drop charges. If you refuse to testify against someone you have accused because you later decide that you don't want him convicted, the military can prosecute you for refusing to testify.

Because you do not decide whether a court-martial will try the case against the accused, you should be free from pressure from the accused to drop the case. You should not even have to talk with the accused, even if he is not in pretrial confinement. If the accused asks you or pressures you not to testify against him or to change your testimony, report it to your commander, to the military police, or to the trial counsel (prosecutor) immediately. It is a crime for an accused person to threaten witnesses.

If you become a victim, you should do the following:

• *Report the crime immediately.* Call the military police, air police, shore patrol, or civilian police—whichever you think is appropriate at the time. Call a law enforcement agency, even if you aren't exactly sure which one ought to investigate the crime; they usually work together and will make sure you get the help you need.

• *Do not touch anything at the crime scene.* In other words, don't clean up the mess left in your room if a burglar tore it up during a burglary. Similarly, if you are the victim of an assault or a sex crime, don't clean yourself off. Even though you may feel unclean and want to wash yourself, you could destroy valuable evidence that would help convict the person who hurt you.

• *Tell the truth about what happened the first time and every subsequent time.* Testify truthfully in court. Perjury, lying under oath, is a crime.

• *Stay away from the accused.* If he threatens to hurt you or someone you love, tell the authorities immediately. The authorities can protect you or your loved ones, so if the accused is not in pretrial confinement, information that he has threatened you will allow his commander to put him in pretrial confinement.

• *Remember that victims have rights, too.* If you are not satisfied with the way the military police or anyone else treats you, tell the chain of command or discuss the problem with the trial counsel or the victim assistance officer.

CONCLUSION

As I said at the end of chapter 7, I hope you never need the advice in this chapter. May you and your family members never get into trouble with civilian law enforcement officials and may you never be a crime victim. If something does happen, though, remember that seeing your lawyer early and often can do a lot to minimize the damage and protect your rights.

Although the prospect of dealing with law enforcement officials is scary, you can do a lot to ensure that you never get into trouble with law enforcement authorities. Good common sense will usually help you avoid doing something wrong. If you do start having problems, however, you need to get help from a lawyer, a chaplain, an accountant, or whoever else has the expertise to help you early on in the area of your problem—before it gets out of hand.

PART IV

Personal Legal Matters

Given the nature of military service, attending to personal legal matters can sometimes be more difficult than it would be for civilians. The military may assign you overseas, for example, or in a state other than your legal residence, so conflicting national or state laws could complicate even the simplest legal problem. And because you're in the military, you may have to deploy anywhere in the world on short notice. If you do not have your personal legal matters in good shape and do not understand the legal aspects of your relationship with your family, a problem could rise quickly and at the worst possible time, such as when you are deployed thousands of miles away. In this area, which is called preventive law, making certain that your legal affairs are in order is a must for you as a servicemember.

Chapter 9 discusses your legal arrangements for any emergency that may arise, especially deployment overseas. The remaining chapters in part IV cover legal matters involving family law: marriage in chapter 10; legal aspects of having family members in chapter 11; and, finally, ending a marriage in chapter 12.

9

Your Legal Survival Kit

Although the military can provide you some help with personal legal matters, keeping your personal affairs in good shape is your responsibility. Having your personal affairs in order is more important in the military than in civilian life because the military could deploy you overseas or send you into combat with very little notice, as many servicemembers learned when ordered to the Middle East in 1990 and 1991. If you do not have a will or a guardian appointed to take care of your children, for example, you may not have time to get one before deployment.

You need to assemble your legal survival kit now, while you have time to think about what you and your family may need. You may want to use this chapter as a checklist to assemble your important papers, to consider all your options, and to talk with your family about what they could expect if the military deployed you suddenly, so that neither you nor they would have so much to worry about in that event.

Putting your legal survival kit in order involves both long- and short-term planning. Planning for the disposition of your property on your death—estate planning—is long-term; planning for when you are away from your family is short-term. It involves having powers of attorney for your family members, guardians for your children, trusts to provide for your family, and joint bank accounts.

ESTATE PLANNING

The law defines your estate as your assets at the time of your death. Your estate consists of your cash, debts owed you, other financial assets (such as bank accounts, stocks, bonds, and so on), and real and personal property.

Claims against your estate, such as funeral expenses, debts, and taxes, reduce the worth of your estate. Estate planning involves deciding how to distribute your assets upon your death, who should get them, and how to preserve them with the least shrinkage because of taxes and attorney's fees. To plan your estate, you *and* your family and your lawyer can review your government benefits, draft wills, and plan insurance coverage and taxes.

Government Benefits

When planning your legal survival kit, you need to understand your military and veterans benefits. If you die while on active duty, your family may receive benefits from the military, the Social Security Administration, and the Department of Veterans Affairs.

Your family could receive the following military benefits if you died while on active duty:

• *Dependency and Indemnity Compensation*. The military would pay a monthly sum of money to your surviving spouse and children if you died on active duty from a service-connected cause. A service-connected cause is an injury or disease that happened or was made worse while you were on active duty. The amount paid would depend on your rank, with additional money available for children, blind spouses, and so on.

• *Death gratuity*. If you, as a servicemember, died on active duty, the military would pay a death gratuity to your spouse or your children. If you had no spouse and no children, the military would pay the death gratuity to your parents or brothers or sisters. The amount of the death gratuity would be your monthly pay (excluding allowances) multiplied by six. The maximum amount is $3,000.

• *Servicemen's Group Life Insurance (SGLI)*. The U.S. government established insurance programs to protect servicemembers because some insurance companies restrict payments to military personnel who die in combat. SGLI insures all servicemembers for $200,000, except those who choose not to be insured or who choose a smaller amount of coverage.

• *Government housing*. The military would give your family members government-paid housing for ninety days after your death if you died while on active duty.

• *Survivor assistance officer*. If you died on active duty, your commander would appoint an officer to help your family with making burial arrangements, getting military and veterans benefits, and completing other necessary paperwork.

• *Burial*. If you died on active duty, the military would help with burial arrangements, including funeral home services, a casket, and military honors. The Department of Veterans Affairs also may provide burial benefits to veterans who served honorably during a war.

In addition to receiving military benefits if you died while on active duty, your family could receive Social Security Administration monthly survivor benefits. A servicemember is insured by the Social Security Administration after he has worked at least six quarters (a quarter equals three months) of the thirteen quarters before his death or disability. Monthly survivor benefits would vary depending on whether you were fully insured (after forty quarters) or currently insured (after six quarters). The Social Security Administration may also pay your surviving family members a lump sum death benefit.

In addition to military and Social Security Administration benefits, if you died on active duty, the Department of Veterans Affairs would provide the following benefits:

- *Survivors' and dependents' educational benefits.* When a veteran dies or is totally disabled from military service, his or her spouse and children may receive tuition assistance for many educational institutions.
- *Burial benefits.* The family of a veteran who served during a war or similar conflict and was discharged under honorable conditions may arrange for the veteran's burial in a national cemetery or receive an allowance to aid in burial in a private cemetery, and receive a grave marker.

Wills

When you plan your estate, you must also have a legal document to put your plan into effect. A *will* is a legal document that specifies how you want your property disposed of when you die. It can also cover other matters such as whom you want to be your children's guardian. Not every servicemember needs a will. If you are single, have no children, and have little property, you probably do not need a will because every state has laws that determine who will receive the property of a person who dies without a will. These laws are called the *law of intestate succession.* Simply stated, if you die without having a will, your property would go to your closest relatives. Because each state has different laws covering the distribution of property of people who die intestate, you should see an attorney to find out the rules in your state.

If you do not want your property to go to the relatives that the state specifies, if you have children, or if you have a lot of property, so that reducing taxes is important, then you need a will. Not only do you need a will, but your spouse needs one too. A legal assistance attorney can prepare routine wills for you and your spouse. But if you have many business interests or want complicated tax planning, a legal assistance attorney may suggest that you consult a civilian attorney who specializes in estate planning.

You may want to include the following considerations in your will:

- *Funeral arrangements.* Although you could include such arrangements in a will, expressing your wishes in a letter to your executor or your family would be better because your family would want to make such arrangements quickly, and probating a will could take a long time.

A SAMPLE WILL*

LAST WILL AND TESTAMENT
OF

_____

I, _____, a legal resident of MONTGOMERY COUNTY, Alabama, Social Security Number _____, now in the active military service of the United States and temporarily residing and/or stationed at FORT LEONARD WOOD, MISSOURI, being of sound disposing mind and memory and not acting duress, coercion or undue influence of any person whomsoever and intending to dispose of my entire estate, do make, publish and declare this instrument as my LAST WILL AND TESTAMENT, hereby revoking all wills, testaments and codicils previously made by me.

GENERAL
FIRST. I declare that I am now married to _____. I have no children now living.

SECOND. I direct that all of my personal debts be paid from my estate prior to distribution of the Personal Representative so desires, otherwise such debts will be apportioned to each devisee and legatee according to his or her share. Unless specifically provided otherwise, debts secured by any property shall not be required to be exonerated, but shall pass with the property.

PROPERTY DISTRIBUTION
THIRD. I give, devise and bequeath all of my estate and property—real, personal or mixed, wherever situated and of whatsoever nature of which I may be seized or possessed or of which I may be entitled or have a power of disposition to at the time of my death, in fee simple absolute, absolutely and forever, to my spouse. In the event that my spouse should predecease me or die within thirty (30) days of my death, I give, devise and bequeath all my estate and property, absolutely and forever, to my FATHER,

_____.

SURVIVAL CLAUSE
FOURTH. Wherever in this my LAST WILL AND TESTAMENT it is provided that any person shall benefit hereunder if such person shall survive me such person shall be deemed not to have survived me if he or she shall die within thirty (30) days after my death or in common disaster with me, or under such cir-cumstances that it is difficult or impossible to determine which of us died first.

PERSONAL REPRESENTATIVE (EXECUTOR)
FIFTH. I hereby appoint my spouse as Personal Representative of this my LAST WILL AND TESTAMENT, and direct that he or she be permitted to serve without bond or surety thereon and without the intervention of any court or courts, except as required by law; I hereby authorize and empower my said Per-sonal Representative in his or her absolute discretion to sell, exchange, convey,

(continued)

*Courtesy of Office of the Staff Judge Advocate, Fort Leonard Wood Missouri.

transfer, assign, mortgage, pledge, lease or rent the while or any part of my real or personal estate, to invest, reinvest or retain investments of my said estate and to perform all acts and to execute all documents which my said Personal Representative deems necessary, convenient or proper in regard to my property; in the event that my designated representative shall predecease me or shall for any reason refuse to or be unable to serve or to continue serving as such hereon, then I hereby appoint _____ of CHARLOTTESVILLE, VIRGINIA, to serve without bond or surety and with the same powers.

SIXTH. I have served in the Armed Forces of the United States. Therefore, I direct my Personal Representative to consult the legal assistance officer at the nearest military installation to ascertain if there are any benefits to which my dependents are entitled by virtue of my military affiliation at the time of my death. Regardless of my military status at the time of my death, I direct my Personal Representative to consult with the nearest Department of Veterans Affairs and Social Security office to ascertain if there are any benefits to which my dependents may be entitled.

IN WITNESS THEREOF, I have at Fort Leonard Wood, Missouri, this 5th day of OCTOBER, 1996, set my hand and seal to this my LAST WILL AND TESTAMENT, consisting of two typewritten pages, this included, the preceding pages hereof bearing my signature.

_____(SEAL)

The forgoing instrument, consisting of two typewritten pages, this included, was at Fort Leonard Wood, Missouri, this 5th day of OCTOBER, 1996, signed, sealed, published and declared by _____, the above-named Testator, to be his or her LAST WILL AND TESTAMENT in the presence of all of us at one time and at the same time, we at his or her request and in the presence of each other hereunto subscribe our names as attesting witnesses, and we do verily believe that the said Testator is of sound and disposing mind and memory at the date hereof.

WITNESSES:
NAME   ADDRESS   SSN

_____   FORT LEONARD WOOD, MO.   _____

_____   FORT LEONARD WOOD, MO.   _____

_____   FORT LEONARD WOOD, MO.   _____

ALABAMA SELF-PROVING CLAUSE

I, _____, the Testatrix, sign my name to this instrument this 5th day of OCTOBER, 1996, and being first duly sworn, do hereby declare to the undersigned authority that I sign and execute this instrument as my last will and that I sign it willingly (or willingly direct another to sign for me), that I execute it as my free and voluntary act for the purposes therein expressed, and that I am eighteen years of age or older, of sound mind, and under no constraint or undue influence.

_____
Testatrix

We, _____, _____, _____, the wit-
nesses, sign our names to this instrument, being first duly sworn, and do hereby
declare to the undersigned authority that the Testatrix signs and executes this
instrument as her last will and that she signs it willingly (or willingly directs
another to sign for her), and that each of us, in the presence and hearing of the
Testatrix, hearby signs this will as witnesses to the Testatrix's signing, and that
to the best of our knowledge the Testatrix is eighteen years of age or older, of
sound mind and under no constraint or undue influence.

_____ FORT LEONARD WOOD, MO. _____
WITNESS   SSN

_____ FORT LEONARD WOOD, MO. _____
WITNESS   SSN

_____ FORT LEONARD WOOD, MO. _____
WITNESS   SSN

STATE OF MISSOURI
COUNTY OF PULASKI
    Subscribed, sworn to and acknowledged before me by _____,
_____, and _____, witness, this _____ day
of OCTOBER, 1996.

(SEAL)   _____
                                 NOTARY PUBLIC IN AND FOR
                                 THE STATE OF MISSOURI

MY COMMISSION EXPIRES: 31 JANUARY 1999.

• *Payment of debts.* Your will should have a clause providing for the
payment of your debts and your funeral expenses.
• *Selection of your executor.* An *executor* is a person or an institution,
such as a bank, that you name in your will to settle your estate. The executor
will manage your estate assets while the court probates the will (processes the
will through a court proceeding to establish that it is valid) and will distribute the estate according to your wishes. You may want to choose an adult
family member as your executor, but you may also choose any other trustworthy adult, lawyer, bank, or trust company. The will or a court may require an
executor to post a bond to guarantee that he does not use the estate assets
improperly, such as for his own benefit. If you choose family members or
friends to be executors, it is customary to specify in the will that they need
not post a bond.
• *Disposition of your property.* You may choose to dispose of your
estate in several ways, including bequests and trusts. A *bequest* is a specific
item of real or personal property or specific amount of money (fixed dollar
amounts or fractions of your estate) left to specific beneficiaries. If you make
a bequest, your executor must, after paying your debts, pay the bequest before

he can distribute your estate to the beneficiaries who share the balance of your estate. If you do not name a particular individual to receive an item of personal property, it will go into the *residue* (remainder) of your estate. You may also leave money or property in trust for specific individuals or to charity. You may leave the remainder or balance of your estate, after specific bequests, to certain beneficiaries, normally by giving them each a percentage of the remaining estate. You may also wish to name alternate beneficiaries, in case the primary ones die before you do.

• *Appointment of guardians for minor children.* If you do not choose a guardian for your children, the court will do so. The guardian the court chooses, however, may not be a person you would want to take your place after your death. Thus, you should choose a guardian in your will. You should also consider establishing a trust to provide the funds for the guardian to take care of the children. It is usually a good idea to have the same person be the guardian and the trustee. If not, and the guardian and the trustee disagreed about how they should use the trust for the benefit of the children, court and attorney's fees could eat up the trust funds if a judge had to resolve the conflict.

Obviously, you must choose a trustworthy person to be a guardian. You may also want to name alternate trustees or guardians in case the primary ones cannot or will not serve in those capacities. In your will you should explain the rights and powers of your executors, guardians, and trustees. If you don't, they may not do what you want, or if they can't decide what they should do, your trust fund could be eaten up by legal fees if a judge has to decide what they should do. You should also talk to the people you want to name as guardians and executors, explain their duties, and ask whether they will accept the responsibility before you execute your will, so that you can choose someone else if they won't do it. Otherwise, if a guardian or trustee refuses to serve in that capacity after your death, a probate court will appoint someone else.

• *Simultaneous death provisions.* If you are married and you and your spouse both have wills, the question of who dies first may be very important to your heirs. For example, if you leave your entire estate to your wife, and, in her will, she leaves half her estate to you and half to her parents, your property goes to her if you die first. Then if she does shortly thereafter, half of her property, including the property she got from you, goes to her parents. If she dies first, however, her parents' share would be smaller, because it would not include any of your property.

But what if you die at the same time, as in an accident? The Uniform Simultaneous Death Act, which is in effect in many states, says that the law presumes that the wife died before the husband when both die in a common accident and no one can determine who actually died first. Because this law may frustrate your wishes regarding how your executor is to distribute your property on your death and because of tax considerations, wills also often contain provisions that the probate court must presume that the husband died before the wife. Complicated situations such as this illustrate your need to consult an attorney instead of using some do-it-yourself will kit.

After you've considered all these factors, have talked with your family and those whom you want to name as your executors, trustees, and guardians, have had a legal assistance officer draw up your will according to your wishes, and have signed it in front of witnesses, you should store your will in a safe place. Let the executor and your spouse know where it is. A safe deposit box is a safe place, but if you keep it in such a location, you must tell your family members where it is. A will does you and your family no good after you are dead if no one left on earth can find it. A good idea is to give a copy of the will to your executor and one to your family and tell them where the original is; the executor usually can submit only the original will to the probate court.

Do not, however, file your will away and forget it. Changes in your situation, such as divorce, new business interests, or more children, or changes in the law may change the effect of your will so that it would no longer fulfill your intentions. Therefore, you should periodically have a lawyer review your will. A good rule of thumb is to take your will to a legal assistance officer at every new duty station you go to on a permanent change of station. If you stay in one place, you should have a lawyer review your will at least every three years. Whenever a major change occurs in your life, such as divorce, new family member, death of a beneficiary, or acquisition of substantial property, you should immediately have a lawyer review your will.

You can make your will reflect these changes in either of two ways: a new will or a codicil. If you have many changes, you probably need a new will. If the change is minor, a codicil will probably suffice. A *codicil* is a legal document that supplements or changes your will. Your legal assistance officer can tell you whether you need to execute a new will or a codicil. When you write a new will, include a clause revoking all previous wills. If you don't, a probate court may have to spend a lot of effort—and a lot of your estate's money—deciding which will is valid.

Probate is a court procedure that determines whether a will is genuine. Your executor must probate your will—show a probate court that it is valid—before the court will allow your executor to distribute your property to the heirs you named in the will. After the probate court finds your will valid, it will supervise the executor to ensure that he distributes your property according to your will and the law.

One major problem servicemembers have, because they move around so much, is which state should probate the will. If you had a *domicile* (your legal, permanent residence) in one state, lived in another (your military duty station), and owned land in a third, a probate proceeding may be necessary in each state. For the title to real property (see chapter 13) to pass to the person you named in your will, the executor must probate the will in the state or county where the land is. Thus, when you make your will, you must tell your attorney your domicile and everywhere you have property and what kind it is. The attorney should make certain that your will is valid in every state where it may have to go through probate court.

Probate begins when the executor files a petition to admit the will to probate with the probate court. When the probate judge hears the petition, the executor must prove that the testator is dead (normally with a death certificate from the state in which he or she died) and that the will is valid. To prove the will's validity, the executor must show three things:

• That the *testator* (the person making the will) was competent. You are competent to make a will if you have a sound mind and are old enough (generally more than eighteen years old). You have a sound mind if you are able to understand what your property is, who should normally get your property, and how the distribution of property after death works.

• That the testator properly executed the will. Every state has laws that spell out how you must execute a will to make certain that the will expresses your wishes regarding the disposition of your property after your death. These laws generally require that the will be in writing, be signed, and be witnessed by two or three people. These witnesses must be able to testify that you were competent and that you were the person whose property the will covered. The witnesses should not be your heirs.

• That the testator intended the document to be a will. You can show that you mean the document to be your will by telling the witnesses that you do, normally when you sign the will in their presence.

In probate court, the testimony of the witnesses normally proves these three things. If the probate judge believes the witnesses' testimony satisfies the three conditions, and if the executor satisfies the judge that the testator is dead, then the judge can admit the will to probate. The judge would issue *letters testamentary* (court orders) that authorize the executor to distribute the testator's property according to the terms of the will. If the judge did not admit the will to probate, and if no other valid will existed, the probate court would distribute the property according to the law of intestate succession, as discussed previously.

Even if the executor is a servicemember and thus has access to legal assistance attorneys, he must hire a civilian lawyer to probate a will because military attorneys normally cannot represent clients in civilian courts. The executor does not have to pay an attorney himself; with the permission of the probate court, or if the will says so, he can use estate assets to pay the attorney.

Living Wills and Healthcare Powers of Attorney

A *living will* is a legal document that you may execute while you are competent that specifies what treatment you will receive if terminally ill, such as that you will not receive any medical treatment that would only artificially prolong the process of dying. Most states provide for such documents but specify the formalities a person must follow when executing one to make it valid.

A *healthcare power of attorney* is a legal document that you execute while you are competent that allows another person, typically your spouse or your parent, to make healthcare decisions for you if you become incompetent. Again, state law specifies the formalities required to execute healthcare powers of attorney. See your legal assistance officer or a civilian attorney if you want to execute a living will or a healthcare power of attorney.

Trusts

Trusts are important in estate planning because they allow you to control your money and other property during your lifetime and after your death. A *trust* is a legal relationship in which one person holds the legal title to property for the benefit of another. The law calls the person holding the legal title the *trustee*. The one for whose benefit the property is used is the *beneficiary*. The person who creates the trust is the *trustor*. You would be most likely to set up a trust in your will for the benefit of your surviving spouse and other family members, but you may also create a trust in a deed, a declaration of trust, or any other legal document that states your intention to create a trust. A trust that you set up in a will is a testamentary trust. A trust you created to be effective while you live is a lifetime trust.

When you create your trust, you may name any competent adult as a trustee. Make certain, however, that the person is experienced in business and financial matters and trustworthy. It is often wise to appoint a bank or trust company as trustee. You normally must pay trustees for managing the trust property and using trust income for the benefit of the beneficiary.

You may set up a trust in many ways for different purposes. You could, for example, set up a trust so that, while alive, your spouse would receive income from trust property and so that your children would receive the trust property after your spouse's death. Or you could provide that your children would receive income from the trust until they reached a certain age and then would receive their share of the trust property. If you have young children, you should consider setting up a trust in your will to take care of them. If you do not have much money, you may make your insurance policies payable to your estate with directions in your will that the trustee use the insurance proceeds to fund a trust with your children as beneficiaries.

Trusts normally provide that only the trust's income (interest, dividends, rents from real property, and so on) may go to the beneficiary, but you may also create a trust that would allow the trustee to use part of the principal, or body of the trust, to meet emergencies or to perform a wish of yours, such as to educate your children. You may also set up a trust with a *spendthrift clause*.

Such a clause prevents creditors from getting money owed them by your beneficiary from your trust and prevents your beneficiary from borrowing money and repaying it out of the principal of the trust before you planned to have the trust funds distributed. No matter what your purpose in setting up the trust, you should carefully explain in the trust papers exactly how the trustee may use the trust principal and income.

Because the legal requirements for a valid trust vary among states and involve income, estate, and gift tax consequences, you must see an attorney to establish a trust. Never use some do-it-yourself trust book or kit, or even a computerized will. If you want a simple trust created by a provision in your will to take care of your family after your death, a legal assistance officer may be able to set it up. If you have substantial property or want a very complicated trust, you should see a civilian attorney who specializes in estate planning.

Life Insurance

Life insurance is an important part of estate planning; few servicemembers are rich enough to be certain that they can leave enough money to care for their family after they die. You can use life insurance, for example, to fund a trust established in your will to take care of your children, or you could have your spouse get the insurance proceeds on your death.

Life insurance is a contract in which the life insurance company agrees to pay money to whomever the insured person or the policy owner has chosen upon the insured's death in return for the payment of money (the *premium*) by the policy owner. Because insurance is a contract, make certain you understand the policy before you buy insurance. If you do not understand the policy, take it to the legal assistance office and have an attorney explain it to you. You need to understand whom you can insure, whom you can name as a beneficiary, and what type of policy you are buying.

Whom can you insure? You can take out a life insurance policy on yourself or on anyone in whom you have an insurable interest. The law defines an *insurable interest* as an expectation of a financial benefit from the continued life of the insured person or a loss if the insured dies. So a spouse could take out a policy on the other spouse or on another family member.

Whom can you name as a beneficiary? A *beneficiary* is the recipient of the life insurance proceeds on your death. You may name anyone you want as beneficiary, without regard to whether that person has an insurable interest, or you may name your estate as the beneficiary. Always consider potential tax effects when you choose a beneficiary. Remember, too, that if you make your estate the beneficiary, instead of a person, your creditors may be able to claim the insurance proceeds. Because of these and other possible complications, you should see a legal assistance officer before you name anyone other than your spouse as the beneficiary. You should also consider naming contingent beneficiaries. A *contingent beneficiary* is one who will receive the insurance

money if the named beneficiary dies before you do or if you both die simultaneously. If no beneficiary you chose survives you, the insurance company
would pay the policy proceeds to your estate.

What type of policy are you going to get? Insurance companies have
developed a bewildering number of policies, but they generally fall within
three major categories: whole life, endowment, and term.

Whole life insurance is insurance plus a savings feature. The cost of whole
life insurance remains constant. (You are actually paying a greater premium
in the early years when the risk of death is less to cover the increased risk as
you get older.) Whole life is more expensive than term insurance because the
insurance company invests a part of your money to build up a cash value,
which is the savings feature. You can take out a loan against this cash value,
or if you cancel the insurance, you can receive the cash value (plus any
accrued interest). If you die with a loan on your policy, the insurance company deducts the outstanding loan from the amount of the insurance proceeds it pays to the beneficiary. This type of insurance has many variations,
such as whole life, for which you pay premiums as long as you live, and
twenty pay life, for which you pay premiums for twenty years.

An *endowment* is another insurance and savings contract. It is more
expensive than other types because it has a savings feature that pays you a
specific amount at a future date, such as when you reach retirement age.
Whole life, on the other hand, pays only your beneficiaries and only when
you die.

Of the three major types of life insurance, *term insurance* is the least
expensive. It protects you for a specific time, without any savings feature.
Term insurance has no cash or loan value. If you do not die during the term
the insurance is in force, no one will collect anything. Nor do you receive
any cash when you end the coverage. In pure term insurance, the cost goes
up, or the benefits go down, as you grow older and the risk of death increases.
Another type of term insurance is level payment, for which you pay the same
amount throughout the policy term. The level payment policy has a higher
premium than does pure term insurance to protect against the risk of death
while the insured is younger and to keep the cost down when the risk is
greater as he or she ages. Servicemen's Group Life Insurance is a level term
insurance program. An indication that SGLI is level term is that the finance
office deducts the same amount from your military pay for your SGLI each
month, regardless of your age, while the amount you are insured for remains
the same.

Annuities are not really life insurance, but insurance companies often
sell them. An *annuity* is a contract between you and the insurance company
in which you pay the company a certain amount of money and the company
agrees to pay you a certain sum each month for a specific period or until your
death. For example, you may pay the insurance company $25,000 for an

annuity. In return, the insurance company would pay you $250 per month for the rest of your life. The amount the company pays depends on how much you pay for the annuity, your age, and current interest rates.

Because life insurance can be so important in the support of family members after the insured dies, the law requires the insurance company and the insured to act in good faith when entering these contracts. You must be honest when you fill out forms about your medical condition, age, or other facts that will determine whether you will get the insurance and how much the premium will be. If you lie on the forms, the company may cancel the contract or refuse to pay death benefits to your survivors.

Before you sign a life insurance contract, have a legal assistance officer review it. Make sure that the contract does not have a war clause or, in the case of aviators, an aviation clause. A *war clause* states that the insurance company will not pay the death benefit if an act of war caused the insured person's death. An *aviation clause* allows the insurance company to withhold death benefits if the insured's death resulted from a plane crash in which he or she was a crew member.

Servicemen's Group Life Insurance (SGLI) provides good, inexpensive, term insurance protection. $200,000 of coverage costs only a few dollars a month, no matter what your rank or age. The government also will pay your beneficiary the death benefits even if you die in a war or aviation accident. You may choose whom you want to be the beneficiary or beneficiaries. If you had not chosen a beneficiary, the insurance company would, according to the law, pay the death benefit to your spouse. If you were single, then your children would receive the proceeds in equal shares. Your estate would receive the proceeds if you had no spouse or children. If you did not have a will, a spouse, or children, your next of kin would be the beneficiary.

If you have a family, you may need to supplement SGLI with commercial life insurance to make certain that they have enough money to live on in the event of your death. To do this effectively, you must make certain you understand the policy's coverage and terms and how it affects your estate planning.

Estate planning is as complicated as it is important. You must review your situation right away to see whether your plan is current and still does what you want it to. Few legal areas require the assistance of an attorney more than estate planning.

POWERS OF ATTORNEY

A *power of attorney* is a written grant of power or authority by one person (the principal) to another (the agent) to act in the place of the principal. The grant may be a general power of attorney, which authorizes the agent to do almost any act that the principal can do. Or it may be a limited (or special) power of attorney, in which the principal authorizes the agent to do only certain acts. For example, you could give a friend a limited power of attorney to

SPECIAL POWER OF ATTORNEY

DATA REQUIRED BY THE PRIVACY ACT OF 1974

KNOW ALL MEN BY THESE PRESENTS:

That I, _____ , a legal resident of _____

have made, constituted and appointed, and by these presents do make, constitute and appoint _____
_____ , whose present address is _____
my true and lawful attorney to act as follows, that is to say:

GIVING AND GRANTING unto my said attorney full power:

FURTHER, I do authorize my aforesaid attorney in fact to perform all necessary acts in the execution of the aforesaid authorizations with the same validity as I could effect if personally present.

AND I HEREBY DECLARE that any act or thing lawfully done hereunder by my said attorney shall be binding on myself and my heirs, legal and personal representatives, and assigns;

PROVIDED, however, that all business transacted hereunder for me or for my account shall be transacted in my name, and that all endorsements and instruments executed by my said attorney for the purpose of carrying out the foregoing powers shall contain my name, followed by that of my said attorney and the designation "attorney-in-fact."

I further declare that this power shall remain in effect even though I am reported or listed, officially or otherwise, as 'missing in action' it being my intention that the designation of such status shall not bar my said attorney from fully and completely exercising and continuing to exercise any and all powers and rights herein granted until this power of attorney is revoked by my death or as otherwise provided herein.

FURTHER, this power of attorney shall remain in full force and effect until the occurrence of the first of the following circumstances: (1) my death; (2) the death of my said attorney; (3) until the revocation of this power of attorney by me; or (4) until _____

IN WITNESS WHEREOF, I have hereunto set my hand and seal this _____ day of
_____ , nineteen hundred and eighty _____ .

WITNESSES:

_____

_____   _____ *(SEAL)*

A sample general power of attorney.

sell your car if you had to rotate overseas before you could sell it. A power of attorney must be in writing and is subject to state laws, so you should go to a legal assistance office to have a lawyer write one for you.

These are some of the reasons you might need a power of attorney:

• So the agent could get your child military medical care. For example, a babysitter may not be able to authorize emergency medical care for your children in your absence without your power of attorney to do so.

• So your spouse or someone else could cash or deposit your paycheck if the military deployed you away from your base.

• So someone could buy, sell, or rent a place for you or your family to live when you're temporarily gone.

• So someone could ship your household goods, after you, say, had to make an unexpected permanent-change-of-station move.

• So someone could clear your government quarters after you had to move.

• So someone could sell your personal property, such as a car, after you had shipped out.

A power of attorney remains in effect until you die or revoke it, unless you make it for a limited time, in which case it will expire. It is always best to make it for a limited time because you don't know how, or whether, the relationship may change between you and the person to whom you have given the power of attorney. You should never make a power of attorney for more than three years. You can always give the agent a new one when the old one expires. The best idea is to limit it to the situation you want it to cover.

Carefully consider whom you make your agent, because you do not want someone to misuse your power of attorney. For example, if you gave your roommate an unlimited power of attorney, your roommate could get all your money from a bank account only in your name. It is also important to be certain that giving someone a power of attorney is necessary. Remember, you will be legally responsible for everything that your agent does using your power of attorney.

If you no longer want the power of attorney to be in effect, you should not only go to legal assistance and revoke it but also give a copy of the revocation to anyone who might enter into a transaction with your former agent, such as your bank, your landlord, merchants, and so on. You should also try to get the power of attorney back from the agent. Some states require recording a revocation of a power of attorney with the county clerk. Ask your lawyer what you must do to make certain the revocation is valid.

GUARDIANSHIP

The question of who will take care of your children if you go away is important to both long- and short-range legal survival planning. If, for some reason, you or your spouse cannot take care of your children, you may need to appoint a guardian.

A *guardian* is a person appointed by a person or a court to take care of someone who cannot take care of himself, such as a minor or an incompetent person. You can appoint a guardian to take care of such a person, his property, or both. Because parents are automatically guardians of their children until the children reach the age of maturity, the law regards a parent as a natural guardian. If you have children, however, you should appoint a guardian in your will in case both you and your spouse die simultaneously or your spouse dies before you. If you have not appointed a guardian and there is no natural guardian to take care of the children, a court will appoint one. If the court appoints a guardian, he may not be someone you would have wanted to take care of your children.

You should choose a guardian with regard to what will be best for the child. Some of the factors you may wish to consider are the child's feelings for the proposed guardian and the guardian's character, financial condition, health, age, religion or lack thereof, attitudes toward schooling, and willingness to perform the duties of a guardian. If you are a single parent in the service, the military may require you to file your guardian plan with your commander so he knows that you are ready to deploy and that your children will be taken care of. Even if the service does not require such a plan, it is only common sense for you to have one.

JOINT ACCOUNTS
If the military deploys you overseas or sends you to sea for an extended time, no one—not even your spouse—will be able to get any money out of your bank accounts unless you have given a power of attorney or the accounts are joint. Joint accounts are in more than one person's name, and most belong to married couples. Both spouses may make deposits and withdrawals from such accounts, and the accounts may be checking or savings. The advantage of such accounts is that either spouse can get money from the accounts in an emergency. If you do not have joint accounts, the only way your spouse could get money from them would be with a power of attorney.

You may also own property, such as your car or stocks and bonds, jointly. If your spouse dies, jointly owned property becomes yours.

PUTTING IT TOGETHER
When you are in the service, you have a greater need to have both your long- and short-term personal legal affairs in order than do civilians. Civilians usually do not need to worry about their employers' deploying them anywhere in the world, about being at sea for months, or about risking their lives in combat. You do. Besides the problems your family will experience if you have not

provided for them, you cannot be effective when you deploy away from your home station if you are worried about your family. The best way to avoid these very real worries is to have your legal affairs in order before you deploy.

How do you get your legal survival kit in order? You must do both long- and short-term planning.

Long-term planning involves estate planning. After you understand your government benefits you can start planning. Further, if you have a family, you and your spouse should each have a will. If you have children or want to control how your beneficiaries use the proceeds of your estate, you may want to set up a trust. You and your spouse's life insurance plans should supplement your wills.

Having your wills and insurance policies in order will protect your family if you die. But you must also make certain that your family can carry on while you are still living, but deployed. So you need to prepare for the short term too.

Provide your spouse with a valid power of attorney, so that he or she can do such things as cash your checks and register your car. If you are not married, you may want to give your parents or a friend a limited power of attorney to take care of such things. If you are a single parent or if both you and your spouse are servicemembers, you must arrange in advance for someone to take care of your children. The services require single parents to have a plan for someone to take care of their children if they are deployed.

Every servicemember needs to consider these parts of a legal survival kit. Even this may not be enough, however. You should also try to foresee special requirements that may come up after you deploy, such as a need to sell a house, and give your spouse or someone you trust a special power of attorney to handle the transaction.

CONCLUSION

The sooner you talk to a military lawyer about your legal survival kit the better. The military provides you many benefits, not the least of which is free legal assistance, and it will help you get your affairs in order. But keeping your affairs in order remains your responsibility. After you have assembled your legal survival kit, you will be ready to deploy and be prepared for any other life situation. Most important, however, you will have taken care of your family and possessions according to your plan and not someone else's.

10

Marriage

The old military feeling about marriage expressed in the statement "If the military wanted you to have a wife, it would have issued you one" has pretty much gone the way of the horse cavalry. The military now recognizes that a spouse can be an asset, not only to the military member but also to the military community.

The potential for problems within a marital relationship, however, increases with the requirements of military life. You may be able to make a happy marriage if you understand the legalities of marriage within the military before marrying. If you are already married, this knowledge may prevent some problems or help you solve them if they do occur.

Marriage is the relationship of a man and a woman who have legally united as husband and wife. Lawyers often call it a contractual relationship, because each spouse agrees to do certain things in return for the promises of the other. Marriage is also a status, however, and has duties imposed by law, such as the duty to support a spouse. Before marrying, you should know several things, such as the legal aspects of marrying either in the United States or overseas, how to handle potential problems in the marriage, and the pitfalls of trying to avoid the legal problems of married life by merely living with someone.

MARRIAGE IN THE UNITED STATES
If you get married while in the military, you will probably marry in the United States, but not necessarily at your permanent home. The state in which you decide to marry will require you to observe its own laws about marriage. Thus, the state in which you marry will do the following:

A military marriage certificate. Note the phrase "united in holy matrimony . . . according to . . . the laws of the state of . . ." This phrase illustrates the requirement for all marriages, including those conducted by military chaplains, to be performed in accordance with the law of the state in which the military base is located.

• Determine the conditions that must exist for you to get married, such as those concerning your age, physical condition, mental competence, and type of marriage ceremony required. Most states permit eighteen-year-olds to marry without the consent of their parents. People less than eighteen but more than sixteen may marry with parental consent. People below the age of sixteen, but more than fourteen years old, must have the approval of a court. The state will not allow you to marry if you have a disease, such as syphilis, that you could transmit to your spouse and children. You must also be mentally competent. The law will not permit insane people or people who cannot understand what marriage is to wed. States may also forbid marriages between certain persons, such as between parents and children, brothers and sisters, and other close relations. The wedding ceremony may be either religious or civil, such as one performed by a justice of the peace. Make certain you check the requirements of the particular state in which you are going to marry.

• Require a license before marriage. All states require you to get a license from a proper licensing official, often the county clerk.

• Require a physical examination. Some states require some form of physical, and most require a blood test that shows you do not have syphilis before the state will issue you a marriage license.

• Specify the duties and responsibilities of the married couple. The duty to support the spouse is one example of such responsibilities.

• Specify the property rights of the marriage partners. A state could, for example, give a spouse the right to take one third to one half of the estate even though the other spouse dies leaving a will that disinherited the surviving spouse.

If you get married without complying with the state's requirements, the marriage is voidable and a court could annul it. An annulment is different from a divorce, which ends a valid marriage. An *annulment* is a legal determination that the marriage was invalid from the state because the couple never properly entered into a marriage. If you qualify for an annulment, it may be better for you than a divorce, because if a court says you were never married, you will not have to pay alimony or divide your property with the other person. If you think you need an annulment, go see an attorney. A legal assistance officer can tell you whether you qualify for an annulment and whether you should get one. In most states, however, you would have to hire a civilian attorney to process the annulment through court channels.

In some circumstances—if you were, say, living with someone—you could end up in a common law marriage without going through a marriage ceremony. A *common law marriage* occurs when a couple live together and act as if they were married. There is no formal marriage ceremony. Although many states do not recognize common law marriages, in those that do, a common law marriage is just as valid as a regular marriage. Before a state recognizing common law marriages will recognize your living arrangement as a common law marriage, you must do the following:

• Have an agreement to take each other as husband and wife.

• Openly cohabit (live together in the same home) as husband and wife.

• Hold yourself out to the world as husband and wife. Holding yourself out as husband and wife means you act as if you are married when you are with others.

Although a formal ceremony is not necessary to have a valid common law marriage, this type of marriage requires a formal divorce proceeding to end the marriage just as a regular marriage does. If you want to end a common law marriage, agreeing not to be married anymore is not enough; you must go to court and get a divorce.

What if, rather than living together, you and your prospective spouse are a great distance apart and you want to get married but cannot be in the same place at the same time? Some states permit *marriage by proxy*. An agent—the proxy—acts for one of the parties and goes through the ceremony for the absent marriage partner. This type of marriage, when valid, can be helpful to a servicemember stationed overseas who wants to marry a person in the United States but cannot attend the ceremony. Once legally married, and if the command will sponsor the new spouse, the new spouse could apply to join the military spouse overseas.

MARRIAGE OVERSEAS

Just as many other servicemembers have, you may want to marry while stationed overseas. If you wish to marry overseas, you must comply with the requirements of the country you intend to marry in, and you may also have to comply with military requirements. If you want to marry while overseas, the military has the right to require you to get your commander's permission to marry. The overseas command may also require you to submit such things as birth certificates, medical examinations, a statement of ability to support a spouse, and any documents required by the foreign country in support of the request. Your command may investigate the background and character of the prospective spouse, too. Further, the military may require both of you to get counseling from military attorneys and chaplains.

Normally, if you follow the required procedure of your command, you will receive permission to marry. If, however, the investigation showed that the person you wanted to marry would not be allowed into the United States or if you could not show that you could support yourself and a spouse, then your commander could deny you permission to marry. Although you could not appeal this decision, you could take some other steps. You could, for example, see the inspector general or file an Article 138, UCMJ, complaint (see chapter 5), if the denial was improper. Or, at the end of your overseas tour, you could try to get a visa for the person you wanted to marry to enter the United States and marry there.

These stringent prerequisites for marrying overseas serve a purpose for you and the military. Many marriages to foreigners do not work well. The differences in background and language, the financial burden, and family disapproval often make the situation difficult. In addition, the investigation to see whether the United States would permit the foreigner to enter the country could prevent you from marrying a foreigner who could not enter the United States.

Even if you thought you could avoid the problems of cross-cultural marriage, the investigation, the financial assessment, and the counseling could only help both of you deal with the pressures you would face. If you marry a foreign national, the best things to do would be to have a long engagement, to learn as much about each other and each other's culture as you can, and to follow the local command's requirements before marrying.

If you want to marry a U.S. citizen overseas, you may still need command approval, but the investigation and counseling requirements should be minimal. The commander could hardly justify denying you the right to marry a U.S. citizen overseas, but you should still follow any local requirement to get prior approval. If the local regulation forbidding marriage without your commander's approval is a punitive one, you could also face disciplinary action under Article 92 of the Uniform Code of Military Justice for violating a lawful general regulation (see chapter 7).

If you did marry overseas without permission, however, the marriage would still be valid if it complied with the local laws. As long as the country where you were married recognized the marriage as being valid, you and your spouse would be eligible for military benefits. But you should go through the required procedure to get permission, both to stay out of trouble and to make certain that your marriage is legal. Besides, a new marriage can be fragile enough without having your commander down on you.

PRENUPTIAL AGREEMENTS

Even if you are in the United States and do not need command approval to marry or do not have to consult anyone, it is a good idea to talk to a chaplain and a military attorney before marriage. You may want to ask an attorney whether you need a prenuptial agreement if, for example, you have children from a previous marriage or a lot of property. A *prenuptial agreement* is a contract between two people who intend to marry, in which they decide how to handle potential problem areas in a marriage, such as money, children, and property. The permissible terms of these premarriage contracts vary among states but may include some of the following agreements:

• Couples with children from previous marriages agree that each spouse will receive only a small inheritance on the other spouse's death, so that their natural children will receive the bulk of their estates.

• Couples agree on how they will divide their property in advance if one of them dies or if they divorce.

• Couples agree about who will get custody of children in the event of a partner's death or a divorce.

• When both partners have separate property and income, couples agree that the property and income will remain separate.

For a premarital agreement to be valid, it must be neither unfair nor unreasonable. In other words, it must not give one spouse a much greater advantage than the other. A court will not enforce the agreement if one party concealed assets, used coercion or undue influence to get the other person's agreement, or had a fraudulent purpose in mind. You must have a lawyer write a prenuptial agreement. The person you want to marry may want to take your proposed agreement to another attorney to review it. Although it may not seem very romantic, if you have substantial property or children from a previous marriage, you should at least see an attorney to find out whether a prenuptial agreement would be advisable.

If you're concerned that the idea of a prenuptial agreement would hurt your future spouse's feelings or indicate reluctance or mistrust on your part, consider that a prenuptial agreement merely means that both of you talk— before you get married—about the things that married couples talk about, such as money and property and children. Talking to each other about how you really feel about these things can only help strengthen your marriage because you'll know for sure how each of you feels instead of wondering or assuming.

Another thing you as a couple need to decide before you marry is what you want your married names to be. Many women want to keep their own names after they marry, or the couple may compromise and hyphenate their surnames. A woman does not have to take the man's name when she marries him. Furthermore, if she keeps her own name when she marries, she does not need to go through any special extra legal proceedings to do so. If, however, she wanted to return to her maiden name after marriage or after divorce, she would have to get an expensive court order.

MARITAL RELATIONS

Although the sexual relationship is an important part of marriage, being married does not permit you to force sex upon your spouse. If your spouse denies you normal sexual relations, your remedy is a divorce or an annulment, not the use of force. Although not all states consider raping your spouse a crime, nor is it the crime of rape under the Uniform Code of Military Justice, any violence you use could be the basis for a prosecution for assault or other similar crime. Even if your spouse refuses to testify against you, your commander could still take an adverse administrative action against you, such as a discharge for misconduct or a termination of government quarters. On the other hand, our society has also seen a recent movement to protect victims of spouse abuse, both in the military and in the civilian community. So if your spouse abuses you, report it.

LIVING TOGETHER

Our society has seen a tendency in the past decade or so for couples to live together without getting married. While this arrangement may be permissible in today's society, you should be aware of some of the legal dangers in doing so, especially if you decide to live with someone while you're in the military.

First, if you live with someone, do not hold yourself out as married when you aren't to get the increased military benefits married couples receive, such as increased quarters allowance. It is a criminal offense—fraud—to do so. And, if you represent yourself as married, you may find that you have taken a common law spouse and are married.

Second, although you are not married, your relationship may make you liable for palimony. *Palimony* is a support allowance you may have to pay to the person you were living with after you break up. The person you lived with can establish a right to palimony in several ways. One way is that you agreed to support the person you lived with in return for such services as companionship, homemaking, and so on. Another method of becoming liable for palimony does not require such an expressed agreement. Rather, if both of you acted as if you expected that one of you, usually the woman, would receive support if the relationship ended, the court could find an implied (unstated) contract and order the other to pay palimony.

Finally, if you are in the process of obtaining a divorce or are merely separated, you could be prosecuted for adultery and also give your spouse evidence to use against you in the divorce action.

Just as you should talk to a minister or an attorney before you get married, you need to consider the legal implications of living with someone before you unpack your toothbrush and your fatigues in someone else's home. Your legal assistance officer would rather discuss with you the pitfalls of living with someone before you end up with a legal problem caused by the relationship.

CONCLUSION

As you can see, marriage has many legal aspects. Although I hope your marriage has no legal problems, your best chance of avoiding difficulties is to prevent them from the beginning. So get married legally and get legal and professional advice before you enter such an important relationship. If you do, perhaps you will never need to read chapter 12, on divorce and separation.

11

Family Members

The military has recently given increased recognition to the importance of the families of servicemembers. One of the reasons for this increased emphasis is that a servicemember who has a family problem is usually not very efficient. The military, however, cannot protect you from every possible family problem. You need to understand the law of family relationships, so you can prevent or solve—perhaps with the military's help—family problems that may arise while you are in the military service.

Servicemembers' questions about legal problems involving family members usually fall into four areas: Is the family member a legal dependent? How do you adopt children? What do you do about children born overseas? What does supporting family members really mean?

WHOM MUST YOU SUPPORT?

The military recognizes the following people as entitled to both your support and military benefits:

- Your spouse.
- Your unmarried children who are less than twenty-one years old.
- Your unmarried children who are more than twenty-one years old but who cannot take care of themselves because of mental or physical reasons.
- Any other relatives you are actually supporting, such as your parents, who live with you.

In chapter 10 you learned about marriage, including about the legal relationship between husbands and wives. You may, however, become responsible for children in many different ways. Because many family problems in the military involve children, you must understand how the law affects your relationship with your children and how children affect your time in the military.

States, not the federal government, determine the laws regarding children, although both the federal government and the military have rules concerning the support of not only children but also all other dependents. State laws classify children in a number of ways, depending on whether the parents were married when they had the child or whether the child was adopted.

Legitimate Children

A legitimate child is one who is born to parents that are lawfully married. Your legal obligation to support a legitimate child arises at birth and normally ends when the child reaches age twenty-one or when he or she becomes emancipated. A child is emancipated when he or she leaves home to live independently. Your support obligation continues past age twenty-one, however, if the child cannot support himself or herself because of a physical or mental condition.

Illegitimate Children

An illegitimate child is the offspring of an unmarried couple. While both parents' legal obligation to support a legitimate child arises at birth, their legal obligation to support an illegitimate child starts at different times. The mother's legal obligation to support an illegitimate child arises at birth, but the father's does not begin until a court decides that he is the child's parent. Such a court action is called a paternity proceeding. If you receive notice that someone is suing you in a paternity proceeding, see a legal assistance officer immediately, even if you are the actual father, because if you don't respond properly to such a notice, a court could order you to pay more support than you are financially able.

Most cases in the military involving illegitimate children happen when the child's mother or a welfare agency tries to get the person believed to be the father to pay child support. The mother or the agency also may try to get government benefits for the child as a servicemember's child. In all states, both parents are liable for support of the child. If a court finds you to be the parent of an illegitimate child, if the court orders you to pay support for the child, or if you admit that you are the parent of the child, the child is eligible for military benefits.

Adopted Children

An adopted child is a child who was born to other parents but whom you make your child through a court proceeding. Once you adopt a child, you have the same legal rights and responsibilities that you would toward your natural children. If you adopt a child, for most purposes under the law, that child becomes your child to the same extent he or she would if you were his or her natural parent. One exception may be in the area of inheritance. So if you adopt a child, you need to review your will to see whether he or she would receive property left to your "children," "heirs," or "issue." A court would probably decide that the terms children and heirs included adopted children, but that the term issue meant offspring of your body and would not include adopted children.

HOW DO YOU ADOPT A CHILD?

Adoption is a legal procedure to establish a parental relationship with a child that is not your offspring. The procedure also ends the parental rights and obligations of the natural parent.

To adopt a child, you must fulfill the requirements of the state you are in. For the adoption to be legal, you must adopt the child in accordance with the state's adoption laws. As is true with all legal questions about children, the welfare of the child is the essential consideration in whether a court will approve the adoption, so the state considers economic status, home environment, age and health of the prospective parents, and so on.

People adopt children in one of three ways, only two of which are legal:

• *Through an adoption agency.* Adoption agencies investigate prospective parents to determine whether they are suitable to adopt a child. Natural parents surrender their parental rights to the agency. The agency then is free to arrange for an adoption. An agency adoption can take a long time because of the thoroughness of an agency's investigation. Agency adoption is often cheaper, however, than a private placement because the government agency's fees are not as high as those of a lawyer.

• *Through private placement.* These adoptions normally happen when the natural parents use an intermediary, such as a doctor or a lawyer, to arrange for an adoption. The couple wanting to adopt the child usually pays any medical bills and legal fees. It is illegal, however, to pay the natural parents any additional money for the child. Even though an intermediary is involved, a court must approve the adoption. Private placements normally do not take as long as agency placements, because they involve little or no investigation into the prospective parents. Private placements can have drawbacks, though. For one thing, usually they are more expensive. Further, because the natural parents may not have surrendered their rights to the child before the adoption proceeding, they could change their minds and back out of the arrangement.

• *Through the black market.* Adopting a child through the black market is illegal. Although the would-be parents may have only the best of intentions, buying and selling babies is a crime. Although it may take longer, use the legal ways to adopt a child. For one thing, you wouldn't be a very good parent while you were in jail for an illegal adoption. Furthermore, the law could refuse to recognize the adoption and order you to give up the child. Also, because the military recognizes only your natural, illegitimate, and legally adopted children, an illegally adopted child would not necessarily qualify for all the benefits servicemembers' children usually enjoy.

As with divorce actions or any other proceeding in the family law area, state laws have several procedural requirements for adoption. The court must have jurisdiction over the child, over the parents-to-be, and either over the natural parents or, if they have previously given up their parental rights, over the child's guardian or custodial institution. If you want to adopt a child, you must give notice of the proposed adoption to all parties that have an interest in the child. The court will often require the consent of the natural parents or the child's guardian for an adoption, unless the parents have lost the right to consent, such as by abandoning the child. Sometimes the court will require older children to consent to an adoption before you can adopt them. Some states require that you have custody of the child for a certain period before the court will permit the adoption. This requirement is to see whether the placement is likely to work out. A judge will ordinarily hold a closed hearing—to keep the adoption confidential—to make certain that the adoption will further the child's welfare.

You or the adopted child would normally have to get a court order to get access to the court records about the adoption. Thus, it is very difficult to find out who the natural parents are. If the court approves the adoption, it will provide a certificate of adoption, which will replace the child's birth certificate.

If you decide you want to adopt a child, go to an attorney to help you with the adoption process. If you do not follow the procedural requirements, the natural parents or some other interested party could try to get the adoption voided.

Servicemembers often consider adopting children when they marry someone who has children from a previous marriage because adopted children are eligible for military benefits, such as medical care. Adopting the child of a divorced parent, however, may end the natural parent's obligation to pay child support, so you need to consider which is more advantageous to the children—the child support or the military benefits. The other natural parent normally also would have to consent to the adoption.

Before you marry someone who already has children, discuss child support, adoption, military benefits, and what would be best for everyone concerned. Then both of you should talk to a legal assistance officer about your concerns for your soon-to-be family, about how all these changes may affect your military service, and about how the military could help you with your new family.

CHILDREN BORN OVERSEAS

If you are married to a U.S. citizen and have a child overseas, he or she is automatically a U.S. citizen. To avoid having a problem proving that the child is a citizen when you return to the United States, however, you should do the following things when the child is born and while you are still overseas:

- Get at least eight copies of the child's birth certificate.
- Register the child's birth at the American consulate.
- Apply for a certificate of citizenship from the Immigration and Naturalization Service.

Under some circumstances, children born overseas may have dual nationality; they may also be citizens of the country they were born in or, if one parent is a foreign national, of the country of that parent's citizenship. Dual citizenship can have important consequences to your child. For example, a male child who is a citizen of both the United States and a European country could be drafted by the European country. It is possible, however, to renounce the other citizenship. You should consult a legal assistance officer to determine whether your child has dual citizenship and what to do about it.

SUPPORT OF FAMILY MEMBERS

Of the problem areas concerning family members, support is probably the biggest. The military expects you to support your family members but tries to help you do so. Legal questions about support involve who must provide it, how much support they must provide, and what happens if a parent doesn't provide adequate support.

Who Must Provide Support?

Years ago the law regarding support of family members was clear—the husband provided financial support to his wife and children, and the wife was the homemaker. In today's society, however, the wife often works and supports the family financially, either totally or partly. Both spouses also must support each other; if your spouse needs support and you can provide it, the law requires you to do so. State laws set the amount of support you must provide, although the military has extra allowances to help servicemembers with families fulfill their obligations. Some states have laws making it a crime to fail to support family members.

All services require servicemembers to support their dependents. Each service, however, implements this DOD policy differently, and their support regulations change frequently. Thus, you should see a legal assistance officer if you need support from a servicemember or if someone tries to get you to pay child support. The accompanying letter is a sample of a Navy letter concerning nonsupport of family members.

LETTER TO NAVY FAMILY ALLOWANCE ACTIVITY
(regarding nonsupport of family members)
(Heading)
(Office Symbol)   (Date)
SUBJECT: Compliance with Bupers Man, Para Section 6210120,
"Support of Dependents"

Commander
Navy Family Allowance Activity
Anthony J. Celebreeze Building
1240 East 9th Street
Cleveland, OH 44199

1. Mrs. _____ has requested my assistance as a military attorney and
has advised me that _____, who is currently assigned to _____,
has failed to adequately provide continuous support for his dependents in
violation of Bupers Man, Para Section 6210120, entitled "Support of Dependents."

2. Request this servicemember's commander be contacted and that this servicemember be counseled as to the Navy Policy and guidelines and the member informed of possible consequences if he fails to comply.

[Paragraphs 3, 4, and 5 are alternate paragraphs that can be used in these letters.]

3. Mrs. _____ has indicated that _____ failed in his duty to adequately support his dependents. Request that you insure that this servicemember is counseled and that he initiates an allotment in the amount of
_____ per month to comply with the appropriate Navy support guidelines. He has the following dependents: _____.

4. The health and welfare of these dependents is being placed in jeopardy.
Mrs. _____ states that she does not wish to jeopardize her husband's
career and that she only desires that her present financial dilemma be corrected with the adequate and continuous support, which is both his legal and
moral obligation.

5. Mrs. _____ has sought my assistance in this matter and it is respectfully requested that _____ be counseled on the urgency of the situation
and of the requirements of Bupers Man, Para Section 6210120. It is further
requested that I be advised of his intentions with regard to this matter and
the remedial action that is being taken in order that Mrs. _____ can be
fully advised. Your assistance in this matter is greatly appreciated.

6. This letter is written in my capacity as a Legal Assistance Attorney of the
Armed Forces acting on behalf of my client, _____. As such, it reflects
my personal considered judgment as an individual attorney at law. It is not to
be construed as an official view of this headquarters, the United States Army
or the United States Government.

CF: Client

If the father of the child is not married to the mother, a paternity proceeding may be necessary. Such a proceeding is a lawsuit to determine whether a person is the father of the child. With today's sophisticated DNA and other tests, it is normally better to save attorney's fees and costs rather than contesting paternity if you are actually the father. If the mother is able to establish paternity, she should be able to get child support.

How Much Support Must You Provide?

Among the things a state court would consider in determining how much support a parent should provide are military pay and other pay, other income, the cost of necessities and other expenses of the family members, whether the family members can contribute to their own support, and other obligations of the parent, such as debts.

The military designed the increased quarters allowance and family separation allowances to help servicemembers with their family support obligations. Generally, if a court has issued an order requiring payment of a support allowance, the military expects the servicemember to pay that amount. If no court has issued an order for support, the military expects that the servicemember will contribute at least the amount of the quarters allowance. In fact, it is illegal to refuse to support dependents while receiving quarters allowances at the "with dependents" rate.

A refusal to provide support to family members could result in a court-martial, nonjudicial punishment, or administrative action, such as a discharge (see chapter 7). If a court has ordered you to pay child support and you refuse, you family members may garnish your military or retirement pay so that the finance center will pay directly to your dependents the amount ordered for support. If you are not certain that a particular person is a legal dependent or that you are required to support a particular person, for any reason, consult a legal assistance officer instead of merely refusing to pay the support.

What If a Servicemember Doesn't Provide Support?

An amendment to a federal law, the Tax Equity and Fiscal Responsibility Act of 1982, provides that the military may take involuntary allotments from a servicemember's pay for support of family members. The military may start such allotments if the servicemember has not made support payments required by a court or state agency order in an amount equal to two months' support.

Family members who want to receive such an allotment do so by serving notice on the servicemember's service finance center along with a copy of the court or administrative agency order requiring the support. The state court or agency may also request such an allotment from the servicing finance center on behalf of the family member. The finance center then notifies the servicemember. Such an allotment cannot start, however, until the servicemember has had the opportunity to consult a staff judge advocate about the situation or for thirty days after the servicemember receives notice of the allotment if such a consultation is not possible.

If you have the opposite problem of supporting a child or children without the assistance of the other parent, the military may also be able to help you. If the other parent is in the military, one problem may be to find him or her. If you do not know where the other parent is, you may use the worldwide locator of his or her service:

Army: Army Active Personnel Locator, U.S. Department of the Army, Worldwide Locator, ELREC, Fort Benjamin Harrison, IN 46249-5301 (317-542-4211).

Navy: For family members, Bureau of Naval Personnel, BUPRS, P-23D Number 2, Navy Annex, Washington, DC 20370-3240. For non-family members, Bureau of Naval Personnel, BUPRS, 02116 Number 2, Navy Annex, Washington, DC 20370-0216.

Marine Corps: Commandant of the Marine Corps, Headquarters Marine Corps, Code MMRB-10, Bldg. 2008, Quantico, VA 22134-0001 (703-640-3942).

Air Force: Air Force Worldwide Locator, AFMPC, RMIQL, 550 C St. W., Suite 50, Randolph Air Force Base, TX 78150-4752 (210-652-5775).

U.S. Coast Guard: Coast Guard Locator, Military Personnel Command, G-MPC-S-3, U.S. Coast Guard, 2100 Second St. SW, Washington, DC 20593-001 (202-267-1340).

For any service, you should first try the Red Cross in case of emergency.

Although the locator service may charge a small fee for finding a servicemember, the fee is minimal when compared with a private investigator's fee. Your request should be in writing and state that finding the servicemember is necessary for you to get child support. You should include the military parent's full name, Social Security number, date of birth, rank, and last known assignment. This service is one of the ways that the military tries to help service family members who need support.

OTHER MILITARY ASSISTANCE FOR FAMILY PROBLEMS

You may encounter other legal problems with your children and other family members besides support problems. Often, the military will be able to help you with these problems. For example, if one of your children is very ill, you may be able to get a compassionate reassignment to a military installation with a hospital that can care for your child. Or, if your child is handicapped, your service will try to assign you where the child can receive the medical care and educational assistance he or she needs. Federal law requires that all states provide educational services to handicapped or disabled children, but the states have the power to determine what programs are available in each state. Check with your base school board to find out what is available in your state.

CONCLUSION

The laws of the state in which you live and the military expect you to support your family members to the best of your ability. Because of the complex laws and regulations in this legal area and the importance of support for family members, you should consult an attorney early and often when support or other family relationship problems arise. It is important not to ignore family problems but to recognize them and get help before they cause legal problems that may be much more difficult to solve.

12

Divorce and Separation

Unfortunately, some marriages end in divorce. It may be more difficult to make a marriage work in the military because of the hardships of military life, such as long working hours, family separations, and so on. If you are having marital difficulties, don't immediately decide you want a divorce. If you and your spouse can't work out your problems together on your own, many sources of help are available in the military. You may wish to consult a chaplain (you don't need to be religious to benefit from a chaplain's marriage counseling) or go to a marriage counseling service.

If you cannot solve your marriage problems, see an attorney. It is not a good idea to go to a country, such as Mexico, that seems to specialize in quicky divorces. Remember, too, that some foreign divorces are not valid in the United States.

When you visit an attorney about a divorce or a separation, you should bring the following documents with you:
1. Copy of your marriage certificate.
2. List of your financial assets.
3. List of your property.
4. List of your debts.
5. List of your monthly income from all sources.
6. List of your monthly living expenses.
7. Your will(s).
8. List of your bank accounts and credit cards.
9. List of your life insurance policies.

The attorney may discuss both separation and divorce with you. If you decide to divorce instead of separate, you will need to discuss grounds for divorce, procedural requirements, and splitting up your assets, including alimony, property distribution, child support, and child custody. This chapter discusses those matters and ends with a discussion of what to do if your spouse sues you for divorce.

SEPARATION

If you cannot solve your marriage problems, you have two options. One is divorce; the other is separation. A *separation agreement* is a contract between the husband and wife that they will live apart from each other. It also divides the couple's property and establishes support and custody rights. Sometimes the separation agreement carries these provisions over into a divorce decree, and often it is a preliminary step to divorce. One reason some military spouses separate, rather than divorce, at least initially, is that the nonmilitary spouse remains eligible for military benefits during a separation. Because the laws of separation and divorce vary among states and because of tax consider- ations, you should see a legal assistance officer if you are considering a separa- tion. Moving out is usually unwise because it could give your spouse grounds for a divorce. More important, however, it would not help you prove to a court that you were responsible enough to get custody of your children.

DIVORCE

If a separation does not solve your marital problems, you may decide to divorce. A *divorce* is the legal ending of a valid marriage. If you end a separa- tion, you remain married. But once you get a divorce, you would have to remarry to continue the marriage with the spouse you divorced. The grounds for divorce vary, but most states now have a form of "no-fault" divorce. If both spouses want the divorce, no matter who is at fault the court will grant a divorce. Grounds for divorce other than no-fault are usually important only in contested divorces. Other legal aspects are important, however, even in uncontested divorces, such as procedural requirements, how to divide your marital property, and child custody.

Grounds for Divorce

Grounds for ending a marriage by a divorce proceeding involve either fault— something one spouse did wrong—or no-fault. Various states recognize some of the following grounds for divorce involving fault:

- *Adultery*. Adultery is voluntary sexual intercourse with someone other than your spouse.
- *Bigamy*. Bigamy is the state of being married to more than one spouse at a time.
- *Cruelty*. This ground is sometimes called "extreme cruelty" or "cruel and inhuman treatment." It may involve physical cruelty, such as violence, or mental cruelty, such as inflicting repeated indignities.

- *Criminal conviction and imprisonment.* A conviction for a serious crime, such as a felony, when coupled with a prison sentence, is a ground for divorce in some states.
- *Impotency.* The law defines impotency as the inability to engage in normal sexual intercourse. Inability to have children is not a ground for divorce, unless it also involves impotency.
- *Insanity.* Mental incapacity, insanity, or commitment to a mental institution is a ground for divorce in some states.
- *Habitual drunkenness and drug use.*
- *Desertion or abandonment of the family.* This ground involves the voluntary separation of one spouse from the other without justification. If you resume living together, even for a short period, you end a desertion or abandonment. A spouse who seriously wrongs the other partner, thereby forcing the other to leave, could, in turn, be found guilty of "constructive desertion," which establishes an abandonment the same as if the guilty spouse were the one who had left.
- *Desertion and abandonment for a specified time, usually six months or more.* For this ground to hold up in court, one spouse would have to show that the other spouse meant to desert or leave. Leaving home to enter the armed forces, seeking a job away from home, or leaving because of a separation agreement, for example, would not be desertion or abandonment.
- *Fraud.* This ground exists when one spouse misrepresents some matter that would have affected the decision to marry that spouse, such as one of these:
  1. Concealment of pregnancy at the time of the marriage when the husband is not the father.
  2. Concealment of a serious illness or venereal disease.
  3. Misrepresentation of previous marital status.

Most divorces, however, involve no-fault grounds. Among the no-fault grounds recognized by various states are the following:
- *Separation.* This ground exists when the spouses live apart for a certain time. It does not matter who was at fault in the separation.
- *Incompatibility.* This ground exists when the husband and wife cannot live together.
- *Irretrievable breakdown of the marriage.* Irretrievable breakdown means that the marriage partners have such differences that the marriage cannot be salvaged.
- *Irreconcilable differences leading to breakdown.* This ground is much like irretrievable breakdown of the marriage. Irreconcilable differences are disagreements that the husband and the wife cannot resolve.
- *Mutual consent.* If both parties consent to the divorce, it does not really matter what caused them to want to end their marriage.

Whatever the reasons for your divorce, you need to see a lawyer. Tell him what is wrong with the marriage and let him tell you which ground or grounds you have for a divorce. If you have grounds and meet the procedural requirements, it should not be difficult for you to get a divorce, even if your spouse does not consent. The old saying "I won't give you a divorce" is an empty threat. If an aggrieved spouse wants a divorce, that spouse can get one. It may be more difficult and more expensive than an uncontested one, but today's courts will not force one spouse to live with another who is mistreating the other or when the marriage is damaged beyond repair.

Procedural Requirements for Divorce

Usually, a bigger problem for spouses in the military than finding a ground for divorce is to satisfy the procedural requirements. Military family members involved in divorce actions face two major problem areas. One is meeting residency requirements; the other is properly notifying the other spouse of the court proceeding.

Most states have a procedural requirement that the person seeking a divorce must be a resident of the state where the divorce action is filed. This residency requirement is often a problem for servicemembers because of the transient nature of military service. You may have just arrived at a military installation when you decide to file for divorce, for example, and have difficulty qualifying for the residency requirements to get a divorce in that state. Or the military may have assigned you overseas, so you are not residents of any state of the United States for divorce court requirements. In such a case, you may have to try to get a foreign divorce. Before doing so, however, check with your legal assistance officer. Many states do not recognize foreign divorces. Divorces from Guam, for example, are not valid in many states.

Federal courts may not grant divorces, so you must go to one of the courts of the state you are in. That court, however, must have jurisdiction— the authority to decide the case. The divorce court gets such jurisdiction by having the spouse suing for divorce establish either domicile or residence in that state. *Domicile* is living in a place with the intent to remain there permanently. *Residence* is less well defined and, when used in divorce jurisdiction, often means domicile. It could, however, mean nothing more than living in the state without the intent to remain there permanently. The word *residence* means one thing in divorce cases and another for tax purposes.

Whether it is called residence or domicile, one of the spouses suing for divorce must live in the state where he or she is seeking a divorce for a prescribed period before that state's court can decide the divorce action. Some states have special laws that allow servicemembers stationed there for a certain period, often one year, to get divorces although they are not legal residents. This special law is another reason to see an attorney—to find out whether you qualify for the local court to grant you a divorce.

Another procedural requirement involves notification of the divorce suit. Not only must the plaintiff (the one suing for divorce) meet the domicile or residence requirements, but also he or she must properly notify the defendant (the spouse being sued) of the divorce suit. There are two types of notice: personal service and constructive or substituted service. *Personal service* means that, for example, someone would deliver the notice of the court case to you in person. Usually, an official would give you a summons or complaint. *Constructive service* means that the plaintiff would, for example, print a notice of the divorce case in a newspaper or mail a notice to your last known address. Generally, constructive notice is sufficient to grant a divorce, but the courts require personal service to determine property and custody rights (see chapter 6 a for detailed discussion of service of process).

A court must also have jurisdiction so that other states will honor the divorce decree. If a court does not have jurisdiction, another state you move to may refuse to honor not only your divorce but also the property distribution and the child custody arrangements. If the court that granted your divorce had jurisdiction based on personal service, then other states should recognize the decree in its entirety, including property division and custody rights. If the court's jurisdiction was based on constructive notice alone, however, then another state could recognize the validity only of the divorce, not of the property settlement or custody determination. If the court ordering child support had jurisdiction, the Uniform Reciprocal Enforcement of Support Act would require other states to enforce the court-ordered payments. In addition, tax refunds may be withheld to pay support obligations.

SPLITTING IT UP

An even bigger problem than getting a court to grant a divorce is the determination of property, monetary, and child custody rights. It is usually not difficult to get a divorce. The problem often is to arrive at an agreement as to the alimony, property distribution, child support, and child custody.

Alimony

Alimony is a monetary allowance one spouse—historically the husband—pays to the other spouse to support the other spouse when they are living apart. Times have changed the way courts handle divorce, however, including awarding alimony. Alimony is now often called *maintenance*. Although previously only husbands had to pay alimony to their wives, the law now provides that a court may require the spouse (husband or wife) who supports the other to pay maintenance to the nonworking spouse during the divorce action and for a period after the divorce is final. Also, not all divorces provide for alimony. If both spouses are able to support themselves, alimony is not necessary.

When a court decides to award alimony, it can be temporary or permanent. Normally, when a spouse files a divorce action with the court, a spouse needing alimony will ask for temporary alimony or support money. That spouse may also request that the other spouse pay attorney's fees and other costs of the case.

If the spouses agreed to these payments, the court would usually grant the temporary alimony request immediately. If, however, the spouses disagreed on such temporary maintenance, the court would listen to all the evidence and their arguments and then decide whether the spouse who is requesting alimony needs it and whether the other spouse can afford to pay it. The court would also consider any prenuptial agreement (see chapter 10) provisions regarding maintenance and enforce those provisions if they were proper.

A court would consider the same criteria in deciding whether to award permanent alimony. Permanent alimony is the support one spouse provides the spouse who cannot support himself or herself for an indefinite period or for the lives of the divorced couple. A court would award permanent alimony as part of the divorce decree to a spouse who is far less able to support himself or herself than the other. The divorce court would also normally consider the contributions the spouse asking for alimony had made to the marriage, such as homemaking, putting the other spouse through school, and so on, when determining the amount of alimony. The court may also consider what sums would be necessary and for how long in order for the spouse receiving the alimony to complete training or education to qualify for a job.

Permanent alimony normally ends when the recipient dies, remarries, or, in some states, lives with a member of the opposite sex. If the circumstances of the ex-spouses change, it may be possible to modify an alimony decree. The most common change occurs when one of the parties' financial situation changes drastically. You cannot, however, relieve yourself of the duty to pay alimony by declaring bankruptcy.

Some states will not award permanent alimony to the spouse who was "at fault" in the marital situation that led to the divorce. For example, if a court finds that one spouse has been adulterous, it may not award that spouse alimony because of marital misconduct. Other courts may consider marital misconduct as a factor in determining the amount of alimony and award less to a guilty spouse than they would to a spouse who had not been at fault.

Another reason to see a lawyer, instead of using a do-it-yourself divorce kit, is that alimony involves important tax considerations. It is normally deductible for the ex-spouse who is paying it and taxable to the one receiving it. Because other circumstances, such as alimony combined with child support, could affect your taxes, you need to discuss all the possible options with a lawyer and, possibly, an accountant.

Property Distribution
Dividing up property can also be a problem in a divorce. How the courts split up marital property varies among states. Generally, each state tries to reach

an equitable, or fair, distribution. More specifically, how the courts split up marital property varies according to whether it is a community property state or a common law property state and according to the state's particular rules.

Community property states (Arizona, California, Idaho, Louisiana, Nevada, New Mexico, Texas, and Washington) would consider that all property acquired during the marriage belonged to both spouses. (The only exceptions in some states may be gifts or inherited property.) Thus, upon a divorce, the court would seek to divide the property either equally between the spouses or in an equitable manner.

In common law property states, the traditional rule was that divorce courts divided only property that was jointly held upon divorce. Few states, however, follow this rule today. Most of these states strive now to make an equitable distribution of the property. The judge tries to give each spouse a fair share, considering such things as length of the marriage, age and health of the spouses, their ability to support themselves, and how much each spouse contributed to the marriage, including nonmonetary contributions.

No matter which type of state you are in when you file for divorce, don't try to hide any of your property so that your spouse can't get it. A judge in a divorce court could take several actions against you, including holding you in contempt of court, for lying about your assets.

Divorce courts divide retirement benefits you earned during the marriage as part of property settlements. The U.S. Supreme Court had ruled that state courts could not divide military retirement pay in a divorce settlement, but, in 1981, Congress changed this situation in the Uniformed Services Former Spouses' Protection Act (USFSPA), which authorized state courts to treat your military retirement pay as community property if state law would do so. The act also authorized the service to pay the ex-spouse's share of your pension directly to your former spouse.

If the court orders the payment of a portion of your retired pay as separate property, your former spouse qualifies for these direct payments if he or she was married to you for ten years or more, during which time you served ten years of military service creditable toward retirement. If the court orders the payment of a portion of your retired pay in the form of alimony or child support, then the USFSPA does not require any number of years of marriage or service for your spouse to qualify to receive these payments. The act limits the amount your former spouse can receive to 50 percent of your military retirement pay. If someone has garnished your retired pay, the total amount may not exceed 65 percent.

The USFSPA does contain some protections for the retired servicemember. Your service cannot, for example, pay your ex-spouse a portion of your pension unless at least one of these requirements is met:

• The court ordering the payment had jurisdiction over you because you resided in the state, other than because of your military assignment.

- You were domiciled within the territorial jurisdiction of the court.
- You consented to the jurisdiction of the court.

If you meet one of these judicial requirements and a court orders a division of your military retirement pay, your ex-spouse may get the payments by mailing a certified copy of the court order to your service's finance center along with proof of the date of marriage unless it is shown in the court order. The order, or accompanying documents, must certify that the court has jurisdiction over you and that the court protected your rights under the Soldiers' and Sailors' Civil Relief Act.

The USFSPA also provides for medical, post exchange, and commissary benefits for former spouses under certain conditions. What benefits are available for a former spouse depends on when the divorce happened. If you are a former military spouse who was divorced before 1 April 1985, you are eligible for commissary and exchange privileges if you were married twenty years or more to a servicemember or military retiree who had at least twenty years of service that qualified for retirement (the years of service and the marriage must overlap, at least in part) and if you have not remarried. If a former military spouse remarried but the remarriage has ended, the former military spouse may again qualify for commissary and exchange privileges.

If you meet those conditions and if you have no employer-sponsored health plan, you are also eligible for medical privileges. If you are a former spouse who meets those requirements except that you got your divorce after 1 April 1985, you are eligible for two years of transitional medical care coupled with a right of guaranteed insurability under a health care plan.

Property transfers between divorcing spouses may be taxable. So it is a good idea to consult not only a lawyer but also an accountant or a tax specialist if you have substantial income or property.

Child Support

As discussed in chapter 11, parents have the duty to support their children, both before and after a divorce. An important consideration in a divorce is how much each parent will contribute to child support. The father used to be the only spouse who would have to pay child support after a divorce. Now the courts have become more willing to impose that duty on either spouse. Most divorce courts now divide the financial responsibility for child support according to the financial situations of the parents and the needs of the children. Because financial situations and children's needs change over time, the courts can change support allowances when circumstances, such as the parents' ability to pay, change. Marital misconduct is not a factor in the decision to award child support because the court will not permit the children to suffer for the wrongs of the parents.

The duty to pay child support usually ends when the child marries or reaches eighteen years of age. A divorce court may order you to pay child support until some later point, such as until the child reaches age twenty-one or graduates from college. Bankruptcy will not relieve you from the obligation to pay child support.

Child support is not tax-deductible to the person who pays it. The parent who provides more than 50 percent of the total support for a child is entitled to claim that child as a personal exemption on his or her federal tax return. In situations where the noncustodial parent is the primary supporter of the child or children, the right to claim the personal exemption should be stipulated in the divorce or custody decree. Also, the custodial parent should sign form 8332 releasing the exemption to the noncustodial parent. In situations where several taxpayers provide support, none of whom provide more than 50 percent of the total support for the child or children, no one may claim the exemption unless all providers sign form 2120 giving one taxpayer the right to claim the exemption.

Child support payments and maintenance payments have serious tax implications. To ensure that the IRS does not receive more than the separating parties intend to pay in taxes, an expert in the field should be consulted. Proper advice will ensure that the payments are structured to reduce the potential tax liability as much as is legally possible.

Child Custody

Perhaps the most traumatic part of a divorce is deciding who gets custody of your children. Child custody is normally not a problem during a marriage unless one or both of the parents abused or neglected the child. In such a case, a civilian court may take the child away from one or both parents to make certain the child receives the care and support he or she needs. But which parent should get custody in a divorce case is one of the areas of greatest concern both to the parents and to the divorce court.

Several questions may come to mind if you consider divorce. Who will get custody? What kind of custody will it be, sole or joint? What, if any, visitation rights will the court grant you? Can the court change its original decision as to who gets custody?

Much as the father used to be the parent the courts usually looked to for child support, the courts used to award custody to the mother. This rule, too, has changed. Although most cases still result in the mother's getting custody, an increasing number of courts have awarded both parents shared custody or have given custody to the father. Among the factors the court would consider in determining who should get custody are these:

1. Age and sex of the child.
2. Health of the child.
3. Health of the parents.
4. Child's wishes.
5. How the child gets along with the parents.
6. How the child gets along in school.
7. Which parent is better equipped to raise the child.

The father is more likely to get sole custody or joint custody if he has been active in rearing the child and has the time to care for the child or if the mother is unfit. The court usually gives the noncustodial parent visitation rights to maintain the relationship between that parent and the child. The court may, in the interests of the child, place limits on visitation rights, such as how long the noncustodial parent can keep the child away from the parent with custody or how far the noncustodial parent can take the child from his or her home. If neither parent is fit to care for the child, the court could give custody to another relative or to a social agency. The welfare of the child is always the primary concern of the divorce court.

Joint custody may consist of several different arrangements. It may be alternating: the child may live first with you for a period and then with the other parent. The child may also live with only one parent, but the other parent may retain the right to help decide how to raise the child.

The courts are willing to reconsider who should have custody upon changed circumstances that affect the child's welfare, such as if your ex-spouse is no longer a fit parent. If the parent who has custody dies, the custody normally goes to the surviving ex-spouse. If the situation changes so that you think you should get custody or greater visitation rights, see an attorney. Don't take matters into your own hands and just take the child. If you do not get custody or joint custody, do not take the child away from the other spouse without a court order, because child snatching is a crime, similar to kidnapping. The U.S. government has passed the Parental Kidnapping Prevention Act to help enforce legal custody and discourage child snatching. In addition, a judge could punish your child snatching as contempt of court. Also, the United States participates in an international agreement to prevent parental kidnapping that is enforceable against military personnel and family members stationed overseas.

You and your spouse must settle many difficult legal and practical questions when you split up your marriage assets. You have to decide about alimony, about splitting up your property, about child support, and about child custody. All these decisions are interrelated, so you cannot really decide on one of them without considering its effect on the others. Therefore, consulting an attorney and, perhaps, an accountant is crucial if you are considering divorce.

IF YOU ARE SUED FOR DIVORCE
If your spouse sues you for divorce, see a legal assistance officer immediately. The legal assistance attorney will tell you whether you need a civilian attorney. If you ignore the *summons*—the papers informing you of the lawsuit—the divorce court may enter a default judgment against you. That bit of legalese means that the court would grant the divorce with any alimony, child support, and property settlement your spouse requested. Even if you do not object to the divorce and if what your spouse requests in terms of alimony, support, and property seems reasonable, you should have an attorney review the summons because of tax and other considerations.

SAMPLE DIVORCE DECREE FOR AN UNCONTESTED DIVORCE

IN THE DISTRICT COURT OF LEAVENWORTH COUNTY, KANSAS

GENERAL CLAIMS DIVISION

vs.　Plaintiff

Defendant   Case Number

DECREE OF DIVORCE

NOW, on this _____ day of April, 1996, the above matter comes before the District Court of Leavenworth County, Kansas, for hearing and trial. Plaintiff appears in person by and through her attorney. Defendant does not appear in person, but consents to this hearing. Thereupon the matter proceeds to hearing and the Court, after hearing evidence and being fully advised in the premises, finds that the relief prayed for in the Plaintiff's petition should be granted.

After examining the files, hearing the evidence, statements, and arguments of counsel, and being fully advised in the premises, the Court finds:

1. The Court finds that it has jurisdiction over the parties and the subject matter of this action.

2. The Court further finds that these parties were married on the 13th day of June, 1979, in Leavenworth, Kansas, and have been since that time and are now husband and wife.

3. The Court further finds that no children were born of this marriage.

4. The Court further finds that the parties are incompatible under the meaning of the laws of Kansas.

5. The Court further finds that the parties have entered into an Agreement concerning a division of both real and personal property; and all the rights, duties, and obligations of the parties to this action; that the terms of the Agreement between the parties is in the best interest of all parties; and that the provisions of the Agreement are fair, just, and equitable under all the circumstances and should be incorporated into the final Decree of Divorce herein.

IT IS THEREFORE, BY THE COURT, ORDERED, ADJUDGED, AND DECREED, that the Plaintiff be divorced from the Defendant on the grounds of incompatibility and that the bonds of matrimony heretobefore existing between the parties be dissolved, set aside, and held for naught.

IT IS FURTHER ORDERED, ADJUDGED, AND DECREED, that the terms of the agreement entered into by and between the parties be, and the same are hereby incorporated into and made a part of this Decree.

IT IS FURTHER ORDERED, ADJUDGED, AND DECREED, that the parties are prohibited from contracting marriage with any other person until thirty (30) days after the decree shall become final. This decree to become effective upon filing of the Journal Entry, this _____ day of _____ 1996.

Judge of the District Court of
Leavenworth County, Kansas

Never go to the attorney that is helping your spouse. For one thing, it is unethical for your spouse's attorney to represent both sides in a divorce. Also, your spouse's attorney owes his undivided loyalty to your spouse, and you need to consult an attorney who owes his undivided loyalty to you.

Divorces are emotional and traumatic events that almost always cause anger and bad feelings. Sometimes these feelings cause both parties to adopt very hard, uncompromising positions about the amount of alimony and child support, who gets various marital property, and so on. Although you may find it difficult to put these bad feelings aside, the divorce will be less painful and expensive if each spouse tries to be reasonable and compromise. Otherwise, much of your marital estate will simply to go pay attorney's fees and court costs.

Your divorce will be much cheaper and usually better for all concerned if you agree on child custody and support, property division, and alimony, and if you present your agreement to the judge for approval instead of fighting it out in court and having the judge decide. The judge's decision may not be the best possible result for either you or your spouse.

CONCLUSION

I hope that your marriage works out so that you do not need to consult this chapter or get a divorce. But if you have marriage difficulties, remember you can ask people both in and out of the military to help you and your spouse solve them. If you can't work them out, however, then remember two rules: try to be reasonable and compromise, so that you avoid making a bad situation worse and losing your assets in court costs and attorney's fees; and see a lawyer early in the divorce process before you end up in a worse condition than necessary.

Although military service may put some strains on your personal life, your service recognizes this possibility and has many professionals, such as legal assistance officers, chaplains, social workers, and so on, to help you. But you must recognize the problem and seek help before your service can help you. If you get your legal survival kit in order and understand the laws of family relationships, you will have gone a long way toward ensuring that your military service is rewarding for you and your family and free from legal hassles.

PART V

Property

Military service complicates the use and ownership of property. Frequent moves, overseas service, lack of family housing, and so on make it more difficult to acquire, keep, and use property without having legal hassles. If you understand the legal concepts of property use and ownership, however, you will still be able to enjoy your property regardless of the conditions of your military service.

Chapter 13 discusses the legal aspects of the real property you live in, whether you rent or own it. Chapter 14 covers personal property, such as cars and stereos.

13

Your Home

My wife cross-stitched a phrase that hung in our kitchen, "Home is where the Army sends you." No matter which service you are in, you have to make a home somewhere. It may be on a military installation or off post. You may own your own home or rent it.

The law calls where you live—the land and the permanent buildings on it—*real property. Personal property* (see chapter 14) is everything else—generally movable objects, such as a car or a stereo set.

Because every piece of real property, every home, every plot of land, is unique, states have special rules about real property. If, for example, a car deal breaks a contract to sell you a car, you can buy the same make and model car from another dealer, but if a homeowner breaks a contract to sell you his house, you cannot buy the same one from another homeowner. Thus, our legal system has unique laws for real property. Different laws also apply when you live on post than when you live off post, and rules change, too, when you rent instead of own a home.

LIVING ON POST
Many service families live on post in government quarters. Although fewer legal considerations are involved in living in military housing than in buying or renting a home, you need to know about the legal aspects of living in government quarters.

Some servicemembers think they are renting government quarters because they give up their housing allowances to the government as if they were paying rent to a landlord. They do not enjoy the legal status of a tenant, however. Instead, they have a status known in the law as *mere licensees*. A *licensee* is a person who has received permission to do something. In this case, the servicemember has received permission to occupy government real property.

The key thing to know about living in government quarters is that the government can determine whether you live in such quarters and under what conditions. Because you do not have the status of a tenant, you have no property right in the quarters, and the military may require you to move out without giving you due process—notice and an opportunity to explain why the government should allow you to remain in the quarters (see chapter 2). Of course, if the military required you to move off post, the move would be at government expense.

The most common reason that the military terminates servicemembers' on-post quarters is that the servicemember or a family member has done something illegal, such as using illegal drugs, in the quarters. A court would not have to convict any of the occupants of a crime for the military to require them to vacate the quarters. Again, however, the military would have to pay for the move and provide any housing allowances due.

Because the quarters are government property, the government may require you to maintain them during your stay. Besides the responsibility to clean them, you must take care not to damage your quarters. If you damaged your quarters beyond "fair wear and tear," you would have to pay the government for the damage. The military defines fair wear and tear as the normal deterioration of properly used property. If you did not agree to pay the amount the housing inspector assessed when you cleared your quarters, the housing office would start a report of survey (see chapter 5). You could go to a legal assistance officer for help in convincing the survey officer that you should not be found liable.

The best thing to do is to treat government property as if it were your own. If you do, you should be able to move from government quarters without any problems.

RENTING A HOME
Often, because of a lack of on-post housing, a wish for more privacy, or some other reason, service families decide to rent off-post quarters. Because the military may reassign you suddenly and because off-post housing may be scarce, you have a greater potential for problems with home rental than does a civilian. Therefore, if you want to rent off-post housing, you need to understand what a lease is, how to rent property, what your and your landlord's duties are, and what protections the law affords both landlords and tenants.

A lease is an agreement to rent real property. It is a contract just as is an agreement to buy a car or to do a job. In a lease, the landlord agrees to allow another person, the *tenant*, to use the property for a specific period, in return for which the tenant agrees to pay the landlord rent. Both the terms of the

SAMPLE MILITARY CLAUSE FOR A LEASE

MILITARY TENANT: The Tenant is a member of the United States Armed Forces and may terminate this lease on 30 days' written notice to the Landlord in any of the following events:

1. If the Tenant receives permanent change of station orders to depart from the area where the premises are located.

2. If the Tenant is released from active duty.

3. If the Tenant has leased the property prior to arrival in the area and his orders are changed to a different area prior to occupancy of the property.

4. If the Tenant receives military orders requiring him to move into on-post quarters.

If the Tenant terminates the lease under this clause and is in compliance with all other terms of the lease, the landlord will refund to the Tenant, within a reasonable time after the Tenant vacates, any and all security or damage deposit held.

_____   _____

_____   _____

         Tenant's Signature   Landlord's Signature

lease and the law of landlord-tenant relationships govern the rights and obligations of the landlord and the tenant.

One of the most important terms in a lease concerns its duration. If you don't understand how long the lease is for, you could end up having to pay rent even after you move. If no lease existed or if the lease did not specify what type of tenancy it was, a court would find that one of the following types of tenancies existed:

• A *periodic tenancy* is one that has no specific agreement as to the term of the lease. The law measures the lease period by the rent payments. If the lease quotes the rent for a year, then it is a tenancy from year to year, even if, for example, you could pay the rent in monthly installments. If your lease quotes a monthly rate, then you have a lease from month to month. A periodic tenancy continues until either the landlord notifies you or you notify the landlord of an intention to end the lease. But neither you nor the landlord may properly end a periodic tenancy nor may the landlord raise the rent until the end of the term. State law determines how far in advance the parties must give notice about ending the lease if such a clause is not in the contract.

•   If you occupied property with the owner's permission but without an agreement as to the length of the rental, the lease would be a *tenancy at will*. Either you or the landlord could terminate this type of lease at any time, without any notice.

•   A *tenancy at sufferance* exists when you occupy rental property under a periodic tenancy and continue to occupy it after the lease ends. A landlord may evict you whenever he wants if you are a tenant at sufferance.

Unless it is contrary to state law, the lease may specify a type of tenancy other than those discussed above or it may have other notice requirements. You should make certain that any lease you sign has a military clause. A *military clause* lets a servicemember whom the military reassigns or requires to move into on-post quarters terminate the lease by giving thirty days' notice. Without a military clause, the lease may require you to pay rent for the term of the lease, even after you've left the rental property. Some states have laws, however, that permit military members to terminate a lease, even without a military clause, if the military transfers them a certain distance away or discharges them.

Regardless of the term of your lease, both you and your landlord have rights and duties specified by the lease and by state laws. The landlord may be responsible to warrant (guarantee) that the leased premises are fit to live in. If a dangerous condition exists on the premises that the landlord is aware of or should know about and that condition harms someone, a court may require the landlord to pay damages to the injured party.

The lease will often state who has the duty to repair the rental property. Some states have laws that make the landlord responsible for keeping the property in good repair. These laws usually require you, the tenant, to notify the landlord of the needed repair before the law requires him to repair it. If, according to the lease or the law, the landlord was supposed to make repairs and did not, you have several options. You could, for example, make the repairs and deduct the cost from the rent, or you could pay the rent and sue the landlord for the cost of the repairs.

Not only is the landlord responsible for the condition of the property, but also you, the tenant, are liable for damage. Leases or state laws often specify that tenants are responsible for damages to the property in excess of fair wear and tear. Many landlords require you as a new tenant to put up a security deposit, which the landlord may keep, in whole or in part, if you damage the property or leave it in an unclean condition. You should make certain that the lease states what the security deposit covers and under what circumstances the landlord must return it. If the security deposit is a sizable amount and if the landlord holds it for a long time, he should pay you interest on it.

Sometimes servicemembers must find a place to live quickly and consequently take what rental property they can get. What happens if you move in and the property is uninhabitable? Some states have a legal doctrine called the *implied covenant of habitability*, which means the landlord is responsible for keeping the property fit to live in. If he does not, you may move out and sue to get back any rent paid in advance, or you can stay in the property and sue for damages. The amount of damages would usually be the difference between the rent due and how much the rent should be considering the condition of the property.

Another legal doctrine that protects you as a tenant is called *constructive eviction*. If your landlord improperly interferes with your use of the leased property and forces you to vacate it, the law will consider the lease terminated and will excuse you from owing more rent. If your landlord forces you to vacate the property, you may also be able to sue for any damages you have suffered. You must move out before a constructive eviction exists. Obviously, you should not move out without consulting a legal assistance officer to make certain that the right conditions exist for a constructive eviction. Otherwise, you may owe rent after you have left the property.

Another duty you, as a tenant, have is to pay the rent when it is due. If you do not, the landlord has several remedies.

Some state laws provide for a *lien* on your personal property. This legal term means that if you do not pay your rent, the landlord may go to court and get permission to sell your personal property and keep the proceeds to pay the rent. Other states allow the landlord to enter the rental property with a court order and seize certain types of your personal property and hold them as security for the unpaid rent. Unless the lease authorizes it, the landlord may not use force to enter and seize your property. The most effective remedies may be to keep your security deposit or any advance rent you paid or to evict you. A landlord usually evicts a tenant by getting a court order and by using a sheriff or policeman to enforce the court order.

If you break the lease without legal justification, the law calls it an *abandonment*. If you abandon the property, the landlord may rent the property to another and sue you for the difference, if any, between what you paid as rent and what the new tenant pays. Or he may let the property remain unoccupied and try to collect the rent from you as it becomes due.

Under most state laws, a landlord must return a security deposit within a specified time, such as thirty days. If the landlord does not return the entire amount, he must give you an itemized list of the amount withheld and why, as for damages to the property in excess of fair wear and tear.

As you can see, the law of landlord-tenant relationships is complicated and varies among states and among leases. Thus, you should always have a legal assistance officer review a lease before you sign it. He can explain the terms of the lease and ensure that the military clause protects you. Do not rely on any oral promises a landlord makes, because another legal rule, the parol evidence rule, will not allow a court to consider oral promises that change a written contract.

If you have any problems with your landlord, see a legal assistance officer before taking any action yourself. Make certain you take a copy of the lease with you when you visit him.

HOME OWNERSHIP

Although military service places some difficulties in the way of home owner-ship, you, like many other servicemembers, may want to own a home. Because making a profit is difficult if you must sell your home within the few years you may spend at a particular duty station, and because you, as a ser-vicemember, may buy and sell many more homes in a lifetime than a civilian, it is important for you to understand the legalities of buying and selling a home, such as legal categories of homes, purchase contracts, closing, financ-ing, and listing with a broker.

Buying a Home

If you decide to buy a home, you may buy a single-family home, a condo-minium, or a cooperative apartment. A *single-family home* is a house designed to be lived in by one family. A *condominium* consists of a number of dwellings that the condominium owners own individually and common areas that they own jointly. If you bought a condominium, you would own the apartment, and you and other apartment owners would own common hallways, entrances, recreation areas, and so forth. A condominium association would manage the condominium. Sometimes the condominium owners manage the association themselves, and sometimes they hire a professional manager. A corporation owns and manages a *cooperative apartment* complex. You, as a shareholder of the corporation, would lease your apartment from the corpora-tion and pay your share of the costs of operating the corporation. Whatever you buy, never sign a contract to buy any home without having an attorney review it first.

Normally you would buy a home, regardless of its type, by entering into a contract with the seller for the purchase of the real property involved. Real estate law requires contracts for the sale of real estate to be in writing and requires all buyers and sellers to sign the contract. Real estate contracts usu-ally specify the following items:

• A *legal description of the property*. The description of the property on the seller's deed normally is sufficient to properly identify the piece of real estate.

• *The purchase price*. The contract should break down the purchase price into its components, such as down payment, assumption of existing mortgages, and balance of the purchase price, and state when the buyer is to pay the purchase price (usually at closing). If you do not assume an existing mortgage, the seller must pay it off before closing. (If he does not, he will transfer the property to you subject to the mortgage, and you will either have to pay it off yourself or you may have a difficult time getting the seller to pay it off after he has sold you the property.)

- *"Subject to" clause.* This part of the contract specifies any conditions the property has, such as zoning restrictions or easements. A *zoning restriction* means that you may not use the property for certain purposes, such as for a business. An *easement* means that someone else has the right to use part of the property for a specific purpose, such as a public road or a utility line that crosses the property.

- *The title that the seller will transfer to you.* The law defines *title* as the proof of ownership of real property. Your deed shows your title to the property. There are two major types of deeds: warranty and quitclaim. A *warranty deed* not only transfers the property but also guarantees that the seller owns the property and that his title is free from liens or conditions other than those listed on the deed. A *quitclaim deed* is usually worse than a warranty deed for the buyer because it transfers only whatever rights of ownership the seller has in the property. With a quitclaim deed, if another party, such as the seller's spouse or a creditor, has a greater right to ownership than the seller does, you could lose the property and have difficulty recovering your purchase price from the seller. Therefore, you should always make certain that your contract to buy a home requires the seller to transfer what is known as *marketable title* by warranty deed. A marketable title is free from limitations on the property, such as a lien or another party's claim to it. Further, you should never sign a contract that offers title only by a quitclaim deed, unless a competent attorney advises you to do so in that particular situation.

- *Contingencies.* A contingency is a condition of the real estate contract. For example, a contingency clause of the contract may make your obligation to go through with the purchase conditional on your getting a mortgage or some other event. If your contract has such a contingency clause, for example, and you cannot get a mortgage, you can cancel the purchase. Without such a contingency clause, the seller could sue you for breach of contract if you didn't get a mortgage and couldn't buy the home. As a servicemember, you should also make your obligation to buy the property contingent on the military's not reassigning you before closing.

- *Personal property the seller will transfer.* If you are to get any personal property from the seller, such as a washer or dryer, as part of the transaction, include it in the contract. You should also make certain the contract states that this personal property must be in working condition at closing time.

• *Inspection.* The contract must list any repairs the seller must make. You should have the house inspected before signing the contract and reserve, in the contract, the right to inspect any repairs the seller has made to see that they are suitable before closing. (Also make certain that the contract provides for a termite inspection.)

• *Adjustments.* This clause apportions various costs, such as electricity, property taxes, and insurance, between the buyer and the seller as of the date of closing.

• *The date and time of closing.* This clause should also state when you get possession of the property. You normally get possession at closing, although you could get possession before or after closing. If you get possession before closing, the contract should state the amount of rent, if any, you would pay to the seller.

• *An attorney's approval clause.* This clause gives the buyer a specified period of time, such as three days, to have an attorney review the contract and either negotiate any necessary changes or allow the buyer to get out of the contract.

You should always ask about hidden or not visible problems with the house. In many states, if the buyer doesn't ask, he is "stuck" with them if he subsequently discovers them. In others, the seller is liable for any defects he or she knows about and fails to disclose.

Now that you've found a home and signed the contract, how do you finalize the transaction? You finalize your home purchase at closing. Real estate law defines *closing* as a meeting in which the buyer gives the seller the purchase money and the seller delivers the deed to the buyer. If the buyer is going to get a mortgage to finance buying the property, the mortgage lender will have an attorney attend the closing to make certain that you properly execute the mortgage documents.

You, the purchaser, normally pay the closing costs, although you and the seller could write the realty contract so that the seller shares these costs. *Closing costs* are the fees for initiating a mortgage, the transfer taxes, the cost of a title search or title insurance, attorney's fees, and the cost of a credit report. Federal law requires that if you get a mortgage that is federally insured (such as one by the Department of Veterans Affairs or the Federal Housing Administration), the lender must inform you in advance of the closing costs.

After the closing, make certain that you properly record the new deed at the county recorder's office. The county recorder will normally stamp the deed showing when he recorded it. If you do not record your deed, someone with a recorded deed to the property could claim the property.

A *title search* proves that the seller has good title to the property and that no one else has a valid claim. A title search cannot eliminate all risks, however, so some mortgage lenders also require a title insurance policy. Such a policy protects you against unknown claimants and the legal costs of defending your ownership. Title insurance has a one-time premium payment, which you usually pay at closing.

Usually, when the seller uses a broker to sell his home (and sometimes when he sells it himself), the buyer and seller use an escrow agreement. A *real estate escrow* is an amount of money that you deposit with a third party (the escrow agent), such as the real estate agent, who holds it as security to make certain that the sale goes through.

The escrow agreement, which is usually part of the real estate sales contract, should explain the conditions under which the escrow agent holds the money. Normally, it states that the agent will return the money to you if the seller cannot provide good title. The escrow agent will deliver the escrow funds to the seller as damages if you break the contract. The seller can take other legal action against you, too, if you break the contract without a proper excuse. Therefore, don't refuse to go through with the transaction without consulting an attorney.

It is important to understand mortgages because few people can pay cash for a home. A *mortgage* is security for the repayment of money you borrow to pay for a house. It is similar to a lien on a car you buy with borrowed money. The bank, savings and loan company, or mortgage company that lends the money is called the *mortgagee*. The borrower is called the *mortgagor*. In some states, a mortgage is called a *deed of trust*. A mortgage or deed of trust must be in writing.

The mortgagee extinguishes (cancels) the mortgage you signed when you pay the debt in full. If you do not make the mortgage payments on time, or if you otherwise default on the mortgage, the mortgagee may sue to foreclose the mortgage. A *foreclosure* is the sale of your mortgaged property to pay off the debt.

When you take out a mortgage to buy a home, make certain it has a *prepayment clause*. Such a clause allows you to pay the mortgage off early without penalty and to refinance your loan if interest rates go down without paying for the privilege of paying the old mortgage off early.

When you take out a mortgage, find out the type and rate of the interest. Mortgage interest rates can be either fixed or variable. A *fixed rate* stays the same throughout the life of the mortgage. A *variable rate* rises or falls with the prevailing interest rates. Mortgage lenders often use the rates on three-month to five-year treasury bills as the index to determine whether, and how much, a variable mortgage rate will change. If you are considering a variable-interest loan, make certain that the mortgage has a limit on how much the interest rate may go up and that you understand how it affects your payment.

Variable interest rate mortgages fall into two categories: (1) fixed payment, variable maturity, and (2) variable payment, fixed maturity. If you had a fixed payment, variable maturity mortgage and if the interest rate went up, then you would make the same payments, but the extra interest would be added to the loan so it would take longer to pay it off. If, on the other hand, you had a variable payment, fixed maturity loan and the interest rate went up, your payments would increase, but you would pay off the loan on the original schedule. If you are thinking about signing a variable rate mortgage, have a legal assistance officer review it because it could have serious legal pitfalls.

Because you are a servicemember, you may want to finance your home with a Department of Veterans Affairs guaranteed home loan or a Federal Housing Administration insured loan.

The VA home loan program is one of the most important veterans benefits. Under the VA loan program, a veteran can borrow as much as he or she wants, so long as he or she qualifies under the lender's terms. The VA will guarantee up to $46,000, which lenders accept for a 25 percent down payment. Thus, a veteran may borrow up to $184,000 before having to put any of his or her money down. VA loans may be used to buy a house or a condominium, to refinance or improve an existing home, or to buy a lot for a manufactured home the veteran already owns. VA loans often have lower interest rates than conventional loans. If you want to apply for a VA loan, the first step is to get a Certificate of Eligibility by filling out Form 26-1880. You can call the VA at 800-827-1000 for more information.

The VA appraises the property to make certain the veteran buyer is paying a fair amount for it. The VA charges you a fee to cover its expenses.

If you are not entitled to a VA guaranteed loan, you should ask your Realtor or lender about a Federal Housing Administration (FHA) insured loan with a veterans preference. This program is similar to the VA guaranteed loan program but requires a down payment, although a much smaller one than conventional financing does.

Another method of buying real property is by a *contract for deed*, also known as a *conditional sales contract* or an *installment sales contract*. In such a contract, you may give the seller a down payment, but regardless of whether you make a down payment, you pay off the balance of the contract in installments. The seller will not transfer the title to the property to you, however, until you have made all the payments. Companies often sell retirement or vacation property this way.

A contract for deed can be dangerous because if you cannot make your payments, you could lose all the money you've paid and have nothing to show for it. Also, if the seller does not own the property outright, he could lose it, so you would be out the property and your money unless you sued to get your payments back. Because of these potential problems, make certain that a contract for deed contains these provisions.

- That the seller will put the property title in trust until you complete the payments or default on them.
- That the seller will write out a deed to the property in your name and give it to the trustee with instructions to give it to you when you complete your payments.

• That your payments will go the trustee, who will pay all taxes and other liens on the land and send the rest to the seller. This provision would help keep the land from foreclosure by someone who holds a mortgage on the property or by a tax official.

• That the seller will record the contract with the registrar of deeds or county clerk.

• That the seller cannot transfer the property to anyone else during the life of the contract.

• That the contract has no prepayment penalty.

• That the seller will provide you marketable title by warranty deed when you have completed the payments.

Before entering into such an arrangement, be certain that you really want the property and that you can make the payments. Then, have a legal assistance officer look over the contract before you sign it.

Buying a house is not simple, so take the time to make certain that you know what you are doing—you can't afford not to. Get a legal assistance officer to help you understand the real estate contract, the closing, and the financing.

When You Sell Your Home

Because the military will probably reassign you after a few years, you may have to sell your home. Two areas that are of special concern to you as a seller are the use of real estate agents to sell your home and what to do if the buyer wants you to help him with financing.

One of the first decisions you must make is whether to sell your home yourself or to use a real estate broker. This decision is not so much a legal one as it is a financial or practical one. But you need to know the rules on how to list your home with a broker.

If you decide to use a Realtor, you can list your home in one of three ways:

• A *multiple listing* lists the home with one broker, who then offers it through other brokers. The listing broker and the broker who actually sells the home then split the commission.

• An *open listing* can be with several brokers, each of whom may try to sell your property. The broker who finds a buyer gets the commission. In this type of listing, if you sell the property yourself, you do not have to pay a commission to anyone.

• An *exclusive right-to-sell listing* is a listing with one broker. No other broker can show the property unless the listing broker agrees.

Read the broker's contract carefully. Many exclusive right-to-sell contracts, for example, require you to pay the broker his commission even if you sell the house yourself.

You may also have to decide whether you should help the buyer with the financing. With the high prices of homes in many areas and high interest rates, sellers sometimes have to help buyers in financing the purchase of the home. If you need to help your buyer, several ways are available to you, including letting the buyer assume your mortgage, giving him a second mortgage, and other financing devices, all of which have potential legal problems you should know about before you offer seller financing.

One way to help the buyer is to allow him to take over your mortgage and then pay you the difference between the amount due on the mortgage and the selling price (known as your *equity*). Allowing the buyer to take over your mortgage instead of taking out a new one can be a good selling tool if your mortgage rate is lower than current interest rates. The pitfall to this arrangement is that you may still be liable for the mortgage debt if you are not careful. If the buyer assumes the mortgage, he becomes liable to pay it off, which releases you from liability. If, however, he only "takes subject" to the mortgage, you and the buyer are both liable, and the mortgage company may seek to collect from you if he does not pay.

If you have a Department of Veterans Affairs insured mortgage, you should include a provision in the sales contract requiring the buyer to substitute his liability for yours with the VA if he is eligible for VA insurance. If he does not substitute his VA liability, your VA mortgage insurance benefits remain tied up with that mortgage, and you cannot use your VA guaranteed financing to buy another home.

Another seller financing tool is a second mortgage. If the buyer does not have enough cash to pay you your equity, you can consent to getting your money in installments by agreeing to a second mortgage, which you would hold yourself as security for repayment of the loan. If you wanted your money immediately, however, you could try to sell the second mortgage to a mortgage institution. Remember, though, that any buyer of a second mortgage will pay you only a fraction of its value because second mortgages are riskier than first ones. If the buyer defaults, the court will order that the proceeds of a foreclosure sale pay off the first mortgage before the remaining proceeds, if any, are applied to the second mortgage. You must be certain that the buyer is financially able to pay you the money secured by the second mortgage.

Agreeing to a second mortgage to sell your home may be necessary, but it is risky. Be certain that a lawyer reviews all mortgage documents, and make sure that you record the mortgage with the appropriate county clerk. If you record it, the person who bought the property will have to pay it off to pass good title if he sells it to someone else. Otherwise, the new buyer would have no notice of the second mortgage, and the person you helped by letting him take the second mortgage instead of paying you cash could sell the property, leave the area, and leave you holding the second mortgage.

Sometimes neither taking over your mortgage nor getting a second mortgage is attractive to the buyer. With high interest rates, Realtors and others have come up with many ways to finance home ownership. While creative financing may be a perfectly valid way to finance a real estate transaction, you must have an attorney review any financing arrangement.

Many states now have laws that require home sellers to notify prospective buyers of any defects in the property. Failure to do so may constitute fraud or at least make the seller liable for any damages resulting from the failure to notify the buyer of the defect.

CONCLUSION
Military service, with its frequent moves, makes finding a place to live more difficult than it is for civilians. But if you understand the legal aspects of living in government quarters, renting, or buying your home, and if you consult an attorney before and during any real estate transactions, you can help make your military home your castle.

14

Personal Property

Not every servicemember will own real property, such as a home, but all servicemembers and their family members own personal property. The law defines *personal property* in several ways. If real property is land and buildings, personal property is everything else, or personal property is all movable property. Such property includes automobiles, boats, motorcycles, furniture and appliances, animals, and money. Legal concerns involving personal property can arise in many ways, such as losing, lending, buying, and insuring property.

LOST PROPERTY

The old saying "Finders keepers, losers weepers" is not accurate. If you find lost property, you do not automatically become the owner. You do, however, get a right to the property that is greater than anyone else's except that of the true owner. If the owner does not claim it, then it becomes yours.

If property is not lost but merely mislaid (intentionally placed somewhere and then forgotten), the person who finds it has no rights of ownership. If the owner abandons the property (throws it away with no intention of retaining ownership), then the person who finds it can keep it. Specific rules about abandoned, lost, or mislaid property vary among states, so consult a legal assistance officer if you find property or if someone else finds yours and will not return it.

ENTRUSTING YOUR PROPERTY TO OTHERS

Often, legal problems arise when you lend your personal property, such as your car, your stereo, or your lawn mower. The borrower may not return it or he may damage it. Special rules apply to property that you lend to another, such as who is liable for its damage, how carefully the borrower must treat it, and what the borrower may use it for. It's important for you to know these rules whether you are the lender or the borrower.

The legal term for the loan or rental of personal property is bailment. A *bailment* is the delivery of personal property to another for some purpose, with the understanding that the borrower will properly use it and return it at the proper time. The person who owns the property and entrusts it to another is the *bailor*. The person who rents or borrows the property is the *bailee*. Bailments come in two kinds: for hire and gratuitous. The law has different rules for legal disputes depending on whether the bailment was for hire or gratuitous.

A *bailment for hire* involves a contract or agreement in which both parties get some benefit from the bailment. Examples of bailments for hire include renting property, such as a car, or a contract to store personal property for money, such as leaving a car in a parking lot. In these situations, both parties benefit because one party gets a service while the other gets money.

Often, the contract for a bailment for hire specifies the terms of the bailment—the rights and obligations of both the bailor and the bailee. If you rent property or leave your property with another, as in a parking lot, for example, carefully read the contract (often the parking ticket) so that you understand your rights. While the ticket may require you to agree that the parking lot owner is not liable for certain things that may happen to your property, the law will not allow him to be free from all liability for damage to or loss of your property. Most states will require him to remain liable for your losses that are the result of his fraud, lack of good faith, or gross negligence. If he cheats you or is very reckless with your property, the law will hold him liable for the loss or damage to your property.

If no agreement in the contract lessens the amount of care that the bailee must take with regard to your property, he must take ordinary care to safeguard it. If he does not, he is liable for the loss of or damage to the property. *Ordinary care* is the care that a prudent person would take of his own property in the same circumstances.

A *gratuitous bailment*, on the other hand, is one that does not have benefits for both parties, such as when you lend your car to a friend. The friend gets the use of your car, but you do not get anything. (The law does not recognize friendship as compensation in this situation.) When the loan of the property is solely for the benefit of the bailee, he must exercise the highest degree of care and be responsible for its loss or damage caused by any negligence on his part.

In either a gratuitous bailment or a bailment for hire, the borrower or renter may use the property only for the authorized purposes and must return it when previously agreed to or when you demand. Failure to return personal property when required may be the crime of wrongful appropriation in violation of Article 121, Uniform Code of Military Justice (see chapter 7).

Of course, the borrower is not the only one who has duties regarding the property. When you lend someone your property, you must tell the borrower about any defects in the property you know of. For example, if your car's speedometer reads twenty miles an hour slower than the car is really going, you need to tell the borrower so that he does not have an accident caused by going too fast. If the bailment is for hire, you have to be even more careful. You must inspect the item you are going to rent and make certain that it is in good working condition before you let anyone use it.

If you have any problems with personal property you have lent, rented, or borrowed, you can get help from legal assistance. Sometimes it may be necessary to go to small claims court or a regular court (see chapter 6) if someone violates your property rights and you cannot work the problem out with the other party. A legal assistance attorney can tell you what you need to do.

GIFTS

A *gift* is a voluntary transfer of property to another without any payment for the property. A gift is not valid unless the *donor* (the person giving the gift) has an absolute intention to make a gift of the property at the time. Your gift is not complete, however, until you transfer the property to the *donee* (the person receiving the gift) and he accepts it. The transfer to the donee may involve physically handing it to the donee, but you can also transfer the property by a *constructive delivery*. For example, if your property is in a safe deposit box, delivering your key to the safe deposit box would be a sufficient transfer of the property in the box to make a valid gift once the donee accepts the property. If the donee already has the property, as may happen when he has borrowed it, all you need to do is to clearly show your intention to make a gift of it.

You could try to get back your property from someone who said you gave it to him as a gift if he got it fraudulently, by force or threats, if the gift was a mistake, or if he took advantage of a special relationship with you, such as a trustee and a trust beneficiary (see chapter 9).

Gifts normally will not have any tax consequences, but if the gift is very valuable you should see an attorney or tax advisor to make certain you understand the tax consequences.

You must know one other legal aspect to gifts. When you are in the military, you cannot always accept a gift from or even give a gift to your boss. Each service has regulations that limit gifts you may give or receive.

Often, servicemembers give gifts to their bosses when the boss moves to another assignment or leaves the service. Such gifts are permissible only when the gifts are voluntary and of nominal value. No one may require you to give a gift to a military superior. A nominal value gift is one that has only a sentimental value, did not cost much, and would not be valuable to anyone but the person who received it. An inexpensive wall plaque, for example, would be a proper nominal gift; an engraved silver coffee service, for example, would not.

Your status as a servicemember also restricts what gifts you may receive. You may receive only nominal gifts from your subordinates. Also, according to the U.S. Constitution, American citizens, including servicemembers, cannot receive gifts from foreign countries without the consent of Congress. Congress has consented to the receipt of foreign gifts of minimal value. Usually, you should refuse to accept a gift from a foreign country or official, but if refusing it would embarrass or offend the foreign country or officer or hurt our relations with the country, you should accept it and then check with your commander to see whether you may keep the gift. If it is not of minimal value, regardless of whether you received it from a subordinate or a foreign government, you would have to turn it over to the U.S. government.

BUYING PERSONAL PROPERTY

When you buy personal property, whether it is a stereo or an automobile, you are entering into a contract. A *contract* is an agreement between two or more parties based upon consideration. *Consideration* is a legal term that means the benefits each party to a contract gets. For example, in a sales contract, the buyer gets the property and the sellers gets consideration in the form of the purchase price.

A contract must have consideration to be enforceable, and the people who enter into the contract must be competent. A competent person is a legal adult who is mentally sound. If you enter into a contract with a minor, the contract will usually be voidable at the minor's option. This phrase means that he can refuse to do his part of the agreement and that a judge would not make him do it if you sued to enforce the contract.

Some contracts must be in writing. The Uniform Commercial Code, which every state has adopted, says that contracts for the sale of personal property of a value of $500 or more must be in writing to be enforceable. If the contract is not enforceable, the other party to the contract could not sue you for breaking it. Contracts that will last longer than one year (such as a four-year installment plan) must be in writing.

Even if your contract does not have to be in writing, a written contract is better for several reasons. First, if you had a dispute, it would show the judge what the actual agreement was. Neither party could say that it was something other than what was written down because the *parol evidence rule* says that the parties to a written contract are not allowed to testify about any oral promises that change a written contract. The court will decide the case *only* on the terms of the written contract.

For the same reason, you must never rely on anything a salesman says, unless it is written in the contract. If, for example, the salesman says that he will make any necessary repairs on the car you are buying from him free for six months, have him write it in the contract and both of you initial it. If he says a handwritten change to a printed contract is no good, he is trying to put one over on you. Insist on his adding it to the contract or take your business elsewhere.

Another reason that a written contract is better than an oral one is that you can take it to a legal assistance officer or a civilian attorney for review before you sign it. Of course, you should read the entire contract carefully yourself and ask a lawyer (not the salesman!) what it means.

It often is necessary to borrow money to buy personal property. Before you sign an agreement to pay for an item over time, read chapter 15, on debt. What appears to be a good buy can be very overpriced if you have to pay a very high rate of interest.

Before you sign a credit agreement, have the merchant sign a certificate of compliance with the Truth in Lending Act (see chapter 15), state law, and the Department of Defense Standards of Fairness. If the merchant does not have such an agreement, you can get one at a legal assistance office. If the merchant will not sign it, you will not be protected by the DOD Standards of Fairness, and the merchant may be trying to cheat you. If the merchant will not sign it and you still want to enter into the transaction, at least take the contract to a legal assistance officer to make certain it is fair to you.

Door-to-Door Sales

It is a rare service family that has not been approached by a door-to-door salesman. While many salesmen are honest and sell good products, door-to-door sales have a high potential for problems. Often, the items are over-priced, the cost of the credit to make the purchase is high, or high-pressure sales techniques result in the purchase of an unwanted item. Because of the dangers of door-to-door sales, the federal government has the Federal Trade Commission Rule to protect potential buyers of products sold door-to-door.

This rule says that in any door-to-door sale or any sale that takes place away from the seller's place of business, the salesman must give the buyer the following documents:

• A complete receipt or copy of a contract covering the sale at the time it is made. The receipt or copy must include the following information:

1. The seller's name and address.

2. A statement that permits the buyer to cancel the sale at any time before midnight of the third business day after the date of the sale. (Business days are days other than Sundays and holidays.) The salesman also has to tell you of your right to cancel.

• A *notice of cancellation* saying in large letters the conditions of the

---

SAMPLE LETTER TO A SELLER
TO CANCEL A DOOR-TO-DOOR SALE

(Name and address of buyer)
(Date)

(Name and address of seller)

Dear Sir or Madam:

This is to notify you that I have decided to exercise my right to cancel our sales contract of (date). Accordingly, please return my payment of $ _____ within 10 business days following your receipt of this rescission notice. I will hold the (goods) for you to pick up at the above address for 20 days from the date of this notice, after which time I will either retain or dispose of the goods without further obligation.

Sincerely,

(Buyer's signature)

---

right to cancel. Normally, if you cancel the sale within the three days, the seller will give you back your money and anything you traded in as part of the transaction within ten days of the cancellation. You must return the property you bought. If you have the property available for the seller to pick up and he does not do so with twenty days after you cancel, you may keep the property or give or sell it to anyone you want. If you do not let him pick up the property or don't send it to him after agreeing to do so, then you remain liable and must pay for it. Finally, the notice of cancellation has to tell you where to mail or send a telegram of cancellation.

Even with this protection, there is no reason for you to sign a door-to-door salesman's contract during his first visit. Ask him to leave a copy of the contract and take it to a legal assistance officer. If the salesman won't do so or says that the deal is a one-day offer, it should tell you that he is trying to put one over on you. No deal is so good that you can't get it elsewhere or a little later.

Mail Order

The federal government has some regulations to protect you when you buy items by mail order. The regulations state that when you buy by mail you must either receive the item by the date promised or within thirty days after you order it. If the firm cannot do either, it must tell you and give you a new delivery date and the option to cancel the order or agree to the new date. If the new shipping date is thirty days or less from the original date and you do not reject it, the regulations say that you have accepted it. If it is more than thirty days or the seller cannot provide a new shipping date, you do not have to do anything: the regulation presumes you rejected the delay and canceled the purchase. These regulations do not apply, however, to magazine subscriptions, mail order seeds and plants, and cash on delivery (C.O.D.) orders.

Sometimes servicemembers receive items through the mail that they did not order. Some companies just send things to people in the hope that the person who receives the item will feel obligated to buy it. This practice is illegal, except if the item is a free sample clearly marked as such or is from a charity asking for donations. When you receive anything you did not order or request through the mail, you can consider it a gift and keep it. You can also complain to the post office if it is not a sample or from a charity.

Receipts

You should always save receipts for valuable items. They will be necessary to substantiate any claim you may have to file, against either the government or your insurance carrier, if the property is lost or damaged, as during a move. If you can't prove what the property cost, the government claims officer or the insurance adjuster may deny the claim or pay a lesser amount.

Warranties

Most new personal property you buy will have a warranty. A *warranty* is a guarantee and may be one of two types: express and implied. An *express warranty* is a written promise about the condition of the property to which it refers. For example, the warranty that comes with your new stereo might say that if it did not work, you could return it for trade-in or repair within six months of the date you bought it. After that, the warranty would expire.

In an *implied warranty* the manufacturer or the seller of the item does not tell you or write down the warranty, but rather the law guarantees the item at least in part. Usually, implied warranties concern merchantability and fitness for the intended purpose. *Merchantability* means that the item is what the seller says it is. An implied warranty of fitness means that the item will do the function it was designed to do. If you bought a portable radio that did not have an express warranty, an implied warranty of merchantability would guarantee that it was a radio instead of a nonworking model radio, for example. The implied warranty of fitness would guarantee that the radio would actually play.

The coverage of implied warranties varies among states, and often an express warranty will state that it is instead of any other warranties, express or implied. If you have a problem with an item you bought, and the seller won't help you, take the warranty to a legal assistance officer. He can also tell you whether any implied warranties will help you and what to do to get the item fixed or to get your money back.

Because warranties can be difficult to understand, Congress passed a law, the Magnuson-Moss Warranty Act, to help you understand warranties on products you buy. The law does not require that the product have a warranty, but if it does, the warranty must specify whether it is a full warranty or a limited warranty. A *full warranty* covers any defect in the product for the period of the warranty. A *limited warranty* covers only certain defects. Under this law, a full warranty requires the manufacturer to repair, to replace, or to refund the cost of a product that is defective. The manufacturer must label any lesser warranty as a limited warranty, so that you are aware that you are not getting a full warranty.

If you do not understand a warranty or if you do not feel that the seller lived up to the warranty, your legal assistance officer can help you. Take a copy of the warranty with you when you go to see him.

PERSONAL PROPERTY INSURANCE
Because you are a servicemember, you may be entitled to have the government reimburse you for loss, damage, or destruction of your personal property if the harm occurred incident to service (see chapter 5). You probably still need personal property insurance for two reason. First, loss, damage, or destruction of the property may not be incident to service, and consequently, the government would not pay a claim. Second, the Military Personnel Claims Act limits reimbursement to the reasonable cost of replacing the item or items, not to exceed $25,000. Thus, the claims system may not fully compensate you, even if the loss, damage, or destruction was incident to service.

AUTOMOBILES
Servicemembers who own automobiles may have more problems with them than do civilians who have cars. Often servicemembers buy cars away from home and have to register them away as well. They also will have to satisfy the military's vehicle inspection and registration requirements in order to have the privilege of driving on military installations, and they must have a valid driver's license and insurance.

Buying a Car
When you buy a car, remember that you enter into a contract just as with the purchase of a stereo. It is especially important to remember that all the oral promises of the car salesman are meaningless unless they are written into the contract. You should also cross out any blank spaces on the contract, so that the salesman cannot later add something to the contract. And it is especially

important to take any contract, sales agreement, or offer sheet to a lawyer if you do not understand it.

You must be even more cautious when buying a used car. Most used cars do not have a warranty. They are sold "as is." If a car is sold as is, and it falls apart after you have driven it five miles, you are stuck unless the state you bought the car in has an implied warranty of fitness and the sales contract does not disclaim the state warranty. You cannot rely on the dealer's saying that if it needs repair within a month he will fix it. Any warranty must be written into the sales contract to be binding.

The Federal Trade Commission has a Used Car Rule to protect buyers, however. It requires all used car dealers to have a large Buyers Guide in the window of each used car for sale. The guide must give the following information:

- Whether the car has no warranty or an implied warranty.
- Whether the car has a warranty and what it covers.
- That you should have the car inspected by a mechanic before you buy it.
- That any promises the dealer makes should be in writing.
- What major problems may happen in a used car.

The considerations discussed in chapter 15 about borrowing money also apply to financing automobile purchases. One legal consideration unique to car financing is that in many states it is illegal to take a car that has a lien on it outside the state without the consent of the lender. This law may cause a problem if you buy a car shortly before being assigned overseas. If you want to ship the car overseas, the lien holder may not grant permission. Then you would have to sell the car, refinance it, pay off the loan, or leave the car behind. Often, if the lien holder agrees to let you ship the car overseas, he will require a large deposit to protect his interests.

Registering Your Car

There are legal consequences to other aspects of getting a car besides buying it. You must also register and license the car. If you have properly registered your car in the state where you are domiciled (your permanent home), the law does not require you to register it in another state where the military has stationed you. This protection for servicemembers is a part of the Soldiers' and Sailors' Civil Relief Act (see chapter 6). The act does not protect servicemembers' spouses, however. Thus, if the car is registered in both your names or in only your spouse's name, the state where you are stationed may require you to follow local registration requirements.

If your car is not registered in your state of domicile but rather in another state, the state where you are stationed may again require you to register it there. For example, if you are a resident of Indiana but are stationed in Virginia, and your car is registered in the state in which you were previously assigned—California—Virginia could require you to register the car in Virginia. Even if you registered your car in the state of your domicile, the state you are in may require you to get local license plates and a safety inspection.

You should check with your legal assistance officer in the state where you are stationed. Many states now require proof of insurance before you can register your car. Most states require all residents of register their cars, usually within thirty to sixty days after becoming a resident. Some states have reciprocity agreements with other states so that a car that has been properly registered in another state will be allowed on the resident state roads without reregistering. Some states have specific exemptions for military personnel stationed therein. Finally, some states require the payment of property taxes on vehicles by all domiciliaries, whether or not they are residents.

Sometimes it may be more advantageous to register your car in the state where you are stationed, especially if, for example, that state does not have a personal property tax as your domicile does. You need to consider such things as sales taxes, personal property taxes, license fees, and inspection requirements when deciding where to register your car.

Your Driver's License
Buying and registering the car are not, however, the only legal problems you need to face. You'll also need a valid driver's license. Many states will allow you to use your home state's driver's license if your car is registered there. Others will allow you to use your home state's license even if you registered your car elsewhere. In most states, however, spouses must get a local driver's license.

Car Insurance
Now that you know about buying and registering your car and getting a driver's license, what about insurance? The state where you register your car can require you to have a certain amount of liability insurance, and many do.

Automobile liability insurance protects you from paying damages you may cause another person or another's property in a car accident. The policy is usually written in three figures, such as $25,000/$50,000/$10,000, which means that the policy would pay up to $25,000 to any one person hurt in your automobile accident, up to a maximum of $50,000 for all people injured, and up to $10,000 for property damage. Regular policies will not pay unless the accident was your fault. Many states, however, require *no-fault insurance*. This type of policy pays victims of accidents no matter who was at fault.

No matter what the state may or may not require, your military base may require you to carry liability insurance as a condition of registering and driving your car on post.

Car Repairs

Unfortunately, cars need repairs. Often, these repairs lead to disputes about overcharging, poor workmanship, and deception. Of course, your best protection against these problems is to find a reputable mechanic or repair shop. You can call the Better Business Bureau or the attorney general of the state you are in to see whether someone has complained about the shop you are considering. You can also ask the shop for the names of some of its customers to contact to see whether they were satisfied.

You should always get a written estimate before you let the mechanic work on your car and tell him to call you if the car requires any additional parts or labor in excess of the amount on the estimate. You should also ask for and get your old parts back. If the charge is much higher than the estimate, work was done without your authorization, or you are dissatisfied with the work, you should question the work and have the mechanic write out the reasons for the difference in cost. Unfortunately, the law often allows the mechanic either to keep the car until you pay or to have a lien on the car so that you cannot sell it without paying him. If you can't work the matter out with the mechanic or his or her boss, you should contact a legal assistance officer or the attorney general's consumer protection or similar office. If your insurance company is paying for the repair, as after an accident, it will help you. Otherwise, you may have to pay the bill and then sue the shop for the return of any excess you were forced to pay.

CONCLUSION

If you follow these rules about personal property and see an attorney when you do not understand a transaction, you should be free to enjoy your property without having legal or financial difficulties.

Military service puts some obstacles in the way of owning property, both real and personal. But it also provides you help, such as the claims system and legal assistance officers, to minimize the obstacles so that you can fully enjoy your property.

PART VI

Financial Matters

Service families have many of the same concerns about money that others do. But being in the military service complicates earning or borrowing money. Paying taxes also is often a greater problem in the military. A good background in the legal aspects of your financial affairs, however, can help you avoid money problems.

Chapter 15 will tell you how to solve legal problems when you borrow money. Chapter 16 discusses the legal pitfalls of earning money and paying taxes of your earnings while you are in the military.

15

Debt

The best advice I can give you is to stay out of debt in the first place. Like alcoholism and drug abuse, compulsive borrowing and spending can ruin careers, break up families, and wreck lives. If you're already at that stage, go get help immediately. Go talk to your chaplain and your military attorney, or you may get the help you need from Debtors Anonymous.

Most servicemembers do borrow money. Some get into financial difficulties as a result of borrowing more than they can repay. If you must borrow money, you need to know the law of debt. If you already have problems with your debts, you need to know the legal procedures, such as bankruptcy, that can help you get out of debt. These legal matters are known as debtor-creditor relations. State law generally controls both borrowing money and attempts by the creditor to get it back if the borrower fails to pay; federal law controls bankruptcy proceedings.

BORROWING MONEY

You can borrow money from any number of places, including a friend, a financial institution (such as a bank or a savings and loan), a loan company, a merchant, a credit card company, or a pawn shop. You may even borrow from another servicemember, but know that it is improper to borrow money from a subordinate, either someone of lower rank or someone who works for you. Your service or unit may also have regulations that prohibit borrowing from certain servicemembers or may set a maximum interest rate. Before you either lend money to or borrow money from another servicemember, be certain you understand any applicable regulations in your command.

Security for Your Loan

Although borrowing money from a friend or a relative may involve no formalities, when you borrow money from a company, such as a loan company or a bank, you usually must sign a promissory note. The law defines a *promissory note* as a written promise in which the maker of the note (the borrower) agrees to pay another (the lender) a sum of money, either when the lender demands it or at an agreed upon time. A promissory note can be either secured or unsecured.

If you sign a secured promissory note, you pledge property, often the property you bought with the borrowed money, as security for repayment of the money. The property you pledge on a secured note is called *collateral*. If you do not pay the money you owe, the lender could repossess this collateral. The lender could then sell the property and keep the proceeds to cover your debt. If the lender could not sell the collateral for enough to repay the debt,

---

SAMPLE PROMISSORY NOTE

For Value Received, I, _____, SSN _____, of
_____ , promise to pay to the order of _____ the sum of
$ _____ on or before _____ 19____.
No interest is being charged on this note.

This note is secured by:
    One   _____
    Body Style   _____
    Identification No.   _____
    Model   _____

    In the event this note is not paid when due, I agree to pay, in addition to principal, all costs of collection including reasonable attorney's fees.

    IN WITNESS WHEREOF, I hereunto set my hand this _____
date of _____ , 19____, at _____ .

                       _____
                            (Promissor)

           (Notary)

however, you would still have to pay the balance of the money you promised to pay. The lender could even sue you in a state or local court to recover the balance you owed (see chapter 6).

If you borrow money with an unsecured note, on the other hand, you would not pledge any property as security for repayment of the money you owed. Whether the lender will require security depends on the amount you want to borrow and whether you are a good credit risk.

Sometimes the lender will not require collateral but instead will require a cosigner. The *cosigner* is liable to pay the debt if the borrower does not. In other words, both are liable for the amount owed. If someone asks you to cosign a note, or in any other way guarantee repayment of the debt, investigate thoroughly and have an attorney review the loan agreement before you sign. If you don't investigate thoroughly and the borrower is a poor risk, for example, you could end up paying the debt if the borrower could not or would not repay the debt. And you would not even have had the benefit of spending the money he borrowed.

A retired military lawyer who now teaches law has defined a cosigner as "an idiot with a pen." One recent study found that three out of four cosigners of finance company loans were asked to repay the loan. A cosigner is being asked to take a risk that the finance company is not willing to take without the cosigner also being liable. If the person you cosign for defaults on the loan, you may be liable not only for the amount owed and interest but also for penalties, late charges, and legal fees. Be especially leery of pledging any of your property as security for a loan you cosign. If, after all this information, you decide to cosign, you should ask the lender to agree, in writing, to notify you if the borrower misses a payment so that you can take care of it before late charges are due or the whole loan becomes due because of a late payment. Also get copies of all the loan paperwork just as if you were the borrower.

Legal Protection for Borrowers

Both federal and state laws protect borrowers. But those laws do not relieve you from the responsibility to protect yourself when you borrow money. You must realize that borrowing money is just as much a business transaction as buying a car or renting a home. If you bought a car, for example, you would look around for the best deal you could get. You should do the same thing when you borrow money.

I think of borrowing money as renting it. I get the use of the money for a time in return for paying "rent" for its use—paying the interest. And I have to give it back to its owner just as I do when I rent a car—repaying the principal. I wouldn't rent a car without reading the lease. You shouldn't borrow money without reading and understanding the loan agreement and making certain that you get the best possible terms.

One of the protections the federal government provides borrowers is the

Truth in Lending Act, which requires the lender to inform you of all the terms of the loan so that you can compare credit terms easily. This law applies when a creditor offers credit to a consumer (a buyer). The act defines a *creditor* as one who regularly extends credit, such as a credit card company or a merchant. The act applies only if the debt has a finance charge or if the borrower must repay the debt in four or more installments. Finally, the credit must be for personal, family, or household reasons, as opposed to business purposes, for the act to apply.

The major protection of the act is its requirement that, before you agree to the loan, the lender give you a paper that tells you both the finance charge and the annual percentage rate. Finance charges (the "rent" for the borrowed money) may include interest, loan fees, mandatory insurance, and so on. The *annual percentage rate* is the ratio of the cost of the credit to the amount borrowed expressed as a yearly percentage rate.

Another protection for you when you borrow money is the Fair Credit Billing Act. It applies to credit card accounts and other revolving charge accounts. It does not apply to one-time loans, even if paid in installments. The act requires stores with revolving credit accounts and credit card companies to do the following things:

• Notify you in writing of your rights if you disagree with the creditor about the amount you owe.

• Acknowledge within thirty days any written notice of an error you provide if you include your name and account number, the amount in dispute, and the nature of the error that caused the dispute.

• Resolve the credit dispute within two billing cycles or ninety days.

Another important protection of the Fair Credit Billing Act is that it prohibits the creditor from sending an adverse report about you to a credit bureau when you dispute an amount you owe him. As a borrower, you also have obligations under the act. You must pay amounts that are not in dispute when they are due, and you must provide the notice specified above when you dispute an amount on the bill.

Credit Bureaus

Like most citizens, servicemembers have credit histories. Many companies, known as credit bureaus or consumer reporting agencies, investigate and report on borrowers' credit histories so that lenders can tell whether they are good credit risks. Their reports on borrowers could include such information as their job, their marital status, their bank accounts, how much they owe, how well they pay their debts, and whether they have ever filed for bankruptcy.

An inaccurate credit history can be very damaging, so Congress passed the Fair Credit Reporting Act to protect borrowers. If any lender has denied credit, insurance, or employment to any servicemember or, indeed, any citi-

zen, because of the information in a credit report, the person harmed by the
report has the following rights:

- To know who prepared the report.
- To know who provided the information used to prepare the report.
- To know who received the report within the last six months.
- To have the credit bureau investigate inaccurate or incomplete
information and, if the bureau finds the information to be wrong, remove it
from the borrower's file.
- To have the credit bureau send the corrected information to anyone who received the incorrect information.
- To have the bureau place your side of any dispute in your file and
include it in any reports the bureau makes to creditors.
- To sue the credit agency for damages if the agency violates the act,
either negligently or on purpose.
- To have a credit bureau not report any adverse information to anyone after seven years have passed, except for bankruptcy. (A credit agency
may report bankruptcy for ten years.)

The Fair Credit Reporting Act does not permit you to actually see your
file, however, but if you were turned down for credit, you are entitled to a
copy of the credit report from the credit bureau.

Another federal law also protects borrowers. The Equal Credit Opportunity Act prohibits discrimination against borrowers based on sex, marital status, race, color, religion, age, or national origin. The act applies to such
lenders as banks, finance companies, stores, credit card companies, and the
federal government. Although it is illegal to deny credit because of any of
these categories, the law does not require lenders to lend money to bad credit
risks. Therefore, as a borrower, you must show that you are willing and able
to repay the loan.

Under the Equal Credit Opportunity Act a lender may deny you credit
only if you are actually a poor credit risk, not because you are female or black
or more than sixty-five years old. You also have the right, under the act, to
your own account, even if you are married, so long as you are creditworthy.
The lender may not even ask your marital status, unless you are in a community property state and are going to use community property as a basis to get
the loan, such as for collateral.

Loan Agreements

Although federal laws provide some protections to you as a borrower, you also
need to understand the loan agreement—the contract you sign to borrow
money. These are some of the items you should look for in any loan contract:

- That it has no balloon payment. A *balloon payment* contract calls
for a number of small payments and then a final, large one to pay off the debt.
Although the small payments may look attractive, if you can't pay off the

large one at the end of the contract period, you could lose the property that was the security for the loan.

• That you can pay off the debt at any time without paying a penalty.

• That any late charge not be unreasonable. An unreasonable late charge is one that is larger than 5 percent of the payment or $5, whichever is less.

• That if the lender sues you for nonpayment of the debt, you do not have to pay more than 20 percent of the outstanding debt in attorney's fees for the creditor's lawyer.

• That it has no *confession of judgment* clause. Such a clause is a statement in which you admit that you are in the wrong if you miss a single payment and that, unless you immediately pay off the entire amount due, you give up all your legal rights. The creditor can then go to court to get a judgment against you without even notifying you and giving you a chance to defend yourself. Fortunately, these clauses are illegal in most states.

Credit Cards

Most Americans use credit cards. These cards can be very convenient but also dangerous. Misuse of credit cards can get you into serious debt problems. Therefore, you must safeguard your credit cards with the same care that you would a large amount of cash. In fact, it could be more damaging to lose a credit card than a hundred dollars, because a criminal could run up thousands of dollars of charges on your card. Federal laws will help protect you if you use credit cards, however.

The Truth in Lending Act also contains provisions to protect credit card holders. The most important one is that if someone illegally uses your card, you are liable only for up to $50 in charges or the amount charged by an unauthorized user, whichever is less, if the following conditions exist:

1.   The credit card company gave you notice of this liability.

2.   The credit card company provided you a means to notify the company of the loss or theft.

3.   The unauthorized use happened before you notified the company. You may notify the company in person, by writing, or by telephoning.

A court can punish a person who illegally uses a credit card to buy things worth $1,000 or travel tickets worth $500 by a fine of up to $10,000 and confinement for up to ten years.

Although the Truth in Lending Act provides you some protection, you need to protect yourself as well. These are some of the things you can do to protect yourself from credit card troubles:

• Get rid of cards you no longer need or use. If the company does not require it back, cut the card into pieces and throw it away.

• Make certain you sign any credit card you get, so that anyone who finds it or steals it must forge your signature to use it.

- Keep a list of your cards in a safe place and check your cards against the list occasionally to see whether any are missing.
- Make certain your card is returned when you use it.
- Don't sign your credit card slip without making certain that the amount is correct and that the total amount is written in the "total" block.
- Don't leave credit cards lying around. You wouldn't leave cash in your motel room or your car's glove compartment. Credit cards are every bit as much money as cash is.
- Ask for the carbons of your charge slip. Criminals can use the carbons to make a card with your name and number.
- Never give your credit card number out over the phone unless you are dealing with a company that you know is reliable.

Although credit cards may be convenient, their high interest rates, the ease with which you can use them to buy things you may not really need, and the danger of loss or theft require that you safeguard them and use them wisely.

Pawn Shops

Just outside the main gate of many military installations is a strip of restaurants and businesses that caters to servicemembers. These areas almost always contain pawn shops, where servicemembers who need quick cash can borrow it. But borrowing money, or even buying property, from a pawn shop has several legal hazards.

The pawnbroker secures the money he lends you by the property that you pledge. But unlike a normal lien, as on your car or a mortgage on your home, you do not get to keep the property at least until you default on the loan and the lender repossesses it. Instead, you must deliver it to the pawnbroker, who keeps it until you repay the loan. If you don't repay the loan within a certain time, perhaps in as short a period as a month or two, the pawnbroker may sell it and keep the proceeds. Besides these disadvantages to pawning your property, the pawnbroker's interest rates will probably be very high, and you will not receive the true value of the property.

Not only do you risk high interest rates and loss of your property at a pawn shop, but you may also find it dangerous to buy property there. Sometimes criminals pawn stolen property. If the police trace the property through a pawn shop to a buyer, they will take it to use as evidence and return it to the true owner. Of course, it is a crime to knowingly receive stolen property.

I don't recommend that you borrow money from a pawnbroker, but if you must, make certain that you completely understand the terms of the loan.

IF YOU CAN'T PAY YOUR BILLS

All the law's protections and all your care when you borrow money may not be enough to keep you from having problems paying your bills. For example, the military could reassign you to an installation with limited on-post housing and very expensive off-post housing where you would have to spend most of your pay and allowances for rent and food and have little left to pay any debts you may have when you arrive. Although the military's policy is that you should pay your debts, if you are unable to do so, the military can help you. If, however, your debt situation is severe, you may have to consider bankruptcy.

The Military's Role in Debt Problems

The military's policy is that servicemembers should pay their just debts in a timely manner. If you cannot pay your just debts, Department of Defense Directive 1344.9, *Indebtedness of Military Personnel*, authorizes your branch of service to take the following actions:

- Review the transaction that resulted in the debt you did not pay.
- Inform you what action you should take to pay the debt if it is just or to contest it if it is not.
- Contact the creditor to notify him that the military has advised you of the policy that servicemembers should pay their just debts.

DOD did not, however, write this directive only for the benefit of people to whom servicemembers owe money. The directive also protects servicemembers by providing that the military will not process claims of nonpayment of debts by creditors against servicemembers unless the creditor abides by the Truth in Lending Act and provides a certificate of compliance with that act. If the creditor is not subject to the act, he must submit a statement that he does not charge a greater finance charge than state law permits before the military will process his letter.

If you have trouble paying your bills, your branch of service will help you. If you have a legal problem with your bills, you can go to your legal assistance officer. A legal assistance officer may be able to use the Soldiers' and Sailors' Civil Relief Act to help you. If you got in debt before you came into the service, for example, and coming into the service hurt your ability to repay your debts, a legal assistance attorney could notify your creditors that they may not repossess any property that is security for the debt, or he could request a delay in making payments or a reduction in the interest rate because of your reduced military pay.

Often, however, the first place to go for help if you can't pay your bills is to a debt counseling service on your installation. A debt counselor will explore such alternatives as persuading your creditors to accept smaller payments over a longer period, having the creditor repossess the property and accept less compensation, debt pooling, and debt consolidation loans.

SAMPLE LETTER FROM A BORROWER
PROPOSING AN ADJUSTED PAYMENT SCHEDULE

(Name and address)

(Date)

(Name and address of creditor)

Reference: Account # _____

Dear Sir or Madam:

    I am writing you in regard to a loan that I got from your company for the amount of $ _____ in _____ , 19 _____ . I have been making monthly payments of $ _____ for _____ years and have reduced the current balance to $ _____ .

    I am now behind _____ payments. The reason(s) for this (is) (are):

(detailed explanation)

    I propose to send you $ _____ per month on the obligation (for months) (until I am able to afford the full normal payments). I have contacted my other creditors with proposals that keep me within my strict budget. I understand the importance of meeting all my obligations, and I hope that you will accept my proposal, made to you in good faith and with the sincere intent to improve my unfortunate financial circumstances.

    Please notify me if you find my proposal acceptable. Your cooperation is appreciated.

Sincerely,

    The debt counselor could help you with the paperwork for the options of persuading your creditor to accept smaller payments or to take the property back and let you off the hook for any remaining balance. In a *debt pool*, a consultant gets your creditors to agree to smaller payments, collects a certain part of your pay, and pays your creditors with it.

    In a *debt consolidation loan*, you borrow a large enough sum to pay off all your debts. With any luck at all it will be at a lower interest rate and payable over a longer period, so that the monthly payments will be within your budget. Be careful of this type of loan, however, for a couple of reasons. First, unless you get such a loan from a reputable bank or other financial institution, you could end up paying much more in finance and other charges than you would have if you had paid off your debts by yourself. Second, when you use a debt consolidation loan to pay off debts that have gotten out of control, you may feel tempted to go out and charge some more because you are out of immediate danger.

If you cannot pay your bills and if a debt counselor or legal assistance officer cannot help you, you may need to consider bankruptcy.

Bankruptcy

The work *bankrupt* means broke, unable to pay debts. *Bankruptcy* is a procedure by which a court relieves a person who cannot pay his debts from liability for those debts. The purpose of bankruptcy is to pay creditors a fair share of whatever funds the debtor has available to pay his debts, and to give the debtor a fresh start.

If you had to file bankruptcy, not all your funds or property would necessarily go to pay your creditors because bankruptcy law exempts certain property, such as some or all of the equity in your home, a car, and household goods. These things are exempt so that you and your family would have a place to live, a car to get to work, and the necessities of life. Generally, the property or portion of property that may be exempt is governed by state law, although bankruptcy itself comes under federal law.

Once you have successfully completed a bankruptcy procedure, you would no longer be liable for unsecured debts—those that do not have any property as collateral. You would, however, still have to repay secured debts, such as a mortgage on your home or a lien on your car. Filing for bankruptcy would also not free you of your other debts, such as alimony, child support payments, and taxes.

If you file for bankruptcy, you will have to, with your lawyer's advice, decide on which type of bankruptcy to use. Of the four different types of bankruptcy, only two, Chapter 7 and Chapter 13, are normally suitable for servicemembers.

In a Chapter 7 proceeding, the bankruptcy court issues an order appointing a trustee to act as the guardian of the debtor's property. The trustee, who represents the unsecured creditors, investigates the bankrupt person's financial affairs, disposes of his nonexempt property, and distributes his assets to creditors.

Chapter 13 proceedings differ from Chapter 7 in that the debtor remains in control of his other assets. The debtor files a reorganization plan that generates sufficient income to pay off his creditors. The bankruptcy court must approve the plan.

Although a legal assistance officer could advise you about whether you should file for bankruptcy, you will normally have to hire a civilian attorney to actually file for it. Remember, you will have to pay your attorney's fees and court costs, and filing for bankruptcy will affect your credit rating for years. Therefore, you should try to manage your finances so that you don't get into credit trouble. If you do have problems, however, seek help early to avoid filing bankruptcy.

CONCLUSION

Borrowing money is sometimes necessary and often helpful. But it can also be dangerous. If you have to borrow money, shop around for a good deal and make certain you understand the loan contract. A legal assistance officer would much rather explain the legal aspects of a loan agreement to you before you sign it than try to "fix it" after legal or financial difficulties happen.

16

Money

Many servicemembers need more money than they receive from the military as pay and allowances. Although it is not wrong to earn and to save money whenever possible, as a servicemember you have certain legal restrictions on your money matters, such as taxes and part-time jobs.

TAXES
Unless federal or state law shelters all or a part of servicemembers' income from taxes, servicemembers have the same tax liability as any other citizen or resident of the United States. Tax laws change often. Thus, when you prepare a tax return, you should consult the current Internal Revenue Service publications and the current state publication or see a tax expert, such as a lawyer, a certified public accountant, or a professional tax preparer. Many military units have unit tax officers to help servicemembers fill out their tax forms. Legal assistance officers may help in cases that are too complicated for unit tax officers. Not only do you need to know the legal aspects of paying federal income taxes, but you may also have to pay state income, personal property, sales, and foreign taxes, depending on where you live.

Federal Income Taxes
Except, as happened during the Vietnam War, and again during Operation Desert Storm, when the government exempts servicemembers who are serving in combat from paying taxes on all or a part of their military pay, servicemembers have the same federal tax liability as anyone else—even if they are serving overseas. Servicemembers do get some tax "breaks," however:

• *Tax forgiveness.* One tax break that I hope you never need is that servicemembers who die because of a military or a terrorist attack against the United States do not owe any federal income taxes for the year they died and for any earlier year in which they suffered from the wounds that led to the death, as long as it was after 17 November 1978.

• *Capital gains deferment on sale of a personal residence.* When home-owners sell their homes, they have to pay capital gains on any profit, unless they reinvest the proceeds in a home of equal or greater value within two years of the sale. As a servicemember, though, you have up to four years to buy another home to defer capital gains. If you were stationed outside the continental United States or your service required you to live on post at certain remote sites and you sold a home after 18 July 1984, you would have until one year after the last day on which you were stationed outside the United States or at a remote site to buy another home. The total period in which you can defer taxes cannot exceed eight years after the sale of your old home.

• *Exclusions from gross income.* Because your federal gross income does not include many military allowances, such as basic allowance for quarters, variable housing allowance, cost of living allowance, basic allowance for subsistence, and family separation allowance, you do not have to pay taxes on them.

• *Filing extension.* If you were outside the United States and Puerto Rico on 15 April, when your return was due, you would automatically get a sixty-day extension to file your return. You would, however, owe interest on any unpaid tax from the 15 April filing deadline until you paid the tax. The Internal Revenue Service also has special rules for filing tax returns when you are serving in combat, are hospitalized because of combat injuries, or are a prisoner of war.

Because specific federal tax rules can change each year, you should get help in filing your taxes. Each service has tax assistance programs, or you can see a legal assistance officer. If, however, you have a personal business or other significant nonmilitary income, you may need to see a professional tax preparer or an accountant.

One thing you must be cautious of is signing your federal income tax refund over to someone else. For example, some loan companies would give you only a small part of your refund and keep the rest themselves as service charges.

State Income Taxes

Not only do you have to pay federal income tax, but you may also be liable for state taxes. Generally, a state can tax the income of its residents, no matter where they earn that income, and can tax nonresidents on any income they earn within the state. Thus, if you were a resident of Oklahoma, for example, and you were stationed in Virginia, you could face double taxation. Section 514 of the Soldiers' and Sailors' Civil Relief Act, however, prohibits double taxation. Under the act, only the state of which you were a resident could tax your military pay. If you had a part-time job, though, the act would not protect this money; you would have to pay taxes to the state in which you had earned the money and to the state of your legal residence. The act protects the military against double state taxation by saying three things:

• That while you are in the service, you do not change your residence for tax purposes solely because the military assigned you somewhere. For example, if you were a resident of California and were assigned to New York, you would not become a resident of New York for tax purposes just because the military had assigned you there.

• That the law does not consider that you earned your military pay and allowances in any state except the state of your legal residence. If you were a California resident stationed in New York, for example, the act would consider that you earned your pay in California, not New York.

• That the law considers your personal property to be located, for tax purposes, in the state of your residence, not where you really are.

States that do not have any income taxes include New Hampshire, Florida, Nevada, South Dakota, Texas, Washington, Tennessee, Connecticut, Alaska, and Wyoming, although several of them tax interest and dividend income or capital gains. The remaining states generally treat the military pay of servicemembers in one of these four ways:

• Some states exempt all resident servicemembers' military pay from taxation. Sometimes they exempt military pay from taxation only when the servicemember is stationed outside the state.

• Some states exempt a part of resident servicemembers' pay from taxation.

• Some states exempt the military pay of servicemembers if they qualify as nonresident domiciliaries (residents who live outside the state). To qualify for the exemption the servicemember must meet the following conditions:

1. Maintain no permanent home in the state.
2. Maintain no permanent home outside the state.
3. Not stay in the state for more than thirty days during the tax year.

• Some states tax military pay the same as any other income.

Because of a federal law, the government may withhold state income taxes from military pay. If the state you are a legal resident of, as shown on your records, has an income tax, the military will withhold state and federal taxes from your monthly pay. You still must file a state tax return, however.

Whether you have to pay state taxes depends on where you are a legal resident. The Soldiers' and Sailors' Civil Relief Act, as stated above, provides that you do not change your legal residence by entering the armed forces and by being assigned away from your home. Thus, you keep the legal residence you had when you entered the service, unless you change it. You change it by living in another state with the intention to make that state your legal residence.

AFFIDAVIT CONCERNING STATE INCOME TAX

STATE OF _____
COUNTY OF _____

I, _____, being first duly sworn on oath, depose and say:

1. That I am not a domiciliary of the state of _____, but that I am a domiciliary of the state of _____.

2. That my residence in the state of _____ is due to my assignment to Fort _____, _____ by the Department of the Army.
                              (state)

_____

(Notarization)

Tax Commissioner (local/state)   _____

DF: Address

Dear _____:

As sworn to above, I am not a domiciliary of the state of _____. Under the provisions of the Soldiers' and Sailors' Civil Relief Act, Section 514, 50 U.S.C. App. §574, my domicile does not change when my residence in another state is due to military orders. Therefore, my income is not subject to taxation by the state of _____.

Sincerely,

_____

If a state tries to tax you as a resident and you claim you are a resident of another state, you need to have some proof of your intention. Such things as voting, registering your car, and owning property in the state you claim as your permanent residence would help show that you were an actual resident. You can use an affidavit such as the accompanying sample form to show a state you are stationed in that you are not a resident for tax purposes. Consult a legal assistance officer if you are thinking about changing your permanent residence so that you will understand the tax consequences and how a change in residence would stand up in court if a state sued you for back taxes.

Even the states that do not tax military pay tax nonmilitary income of both servicemembers and their spouses. The Soldiers' and Sailors' Civil Relief Act does not protect servicemembers' spouses from taxation by the states. If you as a servicemember have a part-time job or if your spouse works, the state in which you or your spouse earns the money may tax it. And if you or your spouse is a permanent resident of another state, that state may tax it as well.

Some states, such as Kansas, have a tax formula that includes the servicemember's military pay with the working spouse's pay and then apportions the tax liability. This results in a higher tax than if the spouse's income were taxed alone but is not a direct tax on the servicemember's military income. This type of formula appears to violate the Civil Relief Act, but no court has so ruled. If your spouse works, you need to be aware of the tax consequences. Therefore, you should consult a legal assistance officer or tax professional to find out the rules in the particular state you are in.

Personal Property Taxes

Section 514 of the Soldiers' and Sailors' Civil Relief Act also exempts servicemembers from paying personal property taxes in the state where they are stationed, unless they are residents of that state. The act protects only servicemembers, however, not their families. Thus, a state other than their legal residence, where a servicemember and his family are living temporarily because of military orders, can require family members to pay personal property taxes on their separate personal property. So, if your spouse was not a servicemember and had personal property that you did not also own, the state you were stationed in could tax it. Some states even tax that part of jointly owned property owned by the nonmilitary spouse. Whenever you are reassigned to another state, therefore, you need to talk to a legal assistance officer before you buy a car or other personal property to find out the tax effects of the purchase and who should have the title.

Sales Taxes

The Soldiers' and Sailors' Civil Relief Act does not protect servicemembers from state sales and similar taxes. Consequently, you have to pay sales taxes on anything you buy in a state where you are stationed, unless the state itself exempts nonresidents from sales taxes.

Foreign Taxes

Status of forces agreements normally provide that servicemembers and their families do not have to pay the foreign country's personal property taxes or income taxes on pay received from the U.S. government. These agreements also permit service families to import personal property for their personal use free from duty. If you or your spouse got a job in the local economy, however, you might have to pay income tax to the foreign government. You would also have to list any foreign income on your U.S. tax return. The Internal Revenue Service, however, would provide a credit against your U.S. tax liability for any foreign taxes you paid.

Aside from the few tax breaks to which servicemembers are entitled, they have the same tax problems as do civilians. And the possibility of double taxation may be greater for service families with their frequent moves. The military does, however, compensate some of the extra tax hassles you as a servicemember may encounter by providing you unit tax officers and legal assistance attorneys to help you make sure you pay only the taxes you owe.

EARNING EXTRA MONEY

Although the military pays servicemembers far better than it used to, many servicemembers, especially those with families, need extra money to support themselves. Although the military recognizes the necessity for some servicemembers to supplement their incomes, federal law places some limitations on how servicemembers can earn extra money. Because you could get into serious trouble for earning money in violation of these laws, you must understand them.

Other Employment

Often, servicemembers have to get part-time jobs to help make ends meet. Although nothing is wrong with needing to get a part-time job, some special rules do apply to part-time employment of servicemembers, such as avoiding conflict with military duties, the possibility of dual compensation problems, the need to follow the standards of conduct, and the requirement for some servicemembers to file reports of their outside income and financial interests.

You cannot allow any part-time job to interfere with the proper performance of your military duties (see chapter 1). Failure to do your duties in an efficient manner can result in criminal charges under the Uniform Code of Military Justice for dereliction of duty. It is not a defense to a charge of dereliction of duty that you could not do your duties well because you were too tired after you had worked all night at a part-time job. You cannot have a

part-time job if it causes you to do your military duties at less than 100 percent of your abilities.

Because of the requirement that part-time employment not affect your
duty performance, you must get your commander's permission to get a part-
time job. If it appears that the job will interfere with your military duties, he
will not grant you permission. If he grants you permission, it will be with the
understanding that the job will not interfere with your duties. If, for example,
you were working as a used car salesman in the evenings, after your normal
duty day was over, and your military supervisor ordered you to work late, you
would have to do so, even if it meant that your civilian boss fired you.

Dual Compensation
Dual compensation involves receiving pay from both the military and
another source for performing military duties. It can be a problem for servicemembers of all ranks, but particularly for officers.

Military personnel of any rank may not accept any pay for anything that
they do as a part of their military duties or may not allow someone to make a
contribution to charity as payment for doing a military duty. For example, if
you participated in a recruiting drive at an off-post shopping center, such as
by showing some military equipment, you could not accept payment from the
owner of the shopping center for attracting business.

Active-duty military personnel may not serve as members of Congress or
hold any office of a foreign government. A servicemember may, however,
work for a foreign company. You, as a servicemember, may accept work with
government contractors without violating dual compensation laws. Such
employment, however, must not violate the standards of conduct discussed
below. Further, your pay for such a job must come from the contractor, not
from the government.

Under federal law, officers cannot accept any pay from the federal government for any outside work that they do. The only federal compensation an
officer may receive is his military pay and allowances. For example, military
doctors who moonlight at civilian clinics cannot receive pay for their services
from federal medical insurance programs, such as CHAMPUS or Medicare.
An officer must also refuse any pay for civilian federal employment. Besides
being subject to criminal penalties if you are an officer and you accept such a
position, you may lose your commission. The only exceptions to this rule are
that your service may permit you to work at a nonappropriated fund activity,
such as tending bar at an officers' club, and that, if you are on terminal leave
before getting out of the service, you may get a civilian federal job.

Standards of Conduct
Until 1993, each service had regulations that made it a criminal offense (violation of a lawful general regulation) to violate the so-called standards of

conduct. In 1993, however, these regulations were made obsolete by the adoption of a single regulation, *Standards of Conduct for Employees of the Executive Branch,* 5 Code of Federal Regulations part 2635, governing the entire federal executive branch, including the military. The general purpose of this regulation is the same as the prior service regulations—to prohibit using one's official position for personal advantage. The Department of Defense has written a regulation to criminalize violations of the *Standards of Conduct.*

Military officers and other federal personnel must adhere to the following standards:

• They may not hold financial interests that conflict with the conscientious performance of duty.

• They may not engage in financial transactions using nonpublic government information or allow the improper use of such information to further any private interest.

• They may not, except as discussed below, solicit or accept any gift or item of value from any person or entity doing business with the government or whose interests may be substantially affected by the performance or nonperformance of the employee's duties.

• They must put forth honest effort in the performance of their duties.

• They may not knowingly make unauthorized commitments or promises of any kind purporting to bind the government.

• They may not use public office for private gain.

• They shall act impartially and not give preferential treatment to anyone.

• They shall protect and conserve federal property and shall not use it for other than authorized activities.

• They shall not engage in outside employment or activities, including seeking or negotiating for employment, that conflict with official government duties and responsibilities.

• They shall disclose fraud, waste, abuse, and corruption to appropriate authorities.

• They shall satisfy in good faith their obligations as citizens, including all just financial obligations, especially those such as federal, state, or local taxes that are imposed by law.

• They shall adhere to all laws and regulations that provide equal opportunity for all Americans regardless of race, color, religion, sex, national origin, age, or handicap.

• They shall endeavor to avoid any actions creating the appearance that they are violating the law or the ethical standards set forth in regulations.

With regard to the prohibitions on soliciting or accepting gifts, a military officer may not accept a gift in return for being influenced in the performance of an official act, coerce the offering of a gift, accept gifts on a basis so frequent that a reasonable person would be led to believe that he or she is using public office for private gain, or accept a gift in violation of a statute. For example, one federal statute prohibits procurement officers from receiving any gift from a competing contractor during the conduct of a federal agency procurement. One may accept gifts, however, other than cash or an investment interest, with a market value of $200 or less if they are bona fide awards given for meritorious public service or achievement by one who does not have interests that may be substantially affected by the performance of his or her duties. One may also accept an honorary degree if an ethics official certifies that the award would not cause a reasonable person to question the officer's impartiality.

Also, one may not make a gift to his or her official superior or solicit a contribution from another for a gift to his or her superior except that items, other than cash, worth $10 or less may be given on occasions on which gifts are traditionally given or exchanged. Gifts may be given to superiors and accepted by them in recognition of infrequently occurring occasions of personal significance, such as marriage, illness, or the birth or adoption of a child, or upon occasions that terminate a subordinate–official superior relationship, such as retirement, resignation, or transfer. The regulations also have other exceptions permitting the receipt of various gifts. These rules are very complex, however, and you should always consult an ethics counselor before accepting a gift.

With regard to prohibited financial relationships, you should be aware that the prohibition extends to financial interests of your spouse; your minor children; your general partner; an organization or entity you serve as an officer, director, trustee, general partner, or employee; and a person with whom you are negotiating for or have an arrangement concerning prospective employment.

Although this new regulation applies by its terms to officers, service regulations extend these general prohibitions to enlisted personnel. Thus, as a practical matter, no one in military service may do the following:

- Use a military job for any personal gain other than your military pay and allowances.
- Give preferential treatment to anyone.
- Harm the government's efficiency or economy.
- Lose independence or impartiality.
- Make a government decision outside official channels.
- Do anything that would make people lose confidence in the integrity of the government.

Not only can you not do anything that would actually violate the above principles, but also you cannot do anything that gives the appearance of violating them.

The government has several rules to help you avoid violating the standards of conduct. One specific prohibition based on these principles is that you cannot use government facilities, property, or personnel for personal business. For example, the standards of conduct forbid you to use a military phone to call long distance to talk to a friend or to use a military truck and driver to transport tomatoes from your garden to the market for sale. Often, such improper use of government property is also a violation of the Uniform Code of Military Justice (see chapter 7). It could be larceny (stealing) or wrongful appropriation (illegal borrowing). Further, any money you earned by the use of government property or personnel would belong to the government. The military even has rules on whether you may keep free tickets and bonus mileage from airline travel when it pays for the travel.

These standards also restrict the use of your military title in commercial enterprises or to endorse a commercial product. For example, if you sold real estate part-time, while still on active duty (assuming you had received permission to have such a job and you did not sell to subordinates), you could not put your military rank and title on your advertisements. You could, however, put your military rank and title on a book or article you wrote if the book was properly cleared for publication by your service. If you are retired, you may use your military title in commercial enterprises under the following conditions:

1.   You show that you are retired.

2.   You do not bring discredit on the military.

3.   You do not make it look as if the military sponsored or approved of your business or product.

The military also restricts whom you can sell things to. These sales, called *personal commercial solicitations*, include selling real estate, insurance, investments, and such things as vitamins and household products. These restrictions apply on or off post, on or off duty, and both in and out of uniform. Generally, you cannot try to sell anything to anyone who is junior in rank or position to you. Nor should your spouse. A few exceptions do apply, however, to this general prohibition:

•   You may work in a retail store, such as a grocery store.

•   You may sell or rent your home to a subordinate.

•   You may sell personal property (see chapter 14) that you do not own for commercial or business purposes. For example, you could sell your car to a subordinate, but you could not sell encyclopedias for a commercial company to him.

Even if you rent a subordinate your house or sell him your car, you still must make sure that you do not use your rank or position to make him do something he wouldn't otherwise do or to pay more for the item than anyone else would. Even so, it's probably best not to enter into such a transaction with a subordinate so as to avoid even the appearance of impropriety.

Another rule about off-duty employment is that while you are in the service, you cannot act as a representative of the government in any matter in which you, a close family member, or a company you are trying to get a job with has a financial interest. For example, you could not negotiate a contract for the government with a company that your wife owned or a company that you were going to work for after you got out of the service.

Negotiating for the government with a prospective employer is not the only danger area you will face when you are ready to get out of the service. Another danger area is simply looking for a job for after you get out of the service. You should not talk to a prospective employer about a job if you have military duties involving that employer. For example, if you were a contracting officer or a clerk who had access to bid information on government contracts, you could not do such things as send a resume to or talk about a job with a company that might enter into a contract with your office. If you did, you would have to disqualify yourself from taking any action that involved that company. Further, if you were involved in hiring people for civilian federal jobs on your installation, you could not consider your family members for any such jobs.

A final requirement of the standards of conduct applies to general or flag officers and other high-ranking officers and civilians. All must file reports of their financial affairs to make certain that they do not have conflicts of interest. These forms are Standard Form 278, *Financial Disclosure Reports*, and DD Form 1555, *Confidential Statement of Affiliations and Financial Interest*. Federal law calls for new general officers to file an SF 278 when they take a general officer position. If you are a general officer, you must file annual reports, as well as termination reports on leaving the position, unless you are moving to another position that calls for filing an SF 278. Officers who do not have to file an SF 278 but who have jobs that affect civilian business, such as contracting officers, must file a DD Form 1555. If you are required to file this form, you must include the following information:

• All companies that you are connected with as an employee, an officer, an owner, or a company stock or bond owner.

• All companies that owe money to you, except normal commercial loans.

• Interests in real property other than a home that you live in, such as an apartment complex you own.

• The names of people who know about your interests that you do not know about. For example, a trustee of a trust of which you are a beneficiary could know what property is in the trust when you do not. In such a case, you should list the trustee on the DD Form 1555.

You must list any such interests of family members as well. You must file these statements with your superior annually. Your superior will review the reports to make certain no interests conflict and will try to resolve them if they do. Military lawyers also review the forms.

CONFIDENTIAL STATEMENT OF AFFILIATIONS AND FINANCIAL INTERESTS
DEPARTMENT OF DEFENSE PERSONNEL
(Including Special Government Employees)
(If additional space is required use separate sheets referencing item numbers below.)

Privacy Act Statement

(Please read Instructions before completing this form.)

1. NAME (Last, First, MI)	2. SOCIAL SECURITY NUMBER
3. TITLE OR POSITION	4. WORK TELEPHONE NO. (Include Area Code)
5. DOD COMPONENT ADDRESS (Include office symbol code letters)	6. GRADE OR RANK

PART I
To be completed by DoD personnel indicated in section F.3.a. and Enclosure 5 of DoD directive 5500.7, or implementing regulations.

7. NON-FEDERAL AFFILIATIONS AND FINANCIAL INTERESTS (See instructions. If none, write "none.")

a. NAME OF ORGANIZATION	b. ADDRESS OF ORGANIZATION	c. YOUR AFFILIATION	d. NATURE OF FINANCIAL INTEREST (Stock, pension, etc.)

8. CREDITORS (List all creditors other than conventional loans on customary terms. If none, write "none.")

a. NAME	b. ADDRESS	c. NATURE OF DEBT

9. INTERESTS IN REAL PROPERTY (List all creditors other than personal residence you occupy. Note any DoD contractor relationships, present or future. If none, write "none.")

a. ADDRESS OF PROPERTY	b NATURE OF INTEREST (Owner, mortgagee, etc.)	c. TYPE OF PROPERTY (Apts., farm, etc.)

DD Form 1555, MAR 87   *Previous editions are obsolete.*   644-07

High-ranking officers may have to file a DD Form 1555, as reproduced here, to show that no conflicts of interest exist between their military duties and their personal financial affairs.

PART II
To be completed only by "Special Government Employees." See Instructions.

10. NUMBER OF DAYS YOU EXPECT TO PERFORM GOVERNMENT SERVICE

a. FOR DOD COMPONENT		d. DAYS WORKED FOR PRESENT DOD COM-PONENT DURING 365 DAYS PRIOR TO PRESENT APPOINTMENT	e. DAYS WORKED FOR ANY DOD COM-PONENT DURING 365 DAYS PRIOR TO PRESENT APPOINTMENT
b. FOR OTHER AGENCIES			
c. TOTAL *(10.a. + b.)*			

11. FEDERAL GOVERNMENT EMPLOYMENT *(List all other agencies with whom you are presently employed.)*

a. AGENCY NAME	b. AGENCY ADDRESS	c. TITLE OR POSITION	d. NO. OF DAYS	e. DATE *(YYMMDD)* (1) FROM	(2) TO

PART III - CERTIFICATION
To be completed by all filers.

12. I certify that the statements I have made are true, complete, and correct to the best of my knowledge and that none of the reported affiliations/financial interests are in conflict with my official duties. I have read and understand DoD Directive 5500.7 "Standards of Conduct" or implementing regulations.

a. SIGNATURE	b. DATE SIGNED

PART IV - EVALUATION AND REVIEW
To be completed by supervisor or superior and Designated Agency Ethics Official or designee. See Instructions.

13. I have reviewed the above statement in light of the present and prospective duties of the individual to ensure that both actual and apparent conflicts of interest are avoided. My evaluation is *(x as applicable)*

a.	No affiliation/financial interests reported.
b.	Reported affiliations/financial interests are unrelated to assigned or prospective duties, and no conflicts appear to exist.
c.	Assigned duties require participation in matters involving or which may involve the highlighted affiliations/financial interests. This conflict will be resolved by *(x as applicable)*
	(1) Change of assigned duties.
	(2) Divestiture of the interests and relief of incumbent from all related duties pending divestiture.
	(3) Disqualification.
	(4) Other. Detailed advice attached. Notice of corrective action will follow.
d.	The highlighted reported affiliations/financial interests are related to assigned or prospective duties, but have been determined by the appropriate appointing official to be not so substantial as to affect the integrity of the individual's services. A copy of the formal determination and rationale is attached.
e.	The prospective employee's duties will require participation in matters involving the highlighted reported affiliations/financial interests and the appointment cannot be consummated until divestiture of these affiliations/financial interests is completed.

f. SIGNATURE	h. OFFICE ADDRESS	i. DATE SIGNED
g. PRINTED NAME		

14. As a Designated Agency Ethics Official or designee, I have examined the foregoing Statement and Evaluation. *(x a. or b.)*

a.	I concur with the supervisor's evaluation
b.	I do not concur with the supervisor's evaluation. Advice attached

c. SIGNATURE	e. OFFICE ADDRESS	f. DATE SIGNED
d. PRINTED NAME		

DD Form 1555, MAR 87

Finally, servicemembers who leave or retire from the military face some restrictions. Retired regular commissioned or warrant officers may not, for example, receive retirement pay within three years after retirement if they sell or try to sell supplies to any agency of the Department of Defense, the Public Health Service, and certain other federal agencies. Nor can a retired regular officer represent anyone trying to sell anything to his service. Many restrictions also apply to helping others prosecute claims against the United States. These restrictions are technical, so you need to see a lawyer before deciding to help someone with a claim after you get out of the service.

Retired regular officers must file a DD Form 1357, *Statement of Employment*, within thirty days after retirement and must update it when the information is no longer accurate. Further, federal law forbids retired officers from accepting jobs from foreign governments. Retired regular officers who go to work for the federal government may have their retirement pay reduced by the provision of the Dual Compensation Act. This act states that retired regular officers who have a civilian federal job may receive the entire salary for the civilian job, but only a part of their retired pay. A similar provision reduces the retired pay of all servicemembers who work for the federal government after retirement. Their civilian federal pay and their retired pay together cannot exceed the basic pay of a Level V of the Executive Schedule ($108,200 as of 1 January 1995). If it does, the government reduces the retirement pay to bring the total to that of a Level V employee.

CONCLUSION

You can obey most of the military's rules about money by using common sense. If you are in doubt about what is proper, however, see a legal assistance officer before getting involved with the transaction. Also feel free to get help with your taxes. That way you will be sure to enjoy the extra money you earn free from legal difficulties and without paying more taxes than you legitimately owe.

Money problems—whether they are debt problems, tax problems, or problems associated with earning extra money—can put a severe strain on both your family life and your military career. Don't let any financial problem get out of hand. Think about your financial transactions, and if you need help, get it early. If you do, you'll improve your chances of having a financially rewarding period of service as well as an emotionally satisfying one.

PART VII

Reserve Components and Mobilization

Events in the Middle East in the early 1990s brought legal issues concerning mobilization of Reserve and National Guard personnel to the forefront. Legal issues may arise concerning reserve status or the particular legal problems of mobilized reserve component personnel. Chapter 17 discusses the composition of the reserve components, rights and duties of reserve component personnel, and the various ways reservists may be activated. Chapter 18 discusses the more common legal problems that reservists face when mobilized.

17

Reserve Components

The reserve components are made up of the Reserves and the National Guard with the mission of providing training units and qualified individuals for active duty during war or other emergencies. Each armed force has three types of reserves: Ready Reserves, Standby Reserves, and Retired Reserves. Inactive status reservists include all reserve personnel who are on an inactive status list of a reserve component and those who are assigned to the inactive Army National Guard or Air National Guard. Military retirees make up the Retired Reserve. All reservists who are not in the Retired Reserve or in an inactive status are in an active reserve status.

RESERVE COMPONENT DUTIES AND BENEFITS

Reserve component personnel have the same responsibilities to the military as active component personnel do (see chapter 1). You have the same responsibility to remain fit and to attend scheduled drills, annual training, and other periods of duty as required. The duty to remain fit means that you, like active component personnel, may be subjected to urinalysis to detect drug abuse and must submit to military medical care. For example, some reserve component soldiers sought legal assistance for help to keep military dentists from removing orthodontic devices—braces—before deployment on Operation Desert Shield. Dental authorities had determined that braces cannot be maintained safely in the desert. Since the military can compel medical treatment, attempts to avoid the removal of these devices were unsuccessful. Nor is the military liable to replace them, although some civilian orthodontists agreed to replace them at no cost.

Reserve component personnel on inactive duty, in annual training, on active duty for training, or on active duty qualify for various military benefits and entitlements, depending on their current status. For example, reservists on inactive duty may shop in the commissary up to twelve times a year and have full commissary privileges while on annual training or active duty. Similarly, reservists have limited exchange privileges, except when ordered to active duty, when they have full privileges. The most important benefits for which reserve component personnel do not qualify, except when on active duty for more than thirty days, are CHAMPUS (the military medical insurance for family members) and military dental care. Nor do reserve component personnel not on active duty qualify for military legal assistance except for premobilization legal assistance, such as preparation of wills and powers of attorney. Reserve component family members' privileges and benefits are also dependent on their military sponsor's status. They have the same benefits as active component family members, such as military medical care, when their sponsor goes on active duty for more than thirty days. The one exception is military dental care, which requires the servicemember to be ordered to active duty for at least two years in order for family members to be covered.

Reservists have certain employment rights under the Veterans' Reemployment Rights Act. Your employer must grant you time off from work to attend military training. Also, your employer may not charge you vacation time for time you spend at military training. If you are away from your job for less than four years for military service, you are entitled to get it back, or be employed in an equivalent job, when you return. While on active duty, you are entitled to keep your job benefits, such as seniority, rate of pay, and so on. You should tell your employer about required training as far in advance as possible and, upon request, provide a copy of your orders. Otherwise, you may lose your reemployment rights.

In a recent federal court case, the court upheld an employer's firing of a reserve soldier who had taken several voluntary extended military leaves of absence for training and extended an annual training (AT) tour for 140 days during a period when the employer had a critical need for him. To prevent this from happening to you, you should notify your employer well in advance of a requested leave period; try to coordinate the specific leave period with your employer if it is voluntary training; explain your inability to reschedule the training if that is the case; coordinate extensions with your employer as early as possible; and, if the military leave is for more than two weeks, specify a definite end date to the service, if possible. You should also consider whether taking a lengthy military leave puts an unreasonable burden on your employer, taking into account such things as your position in the firm, the difficulty of finding a replacement, the workload, and so on. If those factors indicate that the burden on your employer is unreasonable, you probably should not take any voluntary, lengthy leave. This is the type of problem that a military lawyer can, and should, help you with.

CALL-UP FOR TRAINING

Simply stated, each Ready Reservist, unless excused by the Secretary of Defense, is required to participate in at least forty-eight scheduled drills or training periods, commonly known as inactive duty training. Ready Reservists also must perform active duty for training for between fourteen and thirty days a year. The United States Code provides for an involuntary order to active duty for training for not more than forty-five days per year for reserve personnel who do not satisfactorily perform their training obligation. National Guardsmen have similar training duty requirements.

The United States Code also authorizes the service secretaries to involuntarily order any reserve component unit or any active-status member not assigned to a unit to active duty for not more than fifteen days per year for training or operational missions. Call-up of Guard personnel under this provision requires consent of the state governor, except that under the Montgomery Amendment, the federal government may require Guard personnel to serve up to ninety days to augment operational missions outside the United States without state approval. Another portion of this law provides for voluntary call-up of reserve component personnel for more than the fifteen days of the involuntary call-up discussed above. Guard call-up under this provision requires state approval as well.

SPECIALIZED CALL-UPS

Reservists are subject to the Uniform Code of Military Justice. In 1986, Congress revised the Uniform Code of Military Justice to allow the services to order a member of the reserve components to active duty for investigation, nonjudicial punishment, or court-martial for offenses committed on prior active duty or inactive duty training. If one of these situations happens to you, read chapter 7.

As discussed above, the president may order any member of the Ready Reserve to active duty for failure to satisfactorily fulfill his or her obligations, but federal courts have upheld a reservist's mobilization when his unit had been abolished through no fault of his own under this law.

Finally, another 1986 Congressional amendment allows the military to involuntarily order reserve component members to active duty who have been captured or injured as a result of their military duties or affiliation. The military must release such personnel from active duty thirty days after their captive status ends, unless they consent to a longer period. This provision is intended to extend military benefits in such circumstances.

MOBILIZATION

In periods of national emergency, the president or Congress may mobilize reservists. The type and degree of the emergency determines which level of mobilization will be used.

The president has the authority to activate two hundred thousand reservists for up to ninety days, with a ninety-day extension if necessary, for any operational mission without declaring a national emergency. The president used this authority to mobilize the first units and individuals for the Persian Gulf crisis in 1990. This type of mobilization is called presidential call-up.

Four types of mobilization exist: *selective mobilization, partial mobilization, full mobilization,* and *total mobilization. Selective mobilization* is the activation of reserve component units and Individual Ready Reservists to respond to a domestic emergency, such as an earthquake, that does not threaten national security. *Partial mobilization* is the presidential activation of not more than one million Ready Reservists, both individuals and units, for not longer than twenty-four months in cases of national emergency. *Full mobilization* is the activation of all reserve component units, all individual and standby reservists, and retirees for the duration of the emergency plus six months in cases of national emergency. Under a partial emergency, servicemembers on an inactive status list or in a retired status may not be ordered to active duty unless the service secretary, with the approval of the Secretary of Defense, determines that not enough qualified reserves in an active status or in the inactive National Guard are available. Members of the Navy Fleet Reserve and Marine Corps Fleet Reserve, however, are subject to call-up notwithstanding whether sufficient qualified reservists are available. Congress must authorize a full mobilization. *Total mobilization* goes beyond full mobilization and consists of an expansion of the armed forces by Congress and the President to get additional units or personnel in cases of national emergency. Once the Congress and/or the president authorizes the mobilization, the Secretary of Defense directs the mobilization of units and individuals.

The preferred order of mobilization is to first call up the most recently trained units in the Ready Reserve, preferably as units, followed by the Standby Reserve and the Retired Reserve, in that order.

Court challenges to the legality of various types of call-up or mobilization by reserve component personnel who do not wish to go on active duty have, generally speaking, not been very successful. If you do not want to be called up, you need to take steps to sever your connection from the military before a mobilization. See chapter 4 for the types of discharges for which you may qualify.

CONCLUSION

Understanding your reserve or National Guard status, your rights and responsibilities as a member of a reserve component, and the ways in which the military may activate you will help you both to make the best of your military service and to prepare for a potential mobilization as discussed in the next chapter.

18

Reservists' Legal Concerns

Although reservists who are not on active duty do not qualify for military legal assistance except for "premobilization" legal assistance, they certainly will have the same problems as active-duty servicemembers, or greater, when sent away from their homes to a war zone. See part IV, "Personal Legal Matters," particularly chapter 9, "Your Legal Survival Kit," for an overview of legal problems that all servicemembers, including reserve component personnel, face. This chapter amplifies chapter 9 by discussing particular concerns of reserve component personnel who face mobilization. Of course, after mobilization, reservists qualify for the full range of legal assistance and should use it as needed.

Because mobilization may occur very suddenly, it is critical that you make preparations to protect your family, your financial situation, your civilian business interests, and your reemployment rights.

PROTECTING YOUR FAMILY
Most legal problems during mobilization involve family issues. You must make certain, *in advance*, that you take care of your family in your absence.

Legal assistance officers may draft simple wills for reserve component personnel as part of premobilization legal counseling. If they cannot, such as when you want a very complicated will involving significant assets, you must get a civilian attorney to prepare one for you. If a reserve component servicemember dies on active duty, his or her next of kin would receive the full range of military and Department of Veterans Affairs death benefits, such as the military death gratuity and VA Dependency and Indemnity Compensation.

216

POM CLIENT INTERVIEW FORM

Date: _____

_____
(Rank, name, SSN, and unit)

The servicemember is to check the blocks below that most correctly describe his/her situation.

Marital status:

_____ Single

_____ Married

Children:

_____ None

_____ Child(ren) less than 18 years of age

_____ Child(ren) more than 18 years of age

Property:

_____ Do not own land

_____ Own land in the state of _____

Will and Power of Attorney:

_____ Have a Will that is satisfactory to me

_____ Have a current Power of Attorney

_____ Desire to have a Will prepared for me

_____ Desire to have a Power of Attorney prepared for me

_____ Appointment with SJA for preparation of Will or Power of Attorney not desired

_____ Appointment with SJA for preparation of Will or Power of Attorney made for:

_____   _____
(Date)   (Signature)

THIS FORM TO BE REVIEWED BY SOLDIER EVERY SIX MONTHS.

DISPOSITION: File in Personnel Readiness Folder

A legal assistance officer's Preparation for Overseas Movement client interview form.

MILITARY FAMILY CHECKLIST

ON HAND   IMPORTANT DOCUMENTS   LOCATION

1. Marriage certificate.
2. Birth certificate of all family members.
3. Shot records of all family members.
4. Citizenship papers, if any.
5. Adoption papers, if any.
6. Armed forces identification card
   (for all family members over age ten).
7. Insurance policies (or list of companies,
   policy numbers, type of insurance, address,
   and phone number).
8. Last leave and earnings statement (LES).
9. Power of attorney.
10. Copies of wills (both spouses and parents,
    if you have copies of their wills).
11. Bankbooks.
12. State and federal tax records.
13. Car registration/title.
14. Deed(s) and mortgage(s).

INFORMATION SPOUSES SHOULD KNOW

1. Are all immunizations up-to-date for yourself and your children?
2. Do you know the account numbers, addresses, and names of the banks in which you and your spouse have accounts?
3. Do you have money available to you on a continuing basis in the event your sponsor deploys? (The sponsor is the active-duty service-member.)
4. Do you have and know the location of a strongbox or safety deposit box for important papers and the location of the key or the combination?
5. Do you know the location of all credit cards and whom to notify in case of loss?
6. Do you know of all payments that must be made, to whom and when, such as rent or house payment, telephone, water, electricity, insurance, debt repayment (including banks, finance companies, small loan companies, and credit cards), auto license fees, taxes, gas (house, trailer, car)?
7. Do you know the expiration date of your ID card?
8. Do you know your sponsor's Social Security number and unit of assignment?
9. Do you have names, current addresses, and phone numbers of all members of immediate families of husband and wife? (Immediate family includes father, mother, brothers, and sisters.)

An Air Force Mobility Checklist (adopted from the Preventive Law Series of the Staff Judge Advocate, Whiteman AFB, Missouri).

Reserve component personnel on active duty are automatically covered by Servicemen's Group Life Insurance, unless they decline coverage or elect a smaller amount.

You also may want a legal assistance officer to draft a power of attorney giving your spouse the authority to, for example, cash checks mailed to your home in your name after you leave or to sell your car. Legal assistance officers are authorized to draw up simple powers of attorney covering family matters for reservists. They cannot, however, draft a power of attorney to cover who has the authority to act for you in your business dealings. If you don't already have joint bank accounts, you, like your active-duty counterparts, may want to consider establishing such accounts so that your spouse may withdraw funds as necessary in your absence. If you don't have joint accounts, your spouse would need a power of attorney to access your funds. You should also provide for the direct deposit of your military pay to such a joint account.

Your reserve unit may require that you have a Family Care Plan. Even if it doesn't, you should make one. Such plans are especially important when you are a single parent or when both parents are military members. You must make certain that you have a guardian to take care of your children in the event you are mobilized. A legal assistance officer should be able to help you provide for guardianship of your children as a part of authorized premobilization legal assistance. Also, make certain that all your family members who qualify for a Department of Defense Reserve Family Member ID card have a nonexpired one and are enrolled in the DEERS system, so that when you are called for active duty or active-duty training for more than thirty days they can receive military medical care.

PROTECTING YOUR FINANCIAL SITUATION
Often mobilization results in additional expenses, for which you may have less income because your military pay is less than you earn in your civilian job. The law provides a number of protections for servicemembers so that they are not harmed too much by the change in their financial situation inherent in mobilization.

Pension Plans
Not only does the law protect your job rights while training and give you reemployment rights (see below), it also protects your pension plans. Your employer must count time spent on active duty for purposes of participation, benefit accrual, and vesting of pensions if you return to your civilian job. You also have the right to make catch-up contributions to the plan when you return to work. Employers do not, however, have to make profit-sharing plan contributions for periods when reserve component personnel are on active duty.

SPECIAL POWER OF ATTORNEY FOR DEPLOYMENT

KNOW ALL MEN BY THESE PRESENTS: That I, _____, have made, constituted, and appointed, and by these presents do make, constitute, and appoint _____, whose present address is _____, my true and lawful attorney to act as follows, GIVING AND GRANTING unto my said attorney full power to:

_____ 1. Exercise all rights and powers incident and pertaining to ownership of my motor vehicle, including the power of sale, possession, operation, and registration of the following motor vehicle:

(YEAR)	(MAKE)	(IDENTIFICATION NUMBER)

_____ 2. Authorize and request, in my behalf and name, the shipment and storage of household goods, personal baggage, automobile, and any and all of my other personal property.

_____ 3. Authorize any and all medical, dental, and hospital care and treatment, either preventive or corrective, including major surgery, deemed necessary by a duly licensed physician or dentist for the health and well-being of my child(ren):

NAME	AGE	RELATIONSHIP

_____ 4. Pick up military paychecks from the unit First Sergeant, Mail Clerk, Commander, or anyone designated by the Commander to release said checks. Also, the above Attorney-in-Fact can cash said checks or deposit said checks in my account.

_____ 5. Effect the assignment or termination of U.S. Government Quarters and to procure or return any and all U.S. Government property used in or for such quarters, and to execute all necessary documents, instruments, and papers therewith.

I DECLARE THAT THIS POWER OF ATTORNEY SHALL BECOME VALID AND EFFECTIVE ONLY AT AND FROM THE DATE THAT A COMMISSIONED OFFICER IN THE UNITED STATES ARMED FORCES AT _____ ATTESTS, BY HIS NOTARIZED SIGNATURE IN THE DEPLOYMENT CLAUSE BELOW, THAT I HAVE DEPLOYED FROM _____ IN THE ARMED SERVICE OF THE UNITED STATES. I ALSO DECLARE THAT

(continued)

SUCH NOTARIZED SIGNATURE OF AN OFFICER SERVING AT _____ SHALL ITSELF ALONE BE SUFFICIENT TO MAKE THIS POWER FULLY VALID AND EFFECTIVE. I HEREBY REQUEST AND AUTHORIZE THAT AS SOON AS POSSIBLE AFTER MY DEPLOYMENT THE SAID DEPLOYMENT CLAUSE BE COMPLETED AND SIGNED BY A COMMISSIONED OFFICER SERVING AT _____ AND THEN NOTARIZED.

FURTHER, I do authorize my aforesaid Attorney-in-Fact to sign for me all forms, papers, affidavits, statements of ownership, certificates, and receipts necessary to carry out the aforesaid authorizations and to perform any and all necessary acts in the execution of the aforesaid authorizations with the same validity as I could effect if personally present. Any act or thing lawfully done hereunder by my said attorney shall be binding on myself and my heirs, legal and personal representatives, and assigns.

PROVIDED, however, that all business transacted hereunder for me or for my account shall be transacted in my name, and that all indorsements and instruments executed by my said attorney for the purpose of carrying out the foregoing powers shall contain my name, followed by that of my said attorney and the designation "Attorney-in-Fact."

I FURTHER DECLARE that this power shall remain in effect even though I am reported or listed, officially or otherwise, as "missing," "missing-in-action," or "prisoner-of-war," it being my intention that the designation of such status shall not bar my said attorney from fully and completely exercising and continuing to exercise any and all powers and rights herein granted until this Special Power of Attorney is revoked by my death or as otherwise provided herein.

Notwithstanding my insertion of specific expiration date herein, if on the below specified expiration date, or if at any time within thirty (30) days immediately preceding that specified expiration date, I should be, or have been, carried in a military status of "missing," "missing-in-action," or "prisoner-of-war," then this Power of Attorney shall automatically continue to remain valid and in full effect until sixty (60) days after I have returned to United States military control following termination of such "missing," "missing-in-action," or "prisoner-of-war" status.

FURTHER, UNLESS SOONER REVOKED OR TERMINATED by me, this Power of Attorney shall become NULL and VOID from and after _____, nineteen hundred _____.

IN WITNESS WHEREOF, I have hereunto set my hand and seal this _____ day of _____, nineteen hundred _____.

_____(SEAL)
(SIGNATURE)

WITNESSES AND ADDRESSES: _____ _____

_____ _____

A sample Special Power of Attorney for Deployment.

ACKNOWLEDGMENT

STATE OF _____)
COUNTY OF _____) I, the undersigned, do hereby certify
that I am a duly commissioned, qualified, and authorized notary public in and
for the State of _____; that the grantor in the foregoing
Power of Attorney, who is personally well known to me as the person who
executed the foregoing Power of Attorney, appeared before me this day
within the territorial limits of my authority, and being first duly sworn,
acknowledged that he executed said instrument after the contents had been
read and duly explained to him, and that such execution was his free and voluntary act and deed for the uses and purposes therein set forth.

  IN WITNESS WHEREOF, I have hereunto set my hand and affixed
my seal of office this _____ day of _____, nineteen hundred
_____.

                                    _____
                                    NOTARY PUBLIC

                                    My commission expires_____

If you are called up for longer than ninety days, however, the Internal
Revenue Service considers you an active participant in an employer-provided
retirement plan. This means that your ability to deduct Individual Retirement Account deductions is phased out if your adjusted gross income exceeds
$40,000, and is eliminated if your income exceeds $50,000 and you file a
joint return. The phase-out begins at $25,000 if you file a single return, and
deductibility is eliminated at $35,000.

Health Insurance
Employer-provided health insurance benefits may also become an issue if you
are mobilized. The law requires an employer providing health insurance benefits to make continued coverage available to employees and their dependents who may lose coverage because they lose their jobs unless another
group health-care plan covers the employee. The Internal Revenue Service
has decided that because the military does not meet the law's definition of an
employer, employers cannot avoid making continued coverage available
because a reserve component servicemember receives health-care coverage

while on active duty and his family members come under CHAMPUS. Thus, your employer should offer you continued coverage at your expense. You should get a notice of your rights before your employer terminates your health insurance benefits. In addition, your employer may have tax consequences if he terminates your coverage.

Soldiers' and Sailors' Civil Relief Act

The Soldiers' and Sailors' Civil Relief Act (SSCRA) applies to reservists called to active duty as part of a mobilization. A number of the act's protections are especially important for mobilized reserve component servicemembers. In fact, now that we don't have a draft, the act is probably more helpful to reservists than to active component personnel. Many of the protections of the act are not available to career active-duty soldiers because the obligations involved, such as debts and leases, must predate their military service.

For example, if you entered into a lease before going on active duty, the SSCRA allows you to terminate the lease. All you have to do is show the following: that you entered the lease before being activated; that you or your dependents entered into the lease for dwelling, professional, business, agricultural, or similar purposes; and that you are currently in military service. Other provisions of the SSCRA require that you show that your military service "materially affects" your ability to meet your obligations, but the provision allowing you to avoid leases has no such requirement. You cannot, however, use this provision to terminate a lease that you entered into after you went on active duty, although a few states have laws that do allow termination in such situations. Nevertheless, whether you entered into a lease before or after being activated, the SSCRA protects you and your family members from eviction if your military service is materially affecting your ability to make rental payments and the rent does not exceed $150 per month. In such cases, the act provides for a stay of eviction until up to three months after discharge. Legislation has been proposed that would adjust the $150 rent limitation, which was set in 1966, upward to reflect inflation.

Another protection of the SSCRA that is more helpful to reservists than to full-time active-duty soldiers is the limitation on interest rates, because most servicemembers going on full-time active duty from civilian life make more money than they had been as, say, high school or college students. Reserve component personnel often take a pay cut when activated. The 6 percent maximum limitation on interest that a creditor may charge a servicemember for credit extended before the servicemember goes on active duty requires that his or her service "materially affect" the ability to pay the debt. So, if you borrowed money while you were a reservist, you qualify for this protection, so long as you were not on active duty when you incurred the debt. The burden is on the creditor to show that your military service is not affecting your ability to repay a loan. Nor should the creditor accrue the difference between 6 percent and the stated interest rate and require you to pay it after ending your active-duty period.

The 6 percent limitation applies to credit card balances that you ran up prior to going on active duty. The card issuer may, however, legally charge you the full interest rate on any additional charges you make after entering active duty.

Not all loans qualify for the 6 percent interest limitation. Guaranteed student loans, for example, do not qualify, although you could apply for a military deferment during your period of active service up to three years. Loans for which your spouse is solely liable do not qualify either, although you could certainly negotiate with the lender for reduced or deferred payments if your active duty harms your ability to make payments.

The SSCRA also covers mortgages. If you owned real or personal property before beginning active service; entered into a mortgage or security agreement, such as a lien, before entering active duty; and your military service materially affects your ability to repay, you qualify for a stay in any foreclosure proceedings or a decrease in payments during the active-duty period in addition to the 6 percent interest rate limitation discussed above. For mortgages issued under the Federal National Mortgage Association (Fannie Mae), however, the mortgage holder need not determine whether military service materially affects the servicemember's ability to pay interest at the mortgage's rate.

Because they may lose money—the difference between the loan rate and 6 percent—many creditors try to avoid complying with the SSCRA. For example, some creditors have insisted that servicemembers refinance the loan at 6 percent and charge new loan origination charges. Others refuse to reduce the interest rate until you prove that your premobilization income was greater than your military pay. Such tactics are illegal. The SSCRA covers "service charges, renewal fees, fees, or any other charges" within the 6 percent interest cap. Further, the burden is on the creditor to establish that military service is not affecting your ability to repay a loan or mortgage. Nevertheless, it may be helpful, when putting the creditor on notice of your desire to invoke the protection of the act, to provide reasonable proof of material effect on your ability to make the loan payments. See a legal assistance officer if you have difficulty securing your rights under the SSCRA.

Although the law is a little unclear, probably because no one had thought of automobile leases when Congress last amended the SSCRA, you may be able to get relief from an automobile lease if you leased the vehicle "with a view to purchase" it. An option to purchase the car at the conclusion of the lease may meet this requirement.

Another important protection of the SSCRA is its provisions permitting you to delay civil actions until you return from military service. As discussed in chapter 6, the SSCRA authorizes a stay in a lawsuit in which you are involved if your military service "materially affects"—harms—your ability to proceed with the case. You may also be able to reopen a default judgment if your military service prevented you from appearing. Contact a legal assistance officer if you are involved in any litigation when you are mobilized or after mobilization. See chapters 6, 14, and 16 for more on the SSCRA.

YOUR CIVILIAN BUSINESS INTERESTS
You may have a number of legitimate concerns about what may happen to the day-to-day operation of your civilian business interests. A military legal assistance attorney may counsel you about preparing for mobilization, but this assistance cannot cover business matters, nor does the expanded legal assistance for which you qualify if ordered to active duty cover business matters. Thus, you should consult a civilian lawyer to make certain that you protect your business interests in the event of mobilization.

REEMPLOYMENT
As discussed above, if you are mobilized, you have reemployment rights under the Veterans Reemployment Rights Law. This law protects you whether you voluntarily or involuntarily leave your civilian job to enter active duty. You do not need to request a leave of absence if you are mobilized, but the act does not apply if you quit or were discharged before entering active duty. Your employer must, under the law, reinstate you in your former position, or one of similar status, seniority, and pay. He should also award you any automatic pay raises that others got during your absence. To qualify for these reemployment benefits you must meet the following requirements:

• You must have been released from active duty under honorable conditions.

• You must not have been a temporary employee. Generally, if you had a reasonable belief that you would be continuously employed for an indefinite time, you are not a temporary employee, even if you had a contract for a limited period. Seasonal employment, however, does not qualify as permanent employment.

• You must have left your job only because of a call to active duty.

• You must not have served for more than four years on active duty. The law provides for an extension to five years if the extension was at the request of and for the convenience of the government.

• You must be qualified to perform your old duties. If you became disabled because of service-connected disease or injury that prevents you from performing your old job, you are entitled to the nearest comparable job that you can perform.

• You must apply for your job within ninety days of your termination from active duty. This period is reduced to thirty-one days if you are returning from your initial active duty for training of twelve consecutive weeks or more. Merely asking about getting your job back is insufficient; you must apply to get your job back within the time limit. You should request your job back *in writing*. Never sign any documents waiving your Veterans Reemployment Rights Law rights or accept any employment offering you less pay or seniority than you had before going on active duty.

If your employer does not give you your job back, or you lose seniority or pay, you should contact your union representative, any office of the Veterans' Employment and Training Office, Department of Labor (phone 202-523-8611), or the National Committee for Employer Support of the Guard and Reserve at 800-336-4590. Government employees should contact the Office of Personnel Management. If none of these agencies solve the problem, you can use a U.S. district court to enforce your rights under the Veterans Reemployment Rights Law.

The act does have one exception: your employer does not have to rehire you if reemployment is unreasonable considering all the facts and circumstances. A mere decline in business is not enough to make your reemployment unreasonable, but adverse economic circumstances may qualify. The employer has the burden of proving that the circumstances make your reemployment unreasonable.

Once you get your job back, the law protects you from being discharged without cause for one year.

You should also check with a legal assistance officer to see whether your state or other political subdivision has laws that establish greater job protection or additional reemployment rights.

CONCLUSION

While the Soldiers' and Sailors' Civil Relief Act, the Veterans Reemployment Rights Law, and other laws protect you when you are mobilized, they are nowhere near as effective as prior planning on your part is. You must make certain that you take care of your family, your finances, your business interests, and your civilian job *before* you are mobilized, not after.

Glossary

ABANDONMENT. The act of giving up rights to property. Breaking a lease without justification is an abandonment. The term also refers to one spouse leaving the other spouse without justification.

ABUSE OF PROCESS. A tort (civil wrong) in which the wrongdoer improperly uses a legal proceeding to get a result not intended by the proceeding. For example, if you sued someone using proper grounds for a lawsuit, but really intended to coerce the other to sell his home to you, you would be committing an abuse of process.

ACCUSED. The military term for a defendant in a criminal trial. The person who is facing a court-martial.

ADMINISTRATIVE REMEDY. A method of righting a wrong that does not involving suing in a court. Examples of administrative remedies include Article 138 complaints, the claims system, and discharge review boards.

ALIBI. A defense in a criminal trial in which the accused tries to show he could not have committed the crime because he was elsewhere when it happened.

ALIMONY. The monetary allowance paid by one spouse to the other for support during or after a divorce proceeding. It is also called maintenance.

ANNULMENT. A court order that states that a marriage was of no legal effect.

ANSWER. A legal writing filed by a defendant in reply to a lawsuit to deny the plaintiff's complaint.

APPEAL. A request made to a higher authority to correct an improper decision of the lower authority.

APPELLANT. The party bringing an appeal.

APPELLEE. The defendant in an appeal.

APPREHENSION. The military term for what civilian police would call an arrest. The act of taking into custody a servicemember suspected of having committed a crime.

ARREST IN QUARTERS. A form of pretrial restraint that is less restrictive than pretrial confinement. A commander may impose it by an order restraining a person to specified limits, usually the person's dwelling or barracks room. A servicemember who is in arrest in quarters does not perform duty.

ARTICLE 32 INVESTIGATION. A formal investigation that a commander must conduct before he can try a servicemember by general court-martial. The Article 32 investigating officer makes an impartial inquiry into the truth of the charges and recommends how to dispose of them. The convening authority does not have to follow the recommendation.

ARTICLE 138 COMPLAINT. An administrative procedure in which servicemembers can have wrongs done to them by commanders investigated and remedied if the complaint is valid.

ARTICLE 139, UCMJ, CLAIM. A method of compensating a servicemember when another servicemember has stolen or wrongfully damaged his property.

ASSAULT. An act that threatens or offers harm to another. Raising a clenched fist and pointing a loaded pistol are both assaults.

ATTORNEY. A lawyer. A member of the bar of a state or a federal court.

BAD-CONDUCT DISCHARGE (BCD). A discharge under less-than-honorable conditions. The military may give a BCD to enlisted servicemembers only by the sentence of a court-martial. The military cannot give such a discharge administratively. Also, the court-martial may only sentence the accused to a BCD when the accused has been convicted of crimes that authorize this discharge. A BCD results in the loss of substantially all veterans and military benefits. It is, however, less severe than a dishonorable discharge.

BAILEE. A person that another entrusts with personal property.

BAILMENT. The delivery of personal property to another with the understanding that the other will use it properly and return it promptly and in good condition.

BANKRUPTCY. A court procedure for distributing the property of a person who cannot pay his debts, thus releasing him from them.

BATTERY. A completed assault in which an assailant carries out an offer of violence (see assault). A harmful or offensive touching of another without legal justification or excuse.

BENEFICIARY. A person who receives property from an estate or an insurance policy. Also, a person for whom a trustee manages trust property.

BEQUEST. A provision in a will directing that a beneficiary receive a specific item or a specific amount of money.

BOARD OF CORRECTION OF MILITARY RECORDS. An administrative board that decides whether the military wronged a servicemember in a way that affects his military records, such as an erroneous date of rank or an improper discharge.

CAUSE OF ACTION. A factual situation that entitles the plaintiff to bring a lawsuit and get a court settlement for a wrong someone did to him.

CHILD SNATCHING. The act a parent without custody commits when taking a child away from the parent with custody. This is a crime, similar to kidnapping, in many states.

CIVIL RIGHTS. The rights guaranteed to U.S. citizens by the Constitution.

CLAIM. A written demand for money due the claimant.

CLAIMANT. A person who presents a claim against another.

CLAIMS OFFICER. An officer who has the authority to process and, in some cases, to approve claims against the government.

CLOSING. A meeting in which the buyer and the seller perform the requirements of a real estate sales contract, such as exchanging the purchase price for a deed.

CLOSING COSTS. The costs of completing a real estate sale, such as taxes, expenses of a title search, and attorney's fees.

CODICIL. A document that modifies an existing will.

COLLATERAL. Property pledged as security for the repayment of a debt.

COMMISSION. An appointment as an officer in the armed forces. A document that gives rank and authority to an officer in the armed forces.

COMMUNITY PROPERTY. Property acquired by a husband and a wife during the marriage except that received by inheritance or gift. In community property states, all such property belongs equally to both spouses regardless of whose name it is in.

COMPLAINT. A legal document that starts a lawsuit by setting forth the plaintiff's theory of the case.

CONDOMINIUM. Real property consisting of several individually owned, attached dwellings and jointly owned common areas.

CONFESSION. A statement in which you admit you are guilty of a crime.

CONFINEMENT. A punishment that may be given only by a court-martial that sentences the accused to a military confinement facility.

CONFRONTATION. The right to see, hear, and cross-examine (question) witnesses against you in a criminal trial.

CONSIDERATION. The benefits given to each party to a contract, such as the payment one party receives for the work he does for the other.

CONSTRUCTIVE EVICTION. A legal excuse for breaking a lease and moving out of rental property when a landlord improperly interferes with the tenant's use of the property.

CONSTRUCTIVE SERVICE OF PROCESS. A method of providing the defendant notice of a lawsuit when the plaintiff cannot personally notify him. The plaintiff usually does this by publishing the notice in a newspaper. The defendant is then presumed to have knowledge of the lawsuit against him.

CONTINGENT FEE SYSTEM. A system by which a plaintiff pays his attorney by giving the attorney a percentage of the judgment if the plaintiff wins.

CONTRACT. A formal agreement between two or more parties in which each party agrees to do certain things in return for the promise of the other party or parties to do certain things. A court of law can enforce a valid contract.

CONVENING AUTHORITY. A commander who has the authority to establish a court-martial and refer (send) cases to it for trial. Convening authorities have many powers and duties with regard to courts-martial, including choosing court members (the jury), approving the findings of guilt or innocence and the sentence, and granting clemency (reducing or suspending the sentence).

CORPORATION. An artificial body (entity) with a perpetual lifetime, formed to do business.

CONTRABAND. Items that are illegal to possess.

COUNTERCLAIM. A response by the defendant in a lawsuit to the plaintiff's complaint in which the defendant seeks damages against the plaintiff for a wrong done as a part of the incident that gave rise to the plaintiff's case.

COURT OF MILITARY APPEALS. In the military justice system, the highest court of appeals, consisting of three civilian judges appointed by the president. Servicemembers and the government may appeal decisions of the Courts of Military Review to the Court of Military Appeals.

COURTS OF MILITARY REVIEW. The government has three Courts of Military Review: the Army Court, the Navy-Marine Court, and the Air Force Court. Each consists of senior judge advocates who decide the initial appeal in cases in which a court-martial has sentenced the accused to death, to a punitive discharge, or to confinement for one or more years.

COURT-MARTIAL. A military court that can decide guilt or innocence of the accused and an appropriate sentence if the accused is found guilty in a criminal case.

COURT MEMBER. A military juryperson, a member of a court-martial panel.

CUSTODY. In military criminal law, custody means "held under guard." In family law, it means the care, management, and control of children.

DAMAGES. The money paid, usually by a defendant in a lawsuit, to compensate a victim for harm suffered.

DECEIT. A tort (civil wrong) in which a person withholds, misrepresents, or falsifies facts by which another is misled, thus causing harm to the other.

DEFAULT. A failure to do something that you are obligated to do.

DEFAULT JUDGMENT. A court decision granting the plaintiff the relief he sought because the defendant did not answer the complaint or did not defend himself in court.

DEFENDANT. A party sued by another (the plaintiff). The civilian criminal justice system also uses the term *defendant* for the accused.

DEPRECIATION. The lessening in value of property because of age, wear, and tear.

DERELICTION OF DUTY. The crime of failing to perform military duties properly. It is a violation of Article 92 of the UCMJ.

DESERTION. A voluntary separation from your spouse without legal justification. Also, the crime of leaving your unit with the intent never to return to military service.

DETAILED DEFENSE COUNSEL. A military lawyer whom the military appoints to defend an accused.

DISCHARGE. The termination of military status. A discharge certificate documents a separation from the armed forces and characterizes the service as honorable or not.

DISCHARGE FOR THE GOOD OF THE SERVICE. A voluntary discharge submitted by someone who is facing a court-martial for a charge or charges authorizing a punitive discharge. The accused agrees to accept a discharge that may be other-than-honorable to avoid trial by court-martial. A discharge for the good of the service under other-than-honorable conditions results in the loss of military and veterans benefits.

DISCHARGE REVIEW BOARD. An administrative board that decides whether an ex-servicemember's service should upgrade his administrative discharge.

DISCIPLINARY ACTION. The procedure, such as nonjudicial punishment or a court-martial, that a military superior or court-martial uses to punish a servicemember who has committed a crime.

DISCOVERY. A method by which the parties to a lawsuit can learn what information the other side knows about the case. It is intended to disclose all the facts so that the parties can focus on the actual dispute between the two sides.

DISCRETIONARY ACT. An act of a public official that is based on personal judgment.

DISCRIMINATION. Denying a person something because of prejudice.

DISHONORABLE DISCHARGE. A punitive discharge that a general court-martial may give to enlisted members and warrant officers. It is the most severe discharge an enlisted member may receive and results in the loss of all military and veterans benefits.

DIVORCE. A judicial end to the marriage relationship.

DOMICILE. The location in which a person has established his legal home or permanent residence (see below). It requires both a residence and the intention to remain there permanently.

DON'T ASK, DON'T TELL POLICY. The Clinton Administration policy under which the military will not aggressively seek to discharge gays in the military who don't tell anyone their sexual orientation and don't engage in homosexual behavior.

DUE PROCESS. A term meaning fairness. When the government seeks to take a person's life, liberty, or property, it must give the person due process, which means, as a minimum, notice of the proposed action and an opportunity to explain why the government should not take the action.

EASEMENT. A right to use a portion of real property for some purpose, such as to permit a utility line to cross the property.

ENLISTMENT. The act of voluntarily entering into the military service as an enlisted member.

ENTRAPMENT. A defense in a criminal trial in which the accused admits he did the criminal act but says he would not have committed it if law enforcement officials had not caused him to do so. If law enforcement officials merely provide the opportunity for the accused to commit a crime he is predisposed to commit, however, such action is not entrapment.

EQUAL ACCESS TO JUSTICE ACT. A federal law that provides for the payment of attorney's fees for plaintiffs that sue the government under certain conditions.

ESCROW AGREEMENT. A portion of a real estate contract in which a third party holds a down payment and delivers it to the seller when both the buyer and the seller meet the conditions of the contract.

ESTATE. A person's extent of ownership of property, both real and personal.

EXECUTOR. A person or organization that distributes an estate according to the directions in a will.

EXCLUSIONARY RULE. The law stating that the government may not use evidence against a person in a criminal prosecution if law enforcement officials acquired that evidence in a manner that violated that person's Fourth or Fifth Amendment rights.

EXHAUSTION OF ADMINISTRATIVE REMEDIES RULE. The rule that requires a person harmed by the government or one of its agencies to try to resolve the situation by an administrative remedy before a court will hear a lawsuit about the matter. The government often uses this rule when sued by an individual.

EXTENUATION. Facts and circumstances that make a crime less serious than it would otherwise be.

FAILURE TO REPAIR. The crime of not being at an appointed place of duty when required. It is a violation of Article 86 of the UCMJ.

FAIR WEAR AND TEAR. The normal deterioration of properly used property.

FALSE ARREST AND FALSE IMPRISONMENT. A tort (civil wrong) in which a person restricts another's liberty, through arrest and imprisonment, without authority.

FEDERAL TORT CLAIMS ACT. The law that compensates victims, through either the claims system or a lawsuit, for wrongs committed by the government or its agents.

FELONY. A serious offense that normally carries a punishment of confinement for more than one year.

FERES DOCTRINE. The rule that forbids active-duty servicemembers from suing the government for torts (civil wrongs) committed by the government or its agents when the harm occurred incident to service.

FORECLOSURE. A sale of mortgaged property to pay the creditor when the debtor has defaulted on the loan.

FRATERNIZATION. An inappropriate relationship between a military superior and subordinate.

FRAUD. Any act that enables someone to gain an advantage over another by deceitful or unfair means.

GARNISHMENT. A court order commanding an individual or an organization that owes money to a defendant to pay it to the winner of the lawsuit against the defendant.

GENERAL DISCHARGE. A discharge under honorable conditions when the servicemember did not qualify for an honorable discharge.

GENERAL COURT-MARTIAL. The most serious military court, which may sentence a convicted servicemember to any lawful punishment, including the death penalty, any punitive discharge, total forfeitures of all pay and allowances, and confinement for life, depending upon the severity of the crime.

GIFT. A voluntary transfer of personal property to another without any payment for the property.

GRAND JURY. In the civilian court system, a group of citizens who determine whether enough evidence exists to prosecute a suspect.

GROSS NEGLIGENCE. A high degree of negligence, shown by a reckless or wanton lack of care.

GUARDIAN. A person appointed by a court to care for a person who is incapable of caring for himself, such as a child.

HABEAS CORPUS. A court order commanding an official to bring a person before the court to determine whether the government is legally holding him in custody.

HEALTH-CARE POWER OF ATTORNEY. A legal document that gives another the power to make health-care decisions for you if you become unable to do so.

ILLEGITIMATE CHILD. An offspring of an unmarried couple.

IMPLIED WARRANTY OF HABITABILITY. A law that requires a landlord to keep rental property fit to live in.

INCIDENT TO SERVICE. A phrase to describe the requirement that an injury, a loss, or a damage occur within the boundaries of normal military service before the military will pay a claim for it.

INDICTMENT. A grand jury's written accusation that a person committed a crime.

INDIVIDUAL MILITARY COUNSEL. A military lawyer chosen by the accused.

INJUNCTION. A court order restraining a person or an entity, such as a business or government agency, from doing something that would harm the plaintiff.

INSPECTION. An examination of a military organization to determine whether it can perform its mission.

INSPECTOR GENERAL. A military officer who has the duty to investigate servicemembers' complaints and to investigate and report on a military organization's ability to perform its mission.

INTENTIONAL TORT. A wrong done to another on purpose as opposed to negligently.

INTESTATE SUCCESSION. The laws that specify how to dispose of the property of people who die without wills.

INTERFERENCE WITH CONTRACT RIGHTS. A tort (civil wrong) committed by wrongfully preventing the formation or performance of a contract.

JUDGE ADVOCATE. A military lawyer—that is, a commissioned officer who belongs to the Judge Advocate General's Corps of his service. A military lawyer must be a graduate of a law school and a member of a state bar before he can be commissioned as such.

JUDGE ADVOCATE GENERAL. The chief lawyer of his service. Judge advocate generals are major generals (rear admirals in the Navy).

JOINT CUSTODY. The court's award of care, management, and control of the children of a divorced couple to both parents, usually with a provision stating which parent their principal residence will be with.

JUDGMENT. The decision of a court.

JURISDICTION. The power of a court to hear and decide a case.

LARCENY. The wrongful taking of property with the intent to deprive the owner of it permanently; stealing.

LAWFUL ORDER. A directive that has a proper military purpose, given by the proper authority to do or to cease doing a particular act.

LAWSUIT. A legal proceeding in which the plaintiff petitions a court to redress a wrong committed by the defendant.

LEASE. An agreement to rent property.

LEGAL ASSISTANCE. The military's program to help servicemembers with their personal legal problems.

LEGITIMATE CHILD. The offspring of a married couple.

LIABILITY. An obligation or responsibility.

LIABILITY INSURANCE. An insurance policy that protects a policyholder who loses a lawsuit by paying the damages in a tort case.

LIBEL. An untrue writing that injures another; written defamation of character, usually with negative connotations.

LICENSEE. One who has been given permission or authority to do something.

LIEN. A method of securing repayment of a debt by giving the creditor an interest in property, thus permitting him to seize it and sell it to satisfy the debt if the borrower fails to pay it.

LINE OF DUTY. A means of keeping the government from paying benefits to servicemembers who were hurt while conducting themselves improperly in their role as servicemembers. For example, if you broke a leg jumping off a building while drunk, the military could find your injury "not in the line of duty" and require you to pay for your military medical care.

LIVING WILL. A legal document in which you make the election as to what measures a physician should take to save your life, whether extraordinary measures, minimal effort, or something in between.

MALICIOUS PROSECUTION. A wrongful accusation that a person has committed a criminal or civil wrong that results in a lawsuit and harms the person accused.

MANDAMUS. A court order that commands an individual, a corporation, or a governmental agency to do something.

MANUAL FOR COURTS-MARTIAL. A presidential proclamation containing procedural rules for the administration of military justice, rules of evidence, and maximum punishments. It applies to all services.

MARKETABLE TITLE. Ownership of real property that is free from such limitations as a lien or a mortgage.

MEDICAL CARE RECOVERY SYSTEM. The procedure for the government to recover the costs of the medical care of servicemembers injured by someone other than the government or one of its agents.

MILITARY CLAUSE. In a contract entered into by a servicemember, such as a life insurance contract or a lease, a provision that modifies the contract because of the nature of service life. A military clause in a lease allows a servicemember to break the lease when reassigned. A military clause in life insurance often relieves the insurer from liability if the servicemember's death results from an act of war.

MILITARY JUDGE. A judge advocate trained and certified by a judge advocate general to be a judge at a court-martial.

MILITARY MAGISTRATE. A judge advocate, a military judge, or a commissioned officer who can issue search and apprehension authorizations (warrants) and review pretrial confinement to ensure that it meets legal standards.

MILITARY CLAIMS ACT. A federal law providing for the compensation of victims of torts (civil wrongs) committed by government employees or during "noncombat activities," such as training activities.

MILITARY PERSONNEL AND CIVILIAN EMPLOYEES' CLAIMS ACT. The law that establishes a procedure for servicemembers and federal civilian employees to receive compensation for damages to or loss of personal property.

MILITARY POLICEPERSON. An armed forces law enforcement official—a military policeman (Army), a member of the shore patrol (Navy), or a security policeman (Air Force). Members of the services' criminal investigation units are also military policepersons.

MISDEMEANOR. An offense that is less serious than a felony. Normally, a misdemeanor carries a punishment of not more than a year's confinement.

MISREPRESENTATION. A false statement.

MITIGATION. Factors other than the facts and circumstances of the offense that show that the accused should receive a light punishment. Examples include lack of a past criminal record, good duty performance, and family hardship.

MORTGAGE. An agreement to pay a debt secured by a lien on real property.

NEGLIGENCE. Failure to use due care.

NO-FAULT DIVORCE. A ground for ending a marriage in which the party suing for divorce need not prove the other guilty of marital misconduct.

NONJUDICIAL PUNISHMENT. Article 15 of the Uniform Code of Military Justice gives commanders this method of imposing minor disciplinary punishments without the formalities of a court-martial.

OFFICER. A person who holds a position of trust and responsibility that gives him both rights and duties. Here, a commissioned officer of the U.S. armed forces.

OTHER-THAN-HONORABLE DISCHARGE. The most severe type of administrative discharge. The military may give such a discharge only by an administrative action, not by a court-martial. With the loss of benefits and the stigma it carries, however, it is akin to a bad-conduct discharge.

PERIODIC TENANCY. A lease without any specific agreement as to how long the lease is to run. The law measures the duration of the lease by the frequency of rental payments, such as monthly or annually.

PERJURY. Lying under oath at a judicial proceeding.

PERSONAL PROPERTY. Any property that is movable, such as a car or a stereo. Also, anything that you can own that is not real property.

PERSONAL SERVICE OF PROCESS. The act of notifying a defendant, through the mail or in person, of a lawsuit against him.

PETTY OFFENSE. A minor misdemeanor, usually with a maximum punishment of not more than six months' confinement.

PLAINTIFF. The party that starts a lawsuit by suing the defendant.

POSSESSION. The custody, care, management, or control of property. You may possess property that you do not own, for example, if you borrow a friend's car.

POWER OF ATTORNEY. A written grant of authority for someone (the agent) to act for the grantor (the principal).

PREPONDERANCE OF THE EVIDENCE. The usual legal standard for deciding which side will prevail on an issue in a civil lawsuit or an administrative proceeding. For the plaintiff to prove his case by a preponderance of the evidence, he must have more proof supporting his version of the facts than the defendant has.

PRETRIAL AGREEMENT. Known as a plea bargain in civilian courts. An agreement by the accused to plead guilty to some or all of the charges in exchange for certain benefits, most often a limit on the sentence he will receive.

PRETRIAL CONFINEMENT. Custody in a military stockade, brig, or detention facility pending trial by court-martial.

PROBABLE CAUSE. A reasonable belief that a person committed a crime or that evidence of that crime is where the law enforcement official wants to search.

PROBATE. A court procedure to determine whether a will is valid and to order distribution of the estate according to the will and the law.

PROMISSORY NOTE. A written promise to pay a sum of money.

QUARTERS. A military term for a living place. It may be an on- or off-post house or apartment, a bachelor officers' or enlisted quarters, or a barracks room.

QUITCLAIM DEED. A deed that transfers whatever ownership the seller has in the property, but does not warrant that he has good title to it.

REAL PROPERTY. All land and buildings.

REBUTTAL. Evidence given to contradict the evidence given by the other side in a court case.

REPORT OF SURVEY. An administrative procedure by which the government can recover the cost of military property that a servicemember loses or damages.

REPRIMAND. A formal statement, either oral or written, criticizing a servicemember who does something wrong. A commander may issue an administrative reprimand or give a reprimand as an Article 15 punishment. A court-martial may sentence an accused to a reprimand.

RESIDENCE. A legal term for the permanent home of a person. The definition may vary according to the area of law in question. For example, the residence necessary to give a court jurisdiction in divorce cases may be different from the residence for tax purposes.

RESTRICTION. The least severe form of pretrial restraint, usually an order not to leave a certain area, such as a unit. It may also be a punishment given through nonjudicial punishment or through sentencing in a court-martial. Also, a commander may order an administrative restriction for a military purpose, such as restricting a unit to ensure everyone's presence for an upcoming movement.

SEARCH. A hunt for evidence that the government can use in a criminal prosecution.

SEARCH AUTHORIZATION. The military term for a search warrant; that is, the order from a commander, a military judge, or a military magistrate that authorizes the search for and seizure of evidence of a crime.

SECURITY. Property pledged to guarantee repayment of a loan. If the borrower does not repay the loan, a court may order the property seized and used to satisfy the debt.

SEIZURE. Taking property for the government to use in a criminal prosecution.

SEPARATION. The legal termination of cohabitation between a husband and wife. It may be done by a formal agreement or by a court order.

SERVICE OF PROCESS. The act of bringing a lawsuit to the attention of the defendant so that he may defend himself.

SETTLEMENT. An agreement in which two parties to a claim or lawsuit resolve the conflict by determining what is due from one to the other. The settlement then becomes payment in full.

SMALL CLAIMS COURT. A civilian court for lawsuits involving small amounts of money, often $1,000 or less, with informal procedures.

SOLDIERS' AND SAILORS' CIVIL RELIEF ACT. A federal law enacted to prevent servicemembers from being discriminated against in financial, legal, and tax matters because of their military service.

SPECIAL COURT-MARTIAL. The intermediate military court with greater punishment authority than a summary court, but less than that of a general court. Among its maximum punishments are confinement for six months and forfeiture of two thirds pay per month for six months. In some circumstances, it may sentence enlisted members to a bad-conduct discharge. It has a trial counsel (prosecutor), a defense counsel, a judge, and court members.

SPOKESMAN. In nonjudicial punishment proceedings, a participant who speaks for the individual facing nonjudicial punishment. Servicemembers do not have the right to have a lawyer serve as a spokesman in nonjudicial punishment proceedings.

STAFF JUDGE ADVOCATE. The chief legal officer and adviser of a command. He may supervise the other attorneys assigned to the command (except judges and defense counsel).

STATUS OF FORCES AGREEMENT. A treaty between nations that decides how they will handle legal matters involving visiting forces. It specifies under what conditions the host country will try servicemembers and under what conditions they will be tried by their own military justice system.

STAY. A delay or suspension of a court proceeding.

STRICT LIABILITY. A law that holds a defendant responsible for harm caused the plaintiff—even if he has not been negligent—because of the danger of the act he committed. Sometimes called liability without fault.

SUMMARY COURT-MARTIAL. The lowest military court with the most limited punishments. A summary court officer, rather than a military judge and court members, conducts this type of trial. The summary court officer acts as trial and defense counsel, court, and judge all rolled up in one.

TENANCY AT SUFFERANCE. The continuing occupancy of rental property after a periodic tenancy has expired.

TENANCY AT WILL. The occupancy of rental property with the owner's permission but without an agreement as to the term of the lease.

TENANCY FROM YEAR TO YEAR. A lease that lasts for an entire year.

TENANT. A person who rents real property, such as a home or an apartment.

TESTATOR. A person who executes a will.

TESTIMONY. Giving evidence to a court orally and under oath.

TITLE. The evidence of ownership of property.

TORT. A civil, as opposed to a criminal, wrong other than a breach of contract.

TRAINEE ABUSE. Mistreatment by a trainer, often a drill sergeant, of a servicemember who is undergoing initial training in the service.

TRIAL COUNSEL. A judge advocate assigned to prosecute a case before a court-martial.

TRUST. A property interest in which one person, the trustee, holds title to the property but must use it for the benefit of another, the beneficiary.

UNIFORM CODE OF MILITARY JUSTICE (UCMJ). A law passed by Congress that establishes the military justice system and defines military crimes. The text of the UCMJ is contained in the Manual for Courts-Martial.

UNSWORN STATEMENT. A method by which the accused can provide extenuation and mitigation information to a court-martial. Although this information is not sworn, and although the trial counsel cannot cross-examine the accused, a jury may consider it. The trial counsel can, however, introduce evidence to show that the statement is untrue.

VICTIM. A person harmed by a crime. The harm may be physical, mental, or financial.

WARRANTY. A promise or guarantee that something is as it is represented to be and providing remedies, such as free repairs or a replacement, if it is not.

WARRANTY DEED. A deed that guarantees good title to the land it transfers.

WILL. A legal document in which a person directs what he wants done with his property upon his death.

WITNESS. A person who has knowledge about a crime and provides information about that crime to law enforcement officials. Also, a person who testifies about knowledge of a crime at a legal proceeding, such as a court-martial or an Article 32 investigation.

WRIT OF EXECUTION. A court order telling an official to seize the property of the loser of a lawsuit and to sell enough of it to pay the damages and costs.

WRONGFUL APPROPRIATION. Simply, wrongful borrowing. The wrongful taking of another's property with the intent to deprive him of it temporarily.

Suggested Readings

Berner, J. Kevin, and Thomas Daula. *Armed Forces Guide to Personal Financial Planning*. 3d ed. Mechanicsburg, PA: Stackpole Books, 1994.

Budahn, P. J. *Veteran's Guide to Benefits*. Mechanicsburg, PA: Stackpole Books, 1994.

Cline, Lydia Sloan. *Today's Military Wife*. 3d ed. Mechanicsburg, PA: Stackpole Books, 1995.

Cox, Frank. *Enlisted Soldier's Guide*. 4th ed. Mechanicsburg, PA: Stackpole Books, 1996.

Cox, Frank. *NCO Guide*. 5th ed. Mechanicsburg, PA: Stackpole Books, 1995.

Crocker, Lawrence P. *Army Officer's Guide*. 46th ed. Mechanicsburg, PA: Stackpole Books, 1993.

Henderson, David G. *Job Search: Marketing Your Military Experience*. 2d ed. Mechanicsburg, PA: Stackpole Books, 1995.

Napier, John Hawkins III. *Air Force Officer's Guide*. 30th ed. Mechanicsburg, PA: Stackpole Books, 1995.

1995 Retired Military Almanac. Washington, DC: Uniformed Services Almanac, Inc., 1995.

1995 Uniformed Services Almanac. Washington, DC: Uniformed Services Almanac, Inc., 1995.

Nyman, Keith O. *Re-entry: How to Turn Your Military Experience into Civilian Success*. 2d ed. Harrisburg, PA: Stackpole Books, 1990.

Valey, Wayne A. *Airman's Guide*. 3d ed. Mechanicsburg, PA: Stackpole Books, 1994.

Index

About the Author

Jonathan P. Tomes retired from active military service in 1988 as a lieutenant colonel in the Judge Advocate General's Corps. He currently practices law in Chicago for the law firm of Tomes, Lee & Dvorak, which handles cases in military law, employment law, criminal law, medical malpractice, and personal injury. He is the author of twenty-five books and numerous articles in *Army*, *Military Review*, *The Army Lawyer*, and other publications. Mr. Tomes is also the president of Veterans Enterprises, Inc., a real estate development company.